3C Vision

3C Vision
Cues, Contexts, and Channels

Virginio Cantoni
Università di Pavia

Stefano Levialdi
Sapienza, Università di Roma

Bertrand Zavidovique
Université Paris-Sud 11
Institute for Electronics Fundamentals
Orsay, France

ELSEVIER AMSTERDAM • BOSTON • HEIDELBERG • LONDON • NEW YORK • OXFORD
PARIS • SAN DIEGO • SAN FRANCISCO • SINGAPORE • SYDNEY • TOKYO

Elsevier
32 Jamestown Road London NW1 7BY
225 Wyman Street, Waltham, MA 02451, USA

First edition 2011

Notices
Knowledge and best practice in this field are constantly changing. As new research and experience broaden our understanding, changes in research methods, professional practices, or medical treatment may become necessary.

Practitioners and researchers must always rely on their own experience and knowledge in evaluating and using any information, methods, compounds, or experiments described herein. In using such information or methods they should be mindful of their own safety and the safety of others, including parties for whom they have a professional responsibility.

To the fullest extent of the law, neither the Publisher nor the authors, contributors, or editors, assume any liability for any injury and/or damage to persons or property as a matter of products liability, negligence or otherwise, or from any use or operation of any methods, products, instructions, or ideas contained in the material herein.

British Library Cataloguing-in-Publication Data
A catalogue record for this book is available from the British Library

Library of Congress Cataloging-in-Publication Data
A catalog record for this book is available from the Library of Congress

ISBN: 978-0-323-16509-9

For information on all Elsevier publications
visit our website at www.elsevierdirect.com

This book has been manufactured using Print On Demand technology. Each copy is produced to order and is limited to black ink. The online version of this book will show color figures where appropriate.

Working together to grow
libraries in developing countries

www.elsevier.com | www.bookaid.org | www.sabre.org

ELSEVIER   BOOK AID
            International   Sabre Foundation

Contents

Foreword

Digital images are the product of two technologies: cameras and graphics. This book is about both kinds of images. Images from cameras may be fed into computer vision and image-processing systems; the word "vision" in the title of this book refers first to this kind of analysis, which depends on cues (visual features) and contexts (frameworks and predispositions for interpretation). Images that result from graphical synthesis represent the visions (imaginations) of their creators, and this is the second meaning of "vision" in the title. The prime purpose of the image here is to communicate the vision, and the specific medium (e.g., still image, video, virtual world, game, and so on) is a "channel."

The strength of this book lies in its integration of technical information, application, and reflections on the social consequences of this rapidly expanding aspect of the human experience. Let us consider briefly the two main phenomena that are driving these ideas. First, we have digital cameras rapidly becoming more powerful in three respects:

1. Better imaging, with automatic focus, exposure, high dynamic range, image stabilization, color balance, red-eye reduction, panorama, stereo, and so on.
2. Ubiquity, with cameras appearing as standard items in laptops, cell phones, and automobiles.
3. Connectedness, with many cameras integrated with the Internet via their cell phone hosts. Thus, more than ever before, digital images are being generated in greater numbers, in higher quality, and as part of the Internet.

The second phenomenon in the rise of the image is incredible technologies for producing synthetic images, such as the animation systems that helped produce the 3D film *Avatar*, and the powerful gaming graphics chips from companies like NVIDIA that can turn polygon lists into realistic shaded scenes at high speed.

What does this mean? The mindshare of digital images, rather than text, for most of the population is growing. Daily experience is more image oriented and less text oriented for increasingly more people. It is important, therefore, for educated people to understand what is going on with images and to be familiar with the basic concepts of how the images are processed, how they are sent through the Internet, and how they relate to other media, such as interactive games, and audio.

This book does an admirable job of giving an overview, integrating basic technical concepts of image processing with a discussion of a key class of applications: web search involving images (either as queries or as targets), plus a reflection on the role played by images in current and emerging communication media, such as online virtual worlds.

Another strength of this book is its bringing together of many references, put into context by the narrative, so that the reader can easily dig into the literature to follow up on a topic of particular interest. These references span a wide gamut, from articles and texts on computer graphics and computer vision to works on the philosophy of communication.

Steven Tanimoto
University of Washington

Preface

This book analyzes the visual hints by which both humans and computer programs generally interpret, process, and exploit images. The chapters in this book provide a unified framework in which both biological and artificial vision are discussed through visual cues, the role of contexts, and the available multichannels with which information is delivered. These various subjects are traditionally investigated within different scientific communities producing specific technical literature.

The exponential explosion of images and videos concerns everybody because media are now present everywhere and in all human activities. At this stage, it seems important that scientists, artists, and engineers in all fields be aware of how images are essential information carriers. Images carry a strong evocative power because they quickly bring to mind a number of related pictures of past experiences—or even abstract concepts like pleasure, attraction, or aversion. Analyzing the impact that images have on people is the thread of this book. It puts forward the connection between technical issues that can be extracted from objective measurements and psychological issues that emerge from perception, bound to the context and the time at which such images are observed. In short, the book advocates that, as is commonly stated, "there is more than meets the eye" when a picture, a graphical representation, a sketch, or an icon is looked at; for this reason, it is hoped the reader will acquire a deeper insight into joint computer-vision and human-brain machinery when looking at a picture, be it natural, digitized, or artificially generated.

Images play a fundamental role in many application domains such as video surveillance, biomedical diagnostics, remote sensing, automatic inspection, robot vision, and so on. For this reason, the automatic management, retrieval, and processing of images requires sophisticated tools to effectively perform such tasks. Present techniques in most applications—for example, vehicle autonomy from vision, image-based retrieval, or automatic video management—benefit from a better integration of bio-inspired solutions and advanced information-processing facilities. In this connection, a controlled view on the vision process involves:

- concurrent basic information and relative description (cues from image input);
- intended action, *a priori* knowledge, and common culture (context); and
- media to convey processed information, including the coding scheme (through-channels output).

When targeting artificial vision systems, it is worth considering the perception process in a goal-oriented fashion, therefore including an intention. There is always an action to be performed at the end. For instance, in character recognition, a generic action could be rewriting; in understanding an outdoor scene, the action may be survival. Therefore, the computer vision research community has agreed on a two-stage *analytic strategy*:

- Systems first deal with objects, aiming at capturing their interrelations from current scene analysis. To do that, common sense knowledge is employed, usually based on intuitive geometry (perspective, projections, etc.) or naïve physics (e.g., lighting, shadows, and more generally photometry).
- Systems next discover relations among objects and tackle the question of scene understanding for decision and action planning. For this, elaborate or expert knowledge is necessary: This is usually stored independently from the current acquisition and contingent information, allowing for a larger potential interpretation.

Note that such steps follow the historical evolution in human visual communication. During the Renaissance period, artists studied and began to understand the physical rules of their environment, to enable *faithful rendering*, for instance, of natural landscapes (complying with perspective and light propagation laws). During the last century, the impressionists, although they fully knew the physical laws of light, overcame the relative constraints. This allowed for the *conveyance of abstraction*, for instance, for the viewer's immediate access to feelings based on color or texture that predominate over the structure of the painting as a whole. Later, cubists and their followers even used paradoxes triggered by the fragmented image, enabling enriched and more complex nuances to emerge in the observer's mind.

In this book, the evolution of artificial vision will be considered on the basis of a growing understanding of the human visual system. This does not imply in any way that machines can or should mimic human perception. The computer vision community has been proving, for the last decade, that a *synthesis process* is feasible for *interhuman mediation* through machines or for interfacing machines with humans.

Communication systems employ many information channels and an actual representation of the intended goal. They use multiple media to purposely stress a selective presentation of scene components, favoring the given goal of a human or technological agent. This process currently corresponds to a simplistic version of the basic human information exchange, merging images and sounds with actions, such as made popular over centuries by theater or opera, and more recently by comics, movies, and so forth.

Note that, whether computer vision is considered for solving the inverse (image analysis) or direct (image synthesis) problem, whenever interaction occurs, the more intimate and cultivated people are, the more abstract and subjective the process becomes. Abstraction usually goes hand in hand with flexibility (relaxation of constraints), thus lowering precision and favoring subjectivity (interpretation). In this process, the two analysis steps (cues detection and context exploitation) do not have strict parameters. Moreover, objects can also be described qualitatively, suggesting or triggering the observer's feelings. The pattern of the Mona Lisa's lips has given rise to different interpretations for centuries, and this will probably continue regardless of any response given by anthropometry software used to analyze it. Conversely, detecting objects without directly sensing them, but only by analyzing relationships among them or from physical laws, is the essence of the human evolution by abduction. A recent example is the discovery of remote planets without being able to actually see them.

It is no wonder that human subjectivity turns out to be the real technological challenge in man–machine interaction. In fact, the difficulty lies in correctly interpreting the human goal: Machines cannot capture it and normally do not easily decipher concepts.

One of the primary concerns of an artist in successfully conveying his or her message is that of directing the attention of a viewer and concentrating it on some *salient detail*. In image analysis by computers, the main process is the so-called *attention focusing*, dual of the *pop-out/interrupt* phenomenon that triggers human attention. Artists started to highlight objects through their position: central, aligned with a diagonal, plausible, or unexpected (as the egg above the head of the Madonna in *The Sacred Conversation* by Piero della Francesca); through their dimension, for example, the especially large apple tree seen before the naked bodies upfront in *The Tree of Knowledge* by Lucas Cranach; through lighting, as in the little naked model in *L'Atelier du Peintre* by Gustave Courbet and the gigantic cavity in *The Climbing to Paradise* by Jerome Bosch; or through their genuine importance, as seen in depictions of Jesus Christ in most sacred paintings.

More recently, creators work at a conceptual level by exploiting the idea of disruption. For instance, René Magritte painted faces having birds, apples, eggs, and such, to describe their inner personalities; Fernando Botero made a specialty of fat bodies; Maurits Escher played with laws of perspective and gravity; Wassily Kandinsky invented a theory of color effects; and Edvard Munch amplified all movements to evocate missing senses, for example, by actually merging lovers in *The Kiss* or by distorting the features in the melting mouth, face, and scenery in *The Scream.*

A key factor of successful man–machine interaction is *real-time performance*. A natural way to reach real-time image information exchange is to use only the required data at the right time. Biological strategies like attention focusing, smart path scanning, multiresolution analysis, and motion tracking are discussed later in this book. Note that either the significant information is known *a priori* and a predefined sequence of hypothesis test is applied or it must be directly derived from the image data by trivial operators. A number of techniques for simulating biological vision systems and for optimizing limited resources in a "wide field of view" are presented in this text, together with some examples of existing systems based on these principles.

One aim of this book is to trigger curiosity in the reader, introducing him or her to the large world of imagery on which many human activities are based, from politics to entertainment, to technical reports, to artistic creations. To be involved in these creative activities in today's world, it is necessary to understand and use recent technological multimedia tools. In this respect, the book can be seen as a general-purpose guide into the image culture, its development, and potential leverage.

The book is also useful in universities as a comprehensive introductory text for entry-level postgraduate students acquiring a general understanding of image analysis. Our preference not to resort to strictly technical matters will make it easier for most students, whatever their technical skills, to better understand the modern use of computerized images and videos. The book involves an approach to teaching that supports a brief introduction to algorithms and data structures, and does not waste too much of the readers' attention on unnecessary technical details. To that aim, all technical matter—including mathematics and technology-based information or comments—is presented in a smaller, italicized font so that a nonexpert reader can skip it at first reading.

The content of the book is subdivided into four chapters.

Chapter 1: *Natural and artificial vision* discusses differences, analogies, and possible synergies between natural and artificial vision systems. A number of concepts related to the analysis and synthesis of images (*V-schema*) are described. Different strategies for image exploration within artificial vision are explained and presented along with corresponding sketches and figures.

Chapter 2: *Visual cues* explains the different visual cues that can be used both for image analysis and rendering, following three approaches: photometric, morphologic, and spatial. The photometric track provides a general description of light image models, followed by explanations of image synthesis methods and chromatic clues. The morphological track considers different shape representations, transformations, and extraction methods. The spatial track covers 3D vision and modeling, including motion analysis.

Chapter 3: *The role of contexts* considers the various functions that context may play in different communities (artistic, scientific, etc.) and explains how an image can be retrieved and interpreted both in human and computer-based systems. Additionally, a number of methods (statistical, linguistic, structural, etc.) are explained and examples given. The essential link of context with new technologies is illustrated through two generic operations: image retrieval and sensor networking.

Chapter 4: *Channeling the information* deals with the use of different channels for conveying multimedia information thanks to a variety of methods: by using icons and metaphors, using multiple channels, and capitalizing on the network properties. The latest technologies that allow virtual realism, ambient intelligence, and 3D sophisticated animation find a place at the end of the book.

Acknowledgments

We gratefully acknowledge the assistance and support of Alessandra Setti to properly incorporate all the figures in this book as well as the cooperation of Samia Bouchafa and Michèle Gouiffès, who provided advice on different topics covered. Last, thanks are given to the Skype desktop sharing system for all the hours we spent using it during the final revision of our manuscript.

1 Natural and Artificial Vision

Vision can be considered as the activity performed by biological systems to exploit perceived light distributions for building adequate representations of natural scenes in the mind. Such representations can, in turn, be redescribed and presented in a pictorial form, for example, as an artist's rendering on a canvas or on a computer screen. Two main processes are considered here. The former is mainly an analysis task, outlined in [1] as "the process of discovering from images what is present in the world and where it is." The latter is a synthesis task that may be described, by paraphrasing the previous definition, as "the process of rendering, through images, a model of the world." In that sense, these two processes may be considered as dual ones; the first structures the acquired data toward information, whereas the second embodies an internal concept pictorially.

These two tasks may naturally be performed by humans. Nevertheless, in the 1960s, different dedicated systems were designed to execute each task.

Initially, pattern recognition and then image analysis were gradually developed to achieve practical results in different areas of image science (biomedical images classification, optical character recognition (OCR), human signature recognition, remote sensing, automatic inspection, etc.). Further, new methodologies and algorithms for extending and generalizing existing recognition techniques were established. Machine vision has often been divided into computer vision and image understanding; in the former, a correspondence exists with the engineering disciplines, which try to optimize a system performance for a class of specific actions, whereas in the latter the goal is to explain scene contents with reference to a class of models.

Initially, the artificial representations on a screen were graphical sketches made by geometrical primitives (straight lines, circles, and rectangles) using a few gray levels, next a set of packages called *Computer-Aided X* (*X* for design, engineering, manufacturing, etc.) were implemented, igniting the fast explosion in the field of computer graphics. From data visualization to visual realism and pictorial manipulation, a wide number of algorithms have been developed to improve the image quality in texture and color rendering, illumination control, dimensionality, and other areas (see [2]). Today, the possibility of multimedia systems integrating images, sounds, text, and animation allows us to build virtual reality equipment, both in *first* and in *third person*, which enable the user to control and interact with the visualized information.

3C Vision. DOI: 10.1016/B978-0-12-385220-5.00001-2

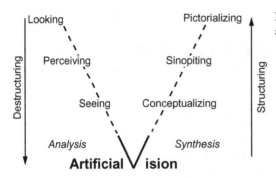

Figure 1.1 Dual aspects of vision: analysis and synthesis.

It is worthwhile to describe, using a functional schema, the characteristics of the vision processes. By looking at Figure 1.1, we may see how the dual aspects of vision can be subdivided into six activities:

- *Looking*: The field of view is scrutinized both for *spread* and for *purposive attention*. In the spread (*diffuse*) instance, the observing system is passively acquiring all the light information from the scene; whereas in the purposive instance, the system actively inspects the visual field pursuing a goal.
- *Perceiving*: A region of interest (ROI) is discovered in space, and/or in time, respectively, on a still frame or on an image sequence: all the computing resources of the system are then concentrated on the ROIs.
- *Seeing*: ROIs are interpreted; the scene components are recognized, locating their position and orientation, and described in a more abstract form, where *symbols* give access to an associated *semantics*. Geometric modeling and then a variety of knowledge representations are used to achieve image understanding [3].

Moving upward along the other arm of V(ision), we find a brief description of the three activities that are dual to the previous ones given:

- *Conceptualizing*: A high-level decision process takes place, by means of which a visual form (concrete or abstract) is conceived to aid reasoning, understanding, and learning.
- *Sinopiting*[1]: A sketching activity that roughly describes the scene spatial (and further spatiotemporal) composition by graphical annotation, indicating placements, shapes, and relationships (and likely further evolutions). This is still a creative activity that may be later modified and refined.
- *Rendering*: The final composition of pictorial elements (using a gray scale or a color palette) designed to visually grasp the concepts and relationships (as in a synthetic molecule, a weather map, or a biomedical image). In some instances, like in many dynamic simulations (e.g., flight simulators), all the laws of physical optics are applied to achieve a visual realism, so providing good three-dimensionality and lifelike computer-generated image sequences. Resulting productions belong to what is now called *virtual reality*.

---

[1] From Sinopite: During the Renaissance period, painters used to indicate the principal elements of their frescoes by preliminary sketches, called *sinopites*, using an ochre earth from the Sinope Harbor on the Black Sea.

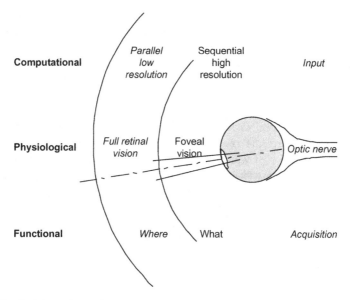

Figure 1.2 Biovision schema for looking.

Natural Vision

Within biological systems, along the phylogenetic evolution of primates, the activity of *looking* has been accomplished through a powerful and reliable system, with a limited amount of resources, that is briefly sketched in Figure 1.2.

Three different facets of the human vision system may be considered, namely, functional, physiological, and computational ones.

The first covers, by means of task-oriented strategies, operations that start from an unconscious attitude. The eye-scanning mechanism is first a random process in a wide visual field (about 180° for a fixed eye position) mainly geared to detect relevant regions (the *where* function). Next, an attentive inspection of such regions is performed (the *what* function): for this purpose the corresponding detailed information is phototransduced and delivered through the optic nerve to the brain (the *acquisition* function).

The second aspect is the physiological one, where the previously mentioned functions are associated to the anatomy of the human visual system. The *where* function is achieved through a full retinal vision, performed with a spatially nonuniform distribution of different photosensors. The *what* function is accomplished by *foveal vision*, operating with some thousands of cone cells, covering a field of view of approximately 2° around the optical axis. Such cones, belonging to red, green, and blue classes, are uniformly distributed, and the minimum visual angle that can be resolved is of 0.5 min of arc [4]. Finally, the last function, the *acquisition*, is obtained by transmitting nervous pulses from each retina to the brain, through 1 million fibers belonging to the nerve. Three levels of preprocessing have been found in the retina that allows a signal data compression of two orders of magnitude.

The third computational aspect is directly connected to the data processing mode that differs for each function. First, a low-resolution process is executed by the full retinal vision, in parallel. There each photoreceptor is able to simultaneously acquire light information, whereas a network of retinal cells performs preprocessing. Second, foveal vision is performed on each relevant region at a time [5], in sequence. There, the resolution is much higher and the analysis is more sophisticated. The order in which the analysis of the ROIs is performed, the *scan path* [6], depends on the task, as demonstrated by Yarbus [7]. A wide number of experiments on eye *fixation points* (the ROIs) over a number of different pictures were reported, to understand causes of ROI saliency. The last function, which essentially provides neurological data to the brain, particularly to its cortical region, has been proven to operate bidirectionally so that, in turn, the brain may send control signals to the eye [8].

Artificial Vision

As for artificial vision, the phylogenetic evolution of machines is condensed into half a century. However, the dramatic concentration of several hundred specific vision projects into the single current PC-based multicore system can be summarized through an historical perspective. By the same token, main activities mentioned in the V-cycle, and corresponding difficulties, are reintroduced within the frame of computer evolution.

Initially, the image analysis was performed by raster-scanning gray-level images (usually having *pixels*[2] with 8 bits[3]). In the same period, the synthesis of images, so-called *computer graphics*, was featuring *vector representation*, where the image components—that is, the lines—were coded by vectors. There was a remarkable difference between the complexity of the images to be analyzed and that of the artificially generated ones, the latter usually of a simple geometrical nature.

At the end of the 1970s, systems had a display-oriented image memory [9] with interactive capabilities and video processing. Such modules were specialized for local convolution (with a limited kernel), template correlation and edge detection, as well as a high-speed address controller for zoom, pan, roam operations, and gray-scale modification.

Currently, special hardware functions can generate vectors and characters on a *graphic plane* [10]. With the addition of these features, plus high-speed central processors, increased bits per pixel,[4] and professional color monitors, today's vision

---

[2] Pixel: Contraction of picture elements, normally considered as the basic digital image unit.

[3] The gray levels of each pixel are usually coded in a computer byte, that is, 8 bits for representing 256 gray levels.

[4] Each bit of an image plane is called a bit plane, and their number corresponds to the bit per pixel number (currently they can reach up to 64).

systems are suitable for both image analysis and synthesis. Finally, new interaction tools like mice, gloves, helmets, spectacles, and multimedia devices enable present workstations to have extremely high performances for all instances of multidimensional image processing.

Destructuring Images

The last five decades have witnessed the historical evolution of systems that have tried to emulate and compete with the visual human system. These will be now described, following the first track of the V-cycle, as may be seen in Figure 1.3.

The first systems for image analysis and pattern recognition were designed around a commercial computer on which a special-purpose interface was built for image acquisition, generally using a standard camera [11]. At that time (1960–1970), serious obstacles were met in image transfer rate and core memory size. Moreover, the processing of raster-scanned images was computationally intensive and slow respective to the tasks that such systems were aimed at: character recognition [12], path recognition in a spark bubble chamber [13], chromosome karyotype classification [14], and so on.

The second decade (1970–1980) may be described as one in which image preprocessing was developed using both *ad hoc* hardware and suitable algorithms [15,16]. Basically, most negative effects introduced by digitization, noise, limited resolution, and such were compensated through enhancement and restoration techniques so that further analysis and recognition could be conveniently performed.

During the third decade (1980–1990), to improve the machine perception strategies, sensing and processing were operating in a *closed loop*, achieving the so-called *active perception* [17,18]. In this way, only the most significant information is considered, facilitating high-level processing. A wide number of new strategies were developed for obtaining only the relevant information from an image. Two of

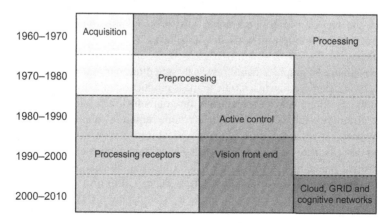

Figure 1.3 Machine vision phylogenesis.

the most significant ones are the synergic exploitation of the spatial and temporal parallelisms [19] and the multiresolution approach for smart sensing [20].

The critical elements of a scene may be captured by means of motion tracking, stereo vision, and change detection, using a front-end processor [21] that may operate autonomously. In this new configuration, besides the peripheral control loop typical of active vision systems, another central control loop, which includes the main vision computer, enables us to sequentially probe the external world (artificial seeing) and compare it with its internal model of the world.

The evolution of the fourth decade (1990–2000) has brought higher computing power to the sensory area; more particularly, *smart artificial retinas* have been built, where the optoelectronic function is combined with moderate processing capabilities [22].

Finally, during the fifth decade (2000–2010), the Internet revolution and wireless technology sparked novel architectures based on a high number of interconnected active elements (*sensor networks, smart dust*, up to *cognitive networks*) that may all process images cooperatively in a natural environment. These new systems are able to provide fast, robust, and efficient image processing. Typical applications include distributed robotics, environment monitoring, emergency management (fire, heart quake, and floods), urban sensing, etc.

Structuring Images

During the 1950s at Massachusetts Institute of Technology (MIT), a system called Whirlwind was developed, having a computer-driven display as output, with some interactivity, and also allowing printouts of the display contents: this may be considered to be the first prototype of a system designed for graphical work [2]. Sutherland's Sketchpad [23] was the first system to enable a user to draw graphical objects (rectangles, circles, etc.) on a screen, imposing some topological constraints and editing the results at any stage of the process: this system may be considered the first example of an *object-oriented* graphical tool. The initial difficulties to the diffusion of graphical systems were the high costs due to the required computing resources, the one-of-a-kind nonportable software, and the complexity of integrating interactive programming with drawing tasks for users proficient in batch environments.

The appearance of graphics-based personal computing introduced a new generation of relatively inexpensive machines (due to mass production and dissemination), which helped in the development of sophisticated programs for easy, interactive drawing of graphical primitives. Interactive graphical systems require a suitable input apart from the conventional keyboard. For nonalphanumerical information, some special-purpose peripheral devices have been designed, such as pen, tablet, mouse, trackball, joystick, touch-sensitive panel, and glove. At the same time, outputs that could be previously seen on a screen by means of a Cathode Ray Tube (CRT) or a direct-view storage tube (DVST) were now delivered on a liquid-crystal display (LCD). The output could also be obtained as hard copies from dot matrix printers, pen plotters, and desktop plotters. From the mid-1960s, and lasting to the mid-1980s for a few specimens, the output devices were vector displays in which the beam was deflected from an end-point to another endpoint for each single drawn segment. Because the scanning order of all the drawing segments was nondeterministic, such systems were based on a technique called *random scan*.

To avoid flicker on the video due to phosphor decay, the image on the screen must be refreshed with a frequency of about 30 full frames per second. This constraint usually limited the complexity of the graphical objects that could be displayed; for this reason, at the end of the 1960s, a new technology called DVST was introduced, which solved both flicker and the need for an extra buffer memory. The next step (1968–1970) introduced a hardware-based refreshed-display, thereby allowing the storage of drawing primitives on the image buffer. Two new hardware controllers were needed: the video controller, which managed the uploading in raster modality of the refresh buffer on the monitor; and the display controller, which stored the primitives (line, characters, patterns, etc.) inside the refresh buffer.

In the early 1980s, personal computers had a bit-mapped refresh memory (where each pixel of the image could be either 1 or 0); it is now common practice to have workstations with 2^n, with $n = 6, 7, \ldots$, single-bit memory planes. Such planes may be subdivided into three groups: a pair of them (each having 2^5 bits) works in a double-buffering mode so that while one buffer is used to update the image, the other is used to refresh it on the screen. 2^5 bits are required to cater for color and control purposes; the remaining 2^5 bits, called the Z-buffer, are used to resolve occlusion and produce depth for a realistic representation of 3D images.

Computing power limitations are due to the tasks that must be carried out by the display and video controllers: the resolution extension in both space (up to mega(s) pixel images) and color (8 bits per primary color component); the realism in animation (moving images); and the short interaction response time and editing facilities. In practice, in the last few years, graphic computer architects have tried to solve such problems, enhancing the controllers' speed by designing multiprocessor rasterization systems. A multitude of projects have been suggested, which may be subdivided into two classes on the basis of the rasterization algorithms: (i) object order and (ii) image order. In the former, the external update cycle is aimed at the representation of each single object (for all objects); whereas in the latter, the external cycle computes the image pixel by pixel. The inner loop of this second case is performed on the objects/primitives. In both cases, the above cycles may be spatially parallelized or pipelined (for a detailed presentation see [2]).

The recent computing power available on modern "workstations" enables us to display high-quality color images with minute details undistinguishable from photographic standards. As a fallout of these techniques, animation spreads everywhere in applications: 2D and 3D solid world animation; simulation of complex rigid and elastic surfaces; and editing of images in video clips, widely used in scientific visualization and in advertising.

The V-Schema

Because of the increase in sophistication, *usability* [24] (see *Social interaction* section in Chapter 4) and computing power of modern machines, the twofold aspects of generating images (graphics) and analyzing images (processing and understanding), may be conveniently solved on one single platform, integrating the corresponding software. This, in turn, facilitates use, portability, distribution, and documentation of image-handling programs independently from the specific application domain.

Images as Information Carriers

Images have been generally considered as information containers. Paintings in an art gallery, photographs in a news agency databank, architectures of buildings, outdoor cityscapes, skylines—they are all examples of *static* information about human activities. The advanced computing facilities available today make it possible to generate, in real time, synthetic images designed to communicate complex messages to different communities. Observers with new professional profiles literally emerge from blending multimedia technologies. The prosecutor of a modern trial may conveniently use, for a complex financial kick-back analysis and description, an image-based system that shows graphs, video interviews with witnesses, and so forth, for delivering a complex information pattern at a glance. Surgeons not only can perform remote operations under visual control but can also check on the patient's entire clinical history through graphics, image radiology, and concurrently audio-monitoring.

Some *dynamic* aspects of a nondeterministic program execution can only be mastered in progressively managing them through human—machine interaction by using a flexible visual environment: for instance, an interface providing immersive virtual reality. In short, while images were previously only used as a static information source, they may be now conceived as convenient real-time information carriers tuned to the requirements of the sender and the needs of the receiver, whether these are humans or machines.

Furthermore, images referred to here may also be used as an aid to the conceptualization of systems and processes, so that by visualizing them, a clearer picture of objects under study can be obtained. Along this way, visual metaphors are increasingly used. They constitute high-level abstractions of processes difficult to describe via natural language because of their complexity and the background heterogeneity of listeners/observers. In a process called *visual reasoning*, rough sketches are employed for fast concept communication.

In [25] some meaningful examples are given: "[T]he teacher draws a diagram on the blackboard. Although the diagram is incomplete and imprecise, the students are able to make inferences to fill in the details, and gain an understanding of the concepts presented. Such diagram understanding relies on visual reasoning so that concepts can be communicated. Humans also use gestures to communicate. Again, gestures are imprecise visual clues for the receiving person to interpret."

Finally, in scientific working environments, images have been largely used as containers of real data (cytological images, spark chamber images, astronomical images, remote sensing, etc.) and also for knowledge instances. In adequately visualizing intermediate results, new hypotheses to be proved can be further generated, triggering novel experiments providing results that may also be visualized. Examples of this last role of images are quoted in [26] and include Friedrich August Kekulè (circular ring of organic components) and Richard Feynman (visual maps for solving complex equations in nuclear physics).

Dissecting Images

Within a traditional image analysis process, a number of different basic stages are considered. The corresponding data flow is shown in Figure 1.4, going from the image sensors down to the final display and interpretation.

The instruments shown at the left represent a sample of image acquisition tools for a number of scientific tasks: video camera, telescope, microscope, and tomograph.

For the scene contents to be fully understood, progressive transformations are necessary to increase the data abstraction level. They can be split into three stages:

1. *Image space transform*: The data space is constrained by the input array of pixels provided by the acquisition device; the purpose is to improve the quality of the data, using some *a priori* knowledge. This knowledge refers to an image context, to the sensor features (like its *point spread function*, the *signal-to-noise ratio*, geometrical distortions, etc.), to the illumination conditions, and to the overall acquisition geometry. This may be seen as an image-to-image transform.
2. *Feature space transform*: The data arrays are now inspected for *segmentation* purposes, and subsequently each image component (*segment*) is described by a suitable set of features. Homogeneous connected components are detected once a given criterion is postulated based on chromatic, morphological, positional, structural, and dynamical cues. For each component, convenient features are selected and evaluated in order to provide the

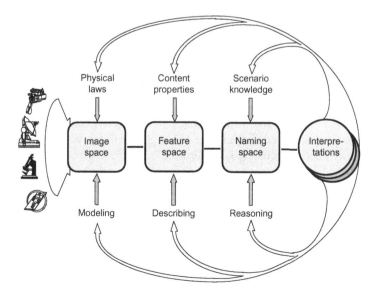

Figure 1.4 The image analysis and interpretation process.

full contextual description of the image segment. This may be seen as an image-to-feature transform.

3. *Naming space transform*: The goal is to label each image component with a name corresponding to the object type. This task is achieved by means of a feature analysis, which is completed by symbol manipulation, usually on a higher abstraction level referring to the intended action, maybe using artificial intelligence techniques. Globally speaking, this may be seen as a feature-to-symbol transform.

The final stage provides the means for accounting what the image contains, that is, an interpretation which, as is well known, may be subjective or at least dependent on a given class of observers (industrial surveyors, astronomers, biologists, etc.) and of their expertise. The knowledge gained from the observation at this last stage is comprehensive enough to support *feedback*. It is used, in turn, for improving and disambiguating the meaning from each and every of the above transforms to reach more stable and robust interpretation.

In particular, at the first stage, the above feedback stemming from the partial results will likely improve *preprocessing* by means of modeling the lighting conditions and the disposition of the scene elements (photometric and geometric modeling). Such preprocessing covers *enhancement* and *restoration* techniques for degraded images.

In the second stage, after having exhibited the first view, image components may suggest better features for their representation. Logical laws may be inferred from the partial results so as to better clarify the component interrelationships, capitalizing on *reasoning*.

The third stage, also known as the process of *consistent labeling*, exploits an integration between the *a priori* knowledge (image bound) and the one derived from the sensed image; in a similar process, the context knowledge may also be logically incremented. Task constraints help reducing the cardinality of allowable image interpretations.

As may be easily understood, a number of iterations of the full process, each one made of the three different stages, will be performed until a stable state with a single satisfactory interpretation is reached. It is worth noting that the data bandwidth on the main horizontal axis (see Figure 1.4) is funneled inversely to the level of abstraction of the image contents, which becomes higher and higher. Yet the external information involved in the whole process is increasing because *a priori* knowledge is modestly used in the image-to-image transform, whereas the opposite is true when symbolic processing is performed.

Artificial Vision Strategies

The necessary condition to reach real-time image processing is to use the required data at the right time. Biological strategies like attention focusing, smart path scanning, multiresolution analysis, motion tracking, and so on can be developed emulating them from natural systems.

Note that, either the significant information is known *a priori* and a predefined sequence of hypothesis-test sets is applied or the information must be directly derived from the image data by trivial operators. A number of techniques for simulating some biological vision features and for optimizing limited resources in a wide field of view will now be described together with some examples of implementations on systems based on these principles.

Refining

The problem of managing attention as a means to optimize computing resources has been widely explored in the last decades through the active perception paradigm, both from an algorithmic and from an architectural point of view. At least two different resolution levels must be considered in order to allow tackling the problem of image analysis in (quasi) real time. Figure 1.5 illustrates this acquisition paradigm applied on two resolution levels only.

Suppose an image contains a number of interesting local areas that must be processed; in this case, the global control will scan the image at a low spatial resolution rate (so ensuring a computation on a relatively small number of data) to detect the interesting regions. The local control, following a given priority-based strategy, will dispatch a new process (of attention), which takes over and analyzes the image at the maximum resolution. The concrete implementation of this strategy has been based on a wide number of different architecture embedding systems that emulate variable visual acuity [27]. Some of these architectures are based on a regular multiresolution organization (such as quadtrees [28] and pyramids [29,30]), and on a nonlinear acuity distribution (usually $1/\theta$, where θ is the angle of displacement with

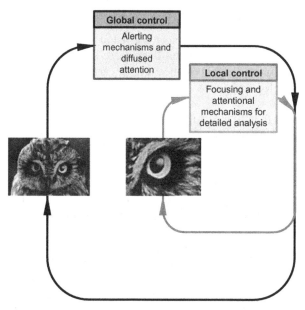

Figure 1.5 The hierarchical control mechanism of the coarse-to-fine acquisition strategy. The outer loop corresponds to the coarse analysis on the full image contents, whereas the inner loop is related to the fine analysis of specific image details.

respect to the optical axis) [31]. Moreover, multiagent systems may also be exploited: at least two agents are required, one for the global control and the other for the local one. Alternatively, a hierarchical control that runs the processes on a mandatory schedule has been suggested. Finally, standard machine implementation can also be effected, for example, through a decimation technique that may be constructed on some *ad hoc* silicon circuitry [32]. *Today's RISC machines and SIMD architectures, multicore, and/or with very long instruction word (VLIW) make it possible to implement such distributed control strategies at no noticeable cost.*

Scanning

Present-day images have sizes ranging typically from 10^4 to 10^6 pixels, with at least 8 bits per pixel (storing the gray-level value) so that the amount of information to be scanned is considerably high. For this reason, when some image regions bear a particular relevance, it is even more necessary to explore them first or, alternatively, to use global strategies for a preliminary rough exploration of the large image. A number of different scanning strategies have been proposed in order to implement the initial inspection process.

Referring to Figure 1.6, a number of different scanning sequences are shown, most of them taken from [33]. Two basic strategies can be considered: (1) deterministic space-filling paths (cases A−I) and (2) random (cases J−L). In the first strategy, after a finite number of steps known *a priori*, all possible cell positions are visited, ensuring that the image space is completely covered. Two basic features characterize the second strategy:

1. The possibility exists of revisiting cells.
2. The finite number of steps does not guarantee exhaustive cell coverage even if such number is much higher than the number of cells.

Cases A and B in Figure 1.6 represent the typical television *raster-scanning* sequence, the second one using interlaced horizontal lines. Case C is also called *corner scanning* because it starts from the left-topmost corner, and all successive cells to be visited lie on right-angled frames that grow until covering the rightmost and bottom edges of the image.

The next three cases, D, E, and F, only visit adjacent cells, on a 4- or 8-connected neighborhood (for neighborhood definition see *Shape representation* section in Chapter 2). In this way, pixels with high autocorrelation values are covered, leading to image compression. In particular, cases E and F are *spiral* based on a 4- and 8-connected neighborhood. Two interesting properties may be noted: the first one, having the scanning sequence starting from the image center; the second one, the higher isotropic nature of case F, where concentric circular approximations may be considered similar to spiral loops.

The following three cases belong to the hierarchical approach. Case G is composed of a *sequence* of *diagonals* initially following the two principal diagonals and next subdividing the quadrants in crosswise mode, each time halving them recursively: diagonals of subquadrants, and so on. In case H, adjacent cells are

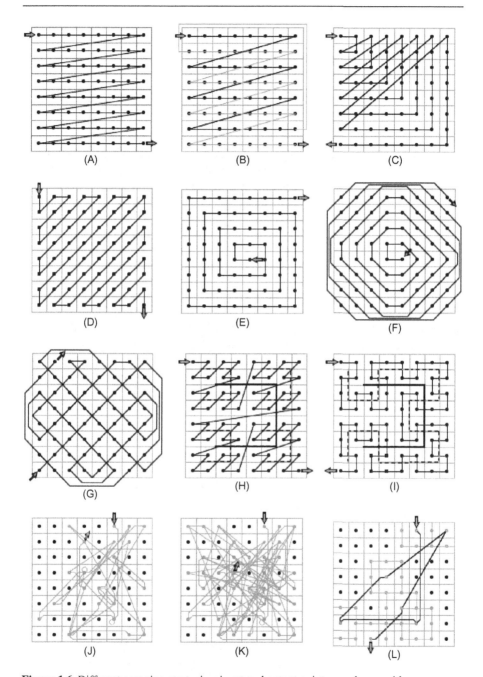

Figure 1.6 Different scanning strategies; input and output points are shown with arrows.

linked by the basic Peano curve (Giuseppe Peano, 1858–1932) that covers recursively the square. Note that the Z-pattern is repeating at progressively larger scales in the same order. Actually, that corresponds to the projection of the known *bin tree* [34] data structure or almost equivalently of the *quadtree* data structure [28], recursively splitting the four quadrants into subquadrants, and so on. The Z-pattern is nothing but the coverage of four neighbors (a, b, c, d) according to the permutation (a, b, c, d); 24 such permutations exist, giving rise to six basic patterns, Z, N, C, U, α, and γ, with their rotated versions, and to as many recursive basic scans [35,42]. In case I, a similar generating process is used, alternating C and U for basic patterns. Resulting curves, a peculiar case of Peano curve of *order 2*, are commonly attributed to David Hilbert (1862–1943) and to Waclaw F. Sierpinski (1882–1969). Note that for cases H and I, hatched lines indicate the sequence of visited quadrants.

The following two cases, J and K, use a *random number generator* to establish the cells to be visited; case J stopped after 32 steps for an 8×8 pixel image. For this instance, with a sample/cells ratio of 0.5, only 21 (about 33% of the total number) cells have been covered, whereas in case K with a ratio of 1 (after 64 steps), 39 cells are covered (about 61% of the total number of cells).

Scan sequences may be generalized to mix deterministic and random strategies. For instance, in [33] a basic regular grid of elements is scanned and a number of randomly chosen neighbors are next visited. Case L inverts the strategies and starts by randomly choosing an element to be visited, and then a deterministic inspection of the local area is performed much in a similar fashion as saccadic eye movements work in natural vision. Attention is the driving force for eye movements and pushes toward *gross centers of gravity* [6]. Next, a detailed analysis is performed via *a searchlight of attention*. In fact, in this last scanning procedure, a first cell is chosen via a random number, and its 8-neighborhood (3×3) is then inspected. Next, another cell is chosen at random, also inspecting its 3×3 neighborhood, and so on. In case L in Figure 1.6, it may be seen that for seven random locations, $7 \times 3 \times 3$ cells would be inspected but, due to the presence of borders, only 37 different cells were effectively considered because 12 were virtual cells, external to the physical image.

Focusing

Focusing may be seen under two different lights: the optical term for *putting into focus* is not of interest here because images are considered always to be in the focal plane of the acquisition device. The second meaning refers to a relevance evaluation of the region within an image, for its subsequent detailed inspection. In fact, from the computational viewpoint, the current region must be quickly analyzed to support the binary decision on whether to continue inspection or leave for another region. The operators for this task must be predefined, considering a finite, reduced set of salient features that generally strongly depend on the application. For instance, typical features are chromaticity, morphology, range, size, and motion, as in domains like robotic vision, industrial inspection, and surveillance.

The focusing process is *goal driven*, and the higher the number of positive alternatives, the higher the computational demand. Yet, humans operate in a different mode from that of computers, as accounted in [5], where the interesting location is found in parallel by the natural visual system, whereas the practical relevance is computed sequentially, location after location.

Tracking

Once an ROI in space, or an event in time, has been detected, the problem is to tie the "attention" to this feature and track it in the image or between successive images. It is worth mentioning that in these cases the attention must be linked to the results of a data analysis; for instance, in a plane figure an x-follower (for x being an edge, a texture, a fixed area, etc.) is a set growing process that will propagate and stop once the condition is satisfied (see *The morphological track* section in Chapter 2). Another case includes a moving object (like a target) to which attention will be coupled, image after image. This coupling may be affected via a correspondence matching between salient features of two consecutive images. In most cases, a prediction about the future position of the moving object is based on the knowledge of the current image followed by an inspection around the expected position (see *Motion via correspondence* section in Chapter 2). A different approach considers a gradient evaluation of the motion analysis, exploiting the *optical flow* technique. In *Motion via local change* section in Chapter 2, motion analysis techniques will be discussed in detail as applied to an image sequence.

Hypothesis Testing

Differently from tracking, with reference to a typical object recognition task, an external pattern model to be matched to the unknown image region is used. During the whole process, there is a continuous interaction between an exploration phase, a computation phase, a new hypothesis generation, and so on. To do this, the *a priori* knowledge of the requested object is used to build both the model and a suitable data structure for the hypothesis-testing mechanism, and then to make them evolve.

There are at least three different approaches to perform this strategy:

- *by means of a pattern tree describing, in a hierarchical structure, the connected components relationships [36,37];*
- *by means of a model feature graph where the main object features and their relationships are represented [38];*
- *by means of production rules within a given grammar where rule satisfaction is checked to test unknown object matching [39].*

All three solutions allow us to easily implement the focus of attention concept granting to sequentialize a complex image task into a number of easily computed steps (see The multiresolution artificial approach section in Chapter 3).

Implementing on the Fly

The last case occurs whenever a person is looking at a picture for the first time; the first goal is to analyze its contents. Typical clues for investigation are critical points on contours, maxima and minima of given functions (gray-level variation, curve features, speed, etc.). The human eye fixation points, when a person is looking at pictures, have been studied [7], and it was shown that for the same figure different humans behave in a similar manner. Some authors [40] have suggested that the extracted information from the scan path approach is also used for storing and recognition purposes. In fact, these can become the building blocks for the hypothesis-test strategy previously described.

Conclusions

In general, an image may be regarded as a rich information source and is gradually becoming the principal communication tool for human−machine−human interaction. This dynamic use of images demands real-time processing involving large amounts of information and, consequently, is computationally intensive. To overcome this difficulty in a way which resembles that of human vision, a computational paradigm that requires at least two different resolution levels has been suggested. In this framework, a set of different activities may be identified like resolution/scale changes and strategies for scanning, focusing, and tracking. Within the recognition task, hypothesis-test strategies must be put forward in order to tackle the real-time constraint. Whenever this is not possible because little information is available about the image content, then coarse on-the-fly strategies must be adopted. A wide technical literature using specific terminology to name all the different processes and algorithms developed for image processing and computer vision can be found in [41].

In all cases, these strategies clearly exploit image transformations. First, transforms are local before spreading over the image. Then multiple decisions occur on the relative and local (both in space and in time) importance of a given intermediate result. As pointed out in this introduction and inspired by human behavior, transformations address the detection of specific points, lines, and regions, and then position (again, in 2D or 3D space and time). Their importance may come from their specific appearance, from interrelations among them, and further from the advance of the analysis toward the completion of an intended action by the system. In Chapter 2, inspired by artists' findings, tools for exhibiting such image features that support attention focusing or some equivalent to a scan path will be presented and discussed from dual point of view: modeling and extracting. Then, a general presentation of usual decision techniques at that context-free level will be detailed independently of their application level (feature selection, feature association, and image scan).

References

[1] D. Marr, Vision: A Computational Investigation into the Human Representation and Processing of Visual Information, W.H. Freeman, New York, NY, 1982.

[2] J. Foley, A. Van Dam, S. Feiner, J. Hughes, Computer Graphics: Principles and Practice, second ed., Addison-Wesley, Reading, MA, 1990.

[3] A. Rosenfeld, Perspectives on vision, in: Proceedings of Seventh ICIAP, Gallipoli, Italy, 1993, pp. 342–347.

[4] D.H. Hubel, Eye, Brain and Vision, Scientific American Books, New York, NY, 1988.

[5] D. Sagi, B. Julesz, 'Where' and 'what' in vision, Science 228 (1985) 1217–1219.

[6] B. Julesz, Early vision, focal attention, and neural nets, in: R.J. Mammone, Y. Zeevi (Eds.), Neural Networks: Theory and Applications, Academic Press, San Diego, CA, 1991, pp. 209–216.

[7] A.L. Yarbus, Eyes Movements and Vision, Plenum Press, New York, NY, 1967.

[8] A. Fiorentini, Neurophysiology of the striate cortex, in: V. Cantoni (Ed.), Human and Machine Vision: Analogies and Divergencies, Plenum Press, New York, NY, 1994, pp. 109–114.

[9] M. Kidode, Image processing machines in Japan, Computer 16 (1) (1983) 68–80.

[10] S. Hanaki, An interactive image processing and analysis system, in: M. Onoe, K. Preston Jr., A. Rosenfeld (Eds.), Real Time—Parallel Computing, Plenum Press, New York, NY, 1981, pp. 219–226.

[11] S. Levialdi, A. Pirri, V. Franchina, An image acquisition device for minicomputers, Comput. Graph. Image Process. 8 (1978) 113–120.

[12] R.L. Grimsdale, J.M. Bullingham, Character recognition by digital computer using a special flying-spot scanner, Comput. J. 4 (1961) 129–136.

[13] H. Gelernter, Data collection and reduction for nuclear particle trace detectors, in: F.L. Alt, M. Rubinoff (Eds.), Advances in Computers, Vol. 6, Academic Press, New York, NY, 1965, pp. 229–296.

[14] D. Rutovitz, Automatic chromosome analysis, Br. Med. Bull. 24 (1968) 260–267.

[15] S. Castan, Image enhancement and restoration, in: J.C. Simon, A. Rosenfeld (Eds.), Digital Image Processing and Analysis, Noordhoff, Leyden, The Netherlands, 1977, pp. 47–61.

[16] B. Zavidovique, P. Fiorini, Control view to vision architectures, in: V. Cantoni (Ed.), Human and Machine Vision: Analogies and Divergencies, Plenum Press, New York, NY, 1994, pp. 13–56.

[17] R. Bajcsy, Active perception, Proc. IEEE 76 (8) (1988) 996–1005.

[18] B.Y. Zavidovique, First steps of robotic perception: the turning point of the 1990's, Proc. IEEE 90 (7) (2002) 1094–1112.

[19] V. Cantoni, S. Levialdi, Matching the task to a computer architecture, Comput. Vis. Graph. Image Process. 22 (1983) 301–309.

[20] P.J. Burt, Smart sensing within a pyramid vision machine, Proc. IEEE 76 (8) (1988) 1006–1015.

[21] P.J. Burt, P. Anandan, K.J. Hanna, An electronic front-end processor for active vision, in: SPIE Conference on Intelligent Robotics, 1992.

[22] B.Y. Zavidovique, T.M. Bernard, Generic functions for on-chip vision, in: Proceedings of Eleventh ICPR, The Hague, The Netherlands, 1992, pp. 1–10.

[23] I.E. Sutherland, Sketchpad: A Man-Machine Graphical Communicating System, Spartan Books, Baltimore, MD, 1963. SJCC.

[24] A.N. Badre, Methodological Issues for Interface Design: A User-Centered Approach. International Report, SI/SD−93/01, Computer Science Department, Sapienza Rome University, 1993.

[25] S.K. Chang, T. Ichikawa, R. Korfhage, S. Levialdi, Ten years of visual language research, in: Proceedings of IEEE Symposium on Visual Languages, St. Louis, MI, 1994.

[26] M.A. Fischler, O. Firschein, The Eyes, the Brain and the Computer, Addison-Wesley, Reading, MA, 1987.

[27] V. Cantoni, Human and Machine Vision: Analogies and Divergences, Plenum Press, New York, NY, 1994.

[28] H. Samet, Foundations of Multidimensional and Metric Data Structures, Morgan-Kaufmann, San Francisco, CA, 2006.

[29] V. Cantoni, S. Levialdi, Pyramidal Systems for Computer Vision, NATO ARW, Springer-Verlag, Heidelberg, 1986.

[30] V. Cantoni, M. Ferretti, Pyramidal Architectures for Computer Vision, Plenum Press, New York, NY, 1994.

[31] M. Bolduc, G. Sela, M. Levine, Fast computation of multiscale symmetry in foveated images, in: CAMP '95, IEEE Computer Society Press, Como, Italy, 1995, pp. 2−11.

[32] G. Van der Wal, M. Hansen, M. Piacentino, The Acadia vision processor, in: CAMP 2000, IEEE Computer Society Press, Padova, Italy, 2000, pp. 31−40.

[33] Y. Tan, H. Freeman, I. Gertner, 1993, Foveation Scanning Strategies Applied to Active Vision, private communication.

[34] A. Merigot, B. Zavidovique, F. Devos, SPHINX, a pyramidal approach to parallel image processing, in: Proceedings of IEEE Workshop on CAPAIDM, Miami, FL, 1985, pp. 107−111.

[35] B. Zavidovique, G. Seetharaman, Z-Trees and Peano Raster for scan adaptive image processing, Int. J. Pure Appl. Math. 38 (1) (2007) 123−151.

[36] P.J. Burt, Attention mechanisms for vision in a dynamic world, in: Proceedings of Eleventh ICPR, Rome, Italy, 1988, pp. 977−987.

[37] P.J. Burt, Smart sensing in machine vision, in: H. Freeman (Ed.), Machine Vision: Algorithms, Architectures and Systems, Academic Press, San Diego, CA, 1988, pp. 1−30.

[38] C.R. Dyer, Multiscale image understanding, in: L. Uhr (Ed.), Parallel Computer Vision, Academic Press, Orlando, FL, 1987, pp. 171−213.

[39] V. Cantoni, L. Cinque, C. Guerra, S. Levialdi, L. Lombardi, 2D object recognition by multiscale tree matching, Pattern Recognit. 31 (10) (1998) 1443−1454.

[40] D. Noton, L. Stark, Eyes movements and visual perception, Sci. Am. 224 (6) (1971) 34−43.

[41] R.M. Haralick, L.G. Shapiro, Glossary of computer vision terms, Pattern Recognit. 24 (1) (1991) 69−93.

[42] H.C. Kennedy, Selected Works of Giuseppe Peano, Allen & Unwin, London, 1973.

2 Visual Cues

The Human Headway

Within natural vision, it can be easily seen from the paintings of the Renaissance (first, by Giotto; next, by Masaccio; and, more technically, by Leon Battista Alberti) that optical laws including lighting, shading, and perspective were carefully followed.

As an example, a fragment of a painting representing *The Holy Marriage* by Raffaello Sanzio is shown in Figure 2.1. In the sequel, sample details of 3D cues are evidenced as specific features deployed by Raffaello to render the environment.

Overlapping objects: Overlapping objects is an old principle that uses occlusion to establish which objects are nearer to the observer. In the example, it is quite evident that the front-robed man is in front of the black-dressed one, and both are in front of the stairs. As a rule, the occluding object is always in front of the occluded object(s).

Quantized scenes: The natural scenario is represented by a small number of "theatrical curtains" that, in decreasing order of crispness and detail, together with an increasing intensity of the blue-sky component, create the perception of depth. In this example, three scenes are shown. As a rule, the sharpest scene is the closest to the observer.

Perspective geometry: Knowledge of the vanishing point and the laws of perspective geometry allow introducing a metric for both representing and perceiving dimensions, including depth. Once the position of the vanishing point is established and the relative sizes of the two doors are given, one may estimate their distance, which, in this case, corresponds to the building dimension. As a rule, the greater the difference of the sizes, the larger is the object depth.

3C Vision. DOI: 10.1016/B978-0-12-385220-5.00002-4

Depth from shading: If the light source position is known or may be easily assessed, when a depicted object is shadowed by another one, it is positioned behind with respect to the light source. Furthermore, shade may be used to delineate shape and attitude of the surface; arches and columns in this example are rendered by variations in the color saturation. As a rule, less shadowed parts are closer to the light source.

Multipresence: Humans appear in different picture locations. When an item appears on different depth planes within a scene and the natural item size is known, a metric-based perspective is introduced. As a rule, different sizes of the same item correspond to the values of different depths.

Depth from textured background: At least two cues based on texture can be exploited to represent depth from texture. The first one stems from the textural element shape (*the texton*) gradient (the staircase step size diminishes with the observer's distance). The second one directly exploits the item position to indicate the relative distance on the textured plane (the two groups of characters are placed on two texture gradient values corresponding to different distances).

The above six 3D cues are already complex even though basic. To capture them, Raffaello honored the optical laws based on his careful observations. Note that the geometric laws, such as perspective or occlusion, were explicit at his time, but colorimetric laws, such as filtering by the thicker or thinner air slice, were not.

Figure 2.1 *The Holy Marriage* (fragment) by Raffaello Sanzio, 1520, Brera Painting Museum, Milan (Italy).

Many physics laws are involved in the creation process; they are grouped into three *tracks*: photometric, geometrical—morphological, and spatial.

Image Computer-Processing Tracks

Natural forms are generally too complex to be automatically video captured as a whole. To achieve image interpretation by knowing physical laws, we must proceed backward from stimuli to the generating sources. This process is, in fact, a reverting one: intermediate models are required with a reduced number of parameters so as to support progressive representations that can be computed on.

Note that the representation problem is considered central to any intelligent activity.

Before tackling the problem of accessing data not explicitly coded, starting with the 3D extension of a 2D image, computer systems must have an adequate data representation. Adequacy has two meanings here:

- For humans, to figure out the result quality in order to design extraction algorithms: this is the reverse process of Raffaello's creation.
- For computers to handle data and climb up the semantic scale. For instance, a contour detection will likely provide a set of pixels through a row scan, whereas the result— ideally the outline of an object—would rather be described as a continuous line in view of its recognition.

The initial models will logically be of the same nature as the image itself. In reference to computers, an image is a function $g = I(I, j)$, relating intensity I to 2D space (i, j) after projections of a scene from the real world onto the photosensor. First, lighting conditions and related constraints (long distance, single source, homogeneous material, etc.) will be assumed to introduce the image formation and subsequent parameters. Then, photometric, geometrical—morphological, and spatial parameters (referred to as the "3D cube") will be presented, making up the basic level of image description; these are exactly the tracks defined earlier.

The Photometric Track

During the Renaissance period, painters started to handle perspective views of the scenes they depicted, as well as using light and shade to denote the 3D nature of physical objects. In Figure 2.2, a sketch is shown in which the three dimensions of a statue are rendered on a flat sheet with a single color by means of shading with different values of brown. In this case, the image synthesis by the human artist, long before computer specialists, anticipates the strategy for image analysis based on photometrical evaluation. The question here is how to formalize such process to provide computers with a capability of similar capture.

Local Rendering

The photometric approach introduced in [1,2] may be seen as a simple and powerful method for *local rendering*. To analyze isolated objects in images, it is

Figure 2.2 Male nude from Michelangelo Buonarroti (1528), showing that the 3D attitude is rendered by local variations of ochre chromatic intensity.

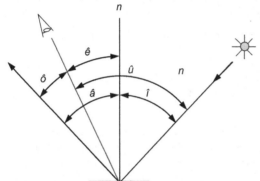

Figure 2.3 Optical geometry of the light-source/eye-receiver system. The beam impinges on the surface from a single light source (sun icon) and is then reflected with an equal angle. Notation: n is the normal to the surface at the incidence point, $\hat{\imath}$ corresponds to the incidence angle, $\hat{o}$ is the mirrored emergence angle, $\hat{u}$ is the phase angle, and $\hat{e}$ is the emergence angle.

considered that the system geometry is known. It consists more specifically of the positions of the light sources versus the acquisition device, as well as the surface physical characteristics of the involved material. In fact, as a starting point, a single point-wise illumination source operates, and the distance of the observer from the object is much larger than the object size, so that an orthographic geometry is enough instead of the projective one. To characterize the object morphology, it is sufficient to consider the local normal vector to the surface on each object point. Under these conditions, for a small patch of the object the full geometrical parameters are those given in Figure 2.3, with the angles $\hat{\imath}$, $\hat{e}$, $\hat{u}$, and $\hat{o}$ as indicated.

From a physical point of view, the light intensity reflected from the object's surface is a function of the material optical properties, of the microscopic structure of the surface, and of the electromagnetic features of the incident light. For several materials, most of these properties may be ignored and the reflectance essentially depends on the system geometry.

Let the surface reflectivity Φ be the ratio between the radiance L (radiation flux emerging from the surface per solid angle and projected area) and the irradiance E (incident flux on the surface per solid angle). Under the above assumptions, Φ only depends on angles $\hat{\imath}$, $\hat{o}$, and $\hat{u}$, making it possible to characterize the materials based on the dependence of Φ from these three angles [3,4].

A Reflectivity Model

The phenomenological analysis of the material reflectivity allows us to consider three different material models: a perfect diffuser, a mirrorlike, and an intermediate material.

In the first case, the reflected light quantity is the same in all directions so being independent from the position of the viewer. The reflectivity only depends on the incident angle $\hat{\imath}$ according to the cosine law (Lambert's law, Figure 2.4A). Analytically, the model may be described as follows:

$$\Phi = \begin{cases} \cos \hat{\imath} & -\dfrac{\pi}{2} \leq \hat{\imath} \leq \dfrac{\pi}{2} \\ 0 & \text{elsewhere} \end{cases} \tag{2.1}$$

Mirrorlike materials mainly reflect along a direction forming, with the normal n, an angle equal to $-\hat{\imath}$: in this case, the reflectivity depends on the position of the viewer with respect to the light beam emergent direction, that is, on the angle $\hat{o}$ (Figure 2.4B). Analytically, the model may be written as follows:

$$\Phi = \begin{cases} \cos^m \hat{o} & -\dfrac{\pi}{2} \leq \hat{o} \leq \dfrac{\pi}{2} \\ 0 & \text{elsewhere} \end{cases} \tag{2.2}$$

where m is the index of *material specularity*, which is a measure of its mirrorlike quality.

Following [1], the third case—the composite one—is a linear combination of the first two models, analytically:

$$\Phi = a \cos \hat{\imath} + b \cos^m \hat{o} + c \tag{2.3}$$

where a is the amount of incident light diffused according to a Lambertian model (isotropic) independent from the receiver's position; b is the amount of incident light specularly reflected by the object, which depends on the phase angle, and m being the exponential specular reflection coefficient; finally, c accounts for the background illumination.

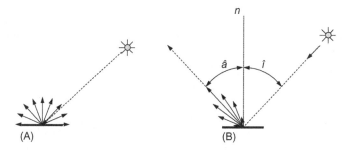

(A)   (B)

Figure 2.4 Two basic reflectivity models: (A) Lambertian and (B) specular.

Reflectivity Maps

For a given physical geometry of the "light source versus receiver" scenario, a particularly convenient way to represent the surface radiance as a function of its orientation is the *reflectance map* [5,6].

A three-dimensional Cartesian reference system is considered, where the optical axis of the acquisition system (the receiver) coincides with the Z-axis. Analytically, the surface described by the function $z = f(x, y)$ has, for every point (x, y), the following normal vector: $(\partial z/\partial x, \partial z/\partial y, -1)^t$. If $p = \partial z/\partial x$ and $q = \partial z/\partial y$, there is a one-to-one correspondence between the plane p, q (called gradient plane), and the normal directions to the surface. According to the schema described in the previous section, the surface radiance, proportional to the object reflectivity, may be determined by the surface normal direction, so that it can be associated univocally to p and q.

The surface reflection map is defined as a function $R(p, q)$ proportional to the image intensity. It can be estimated once the full geometry of the scene and the optical material characteristics are known. The three angles $\hat{\imath}$, $\hat{u}$, and $\hat{e}$ may be computed with the following formulas:

$$\cos \hat{\imath} = \frac{1 + pp_s + qq_s}{\sqrt{1+p^2+q^2}\sqrt{1+p_s^2+q_s^2}} \tag{2.4}$$

$$\cos \hat{e} = \frac{1}{\sqrt{1+p^2+q^2}} \tag{2.5}$$

$$\cos \hat{u} = \frac{1}{\sqrt{1+p_s^2+q_s^2}} \tag{2.6}$$

where $(p_s, q_s, -1)$ provides the light source direction. Based on Eqns (2.1)–(2.3), it is now possible to build the reflectance map. For instance, for the Lambertian reflectivity model, the following formula holds:

$$L(p,q) = \begin{cases} \rho \cos \hat{\imath} & -\frac{\pi}{2} \le \hat{\imath} \le \frac{\pi}{2} \\ 0 & \text{elsewhere} \end{cases} = \begin{cases} \rho \dfrac{1+pp_s+qq_s}{\sqrt{1+p^2+q^2}\sqrt{1+p_s^2+q_s^2}} & -\frac{\pi}{2} \le \hat{\imath} \le \frac{\pi}{2} \\ 0 & \text{elsewhere} \end{cases} \tag{2.7}$$

where ρ is the ratio coefficient between radiance intensity L and surface reflectivity Φ.

Figure 2.5A−C shows the reflectance map where the receiver direction coincides with the Z-axis, respectively, for cases with Lambertian, specular, and composite models. In this third case, the first two models are equally combined and without background diffusion.

Figure 2.6A and B shows the reflectivity map for cases in which the position of the light source is not aligned with the receiver's position. More specifically, in Figure 2.6A, a Lambertian model, the receiver is on the Z-axis and the light source is along the octant's bisector. The reflectivity map is not radially symmetric anymore; isoluminance loci are *conics*, which turn around the point of maximum reflectivity. The reflectivity gradient is sharper and strongly anisotropic, and its

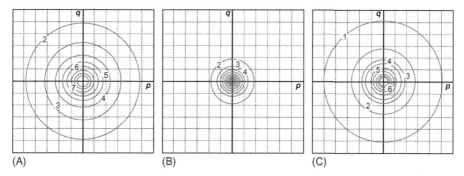

(A)   (B)   (C)

Figure 2.5 (A) Reflectivity map for a Lambertian case having both camera and light source coincident with the Z-axis; eight isoluminance circles with their corresponding ratios are displayed. (B) Reflectivity map for a specular model having both camera and light source coincident with the Z-axis; the specularity index m is 3, nine isoluminance circles with their correspondent ratios are displayed. In this situation, a concentration of isoluminance circles is obtained around the central mirror emergent angle; note that the innermost circle corresponds to $\Phi = 0.9$. (C) Reflectivity map for an intermediate model with $a = b = 0.5$ and $c = 0$, having both camera and light source coincident with the Z-axis; the index of specularity $m = 3$, nine isoluminance circles with their correspondent ratios are displayed. The monotone decrease of luminance is the arithmetical average of the previous two luminance distributions.

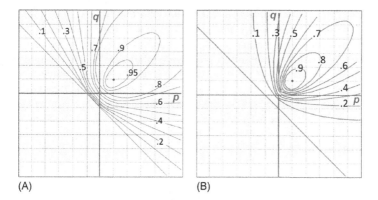

(A)   (B)

Figure 2.6 (A) Reflectivity map for a Lambertian model, having the camera on the Z-axis (0, 0, −1) and the light source positioned at (1, 1, −1). The maximum reflectivity is along the light source direction. The isoluminance patterns are quadrics labeled with their corresponding ratios. More specifically, the incident light source corresponds to the bisector of the first octant in 3D space. (B) Reflectivity map for a specular model, having the camera coincident with the Z-axis (0, 0, −1) and the light source positioned at (1, 1, −1). In this case, the maximum reflectivity is along the light source direction as well. The isoluminance patterns are quadrics labeled with their corresponding ratios. Note that the incident light source corresponds to the bisector of the first octant in 3D space. The specularity index is $m = 3$, nine isoluminance quadrics with their corresponding ratios are displayed. In this situation a concentration of isoluminance quadrics is obtained around the central mirror emergency angle.

maximum and minimum values occur on the straight line $p = q$. Figure 2.6B shows the reflectivity map for a specular model with the same position for light source and receiver. The reflectivity gradient is higher than in the previous case, having the same structure.

Photometric Analysis

Once the geometry of the system as well as the physical characteristics of the object are known, the reflectance map may provide, for each gray level along the surface, all the compatible orientations (p, q, -1) of the elementary facets. If the light source position changes, the gray level will also change, thereby obtaining another locus of possible facet orientations having at most four common intersection points with the previous locus.

As an example of a Lambertian object surface, consider Figure 2.7 where initially the light source is positioned on point 1 (coordinates 1, 1, -1). It may be supposed that for a given pixel (x, y) belonging to the object, the detected gray-level value will correspond to a reflectivity of 0.95, which is represented in Figure 2.7 by the locus labeled a. The second position of the light source coincides with the receiver's position and is indicated with point 2 (coordinates 0, 0, -1), having a reflectance value of 0.3 on the considered pixel (x, y): the corresponding locus is a circle labeled b. Now two real intersection points A and B (coordinates 2, 2.4, -1 and 2.4, 2, -1, respectively) occur. Finally, the light source is further moved to position point 3 (coordinates -1, 1, -1), producing a reflectance value 0.1 on the considered pixel, thereby obtaining the locus c intersecting the previous loci a in B and C, and b in B and D. Only one common point B is among the three loci.

This process may be implemented in a very effective way. Reflectance maps can be built offline once the system geometry and the physical features of the object's surface are known (using Eqns (2.3)–(2.6)). Given three gray-level values, the facet orientation can be obtained directly through a look-up table containing the attitudes corresponding to those reflectance values. A general strategy is presented in [7], where the first considered couple of loci corresponds to the highest reflectance values (and therefore to a high gradient in the reflectance map, so providing a sharper location), while the third locus, having the lowest reflectance, is used to select one of the two attitude candidates. Even if this last locus would be less precise in selecting exact values of p and q, their accurate value was already obtained by the previous precise intersections.

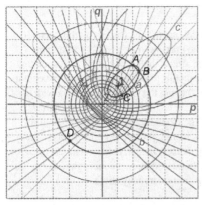

Figure 2.7 Overlapped isoluminance patterns for the Lambertian model, with three different positions of the light source used for determining the attitude of an object's facet.

In *The morphological track* section, how to find the 3D attitude of an object's surface will be discussed. Actually, there are alternative methods to the inverse use of the reflectivity map; one of the most effective is stereovision based on two separate points of view. In stereovision, singular points must be defined and detected in both images. This process is known as the *correspondence problem*, an *ill-posed* problem too [8]. It is not always possible to find the same points on both images because they come from two different viewing points; furthermore, correspondences require intensive computing, thereby making this process a cumbersome one. In the photometric approach, such restrictions do not hold because only one viewpoint is considered. As this approach is based on point-wise processing, it is computationally fast and often provides an adequate approximation. However, a controlled illumination environment is required to activate different light sources. Other strategies are to work with specific illumination patterns, as in automatic inspection systems (typically using structured light) or applying shape-from-shading techniques [9,10], which are not point dependent. Eventually, note that reflectivity maps would hold inside homogeneous regions of the image, whereas singular points founding stereo reconstruction lie instead on their frontiers.

Image Synthesis Following the Phong's Model

Another more interactive way to check the validity of the above analysis consists in image synthesis to be tested for realism by humans. An example of a synthetic image is displayed in Figure 2.8.

In the local approach, each object of the scene is rendered independently from the others; no mutual interactions are considered. It has the advantage of being straightforward; it is easily implemented (with common parallelism at object level) but is severely limited because reflection, shadowing, and transparent and translucent refractions among objects and complex light sources are not considered.

Global Rendering

By the late 1960s, a global rendering approach had been introduced with the *ray tracing* technique [11], but the accurate simulation of reflection, shadowing, and

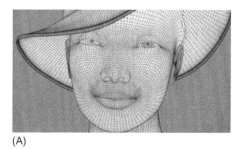

(A)   (B)

Figure 2.8 The "Digital Marlene," created as an experimental project for the benefit of Virtual Celebrity Productions, which is a digital cloning studio. In (A), the "wire frame" model of the face attitude is depicted and in (B), the subsequent achieved rendering.

refraction was achieved only in the 1980s [12]. This technique analyzes the light ray paths and models their interaction with the scene: when a ray intersects an object, it sends off secondary rays, following the laws of reflection, refraction, and transmission that determine the shadows. Obviously, this method is more time consuming than the local one; nevertheless, its most important weakness remains not accounting for diffuse reflections (color bleeding).

Another method developed in the 1980s [13] is called *radiosity*. In this method, spatially extended light sources with arbitrary shapes are considered, and the luminance model incorporates diffused interreflections (glossiness) among objects in the scene.

The Ray Tracing Approach

A first implementation of this approach followed the physics: the light source *forwards* the rays that can be traced through potentially many scene interactions. Most rays will never even get close to the eye: the implementation is thus very inefficient because it computes many useless paths of rays (Figure 2.9A). Ultimately it is more efficient to trace the ray *backward,* from the eye, through every point on the screen (Figure 2.9B). This is indirectly physically based and cannot properly model diffuse reflections and all other changes in light intensity, or color, due to refractions and nonspecular reflections. Originating from the eye, the algorithm computes only visible rays—one per pixel— and achieves an efficient simulation on the average, finally obtaining realistic images.

From the computational viewpoint, despite many suggested optimized implementations, ray tracing is obviously still very expensive compared to local rendering. A ray sent from the eye to the scene through the image plane (Figure 2.10) may intersect an object; in this case, secondary rays are sent out, and three different lighting models ensue:

- *Transmission*: The secondary ray is sent in the direction of refraction, following Descartes' law.
- *Reflection*: The secondary ray is sent in the direction of reflection, and the Phong model is applied.

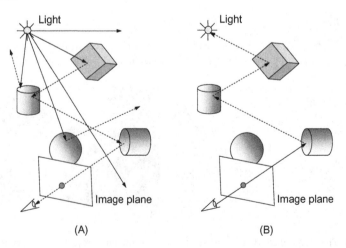

(A)   (B)

Figure 2.9 The two basic schemes of forward and backward ray tracing in (A) and (B), respectively.

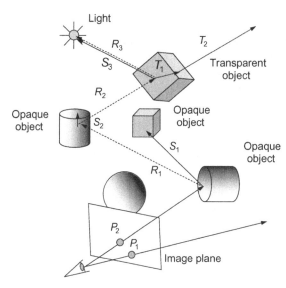

Figure 2.10 A background pixel corresponding to the ray P_1 and a pixel representing an object (ray P_2). The secondary rays triggered by the primary ray P_2, according to the three models: transmission (T_1 and T_2), reflection (R_1, R_2, and R_3), and tentative shadowing (S_1, S_2: true shadows, and S_3).

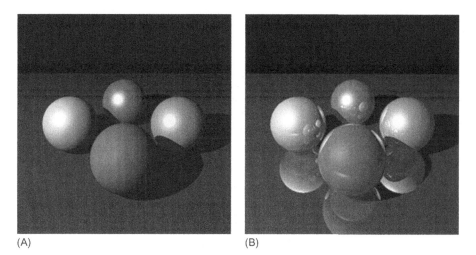

(A)   (B)

Figure 2.11 Synthesized images created by David Derman (from Mani Thomas): (A) following Phong's model and with shadows; (B) with internal iterative reflections (three bounces).

- *Shadowing*: The secondary ray is sent toward a light source. If intercepted by an object, the point is shadowed; if it reaches the source, the ray is not considered anymore.

If the ray does not intersect any object, the pixel is set to the background color.

Each new intersection spans secondary rays recursively, until the ray does not intersect any object or until a predefined maximum intersection depth (or minimum light value) is reached. A practical example may be seen on Figure 2.11.

The Radiosity Approach

The *radiosity* method has been developed to model the diffuse—diffuse interactions, thereby gaining a more realistic visualization of surfaces.

The diffused surfaces scatter light in all directions (i.e., in a Lambertian way), so objects appear the same independently from the direction from which they are looked at. Thus a scene is divided into *patches*—small flat polygons. The goal is to measure energies emitted from and reflected to each patch.

The radiosity B_i of patch i is given by:

$$B_i = E_i + \rho_i \sum_{j=1}^{n} B_j F_{ij} \tag{2.8}$$

where E_i represents the energy emitted by patch i; ρ_i, the reflectivity parameter of patch i; and $\sum_{j=1}^{n} B_j F_{ij}$, the energy reflected to patch i from the n patches j around it, depending on the form factors F_{ij}.

A scene with n patches follows a system of n equations for which the solution yields the radiosity of each patch.

The form factor represents the fraction of light that reaches patch i from patch j. It depends on the distance and orientation of the two patches (Figure 2.12). Between differential areas, the form factor is given by:

$$F \, dA_i \, dA_j = \frac{\cos \varphi_i \cos \varphi_j}{\pi |r|^2} \tag{2.9}$$

where $dA_i \, dA_j$ are the differential areas of surface i, j; r is the vector from dA_i to dA_j; φ_i is the angle between the normal N_i and r; and φ_j is the angle between the normal N_j and r. The overall factor F_{ij} between patches i and j is calculated by integrating:

$$F_{ij} = \frac{1}{A_j} \int_{A_i} \int_{A_j} \frac{\cos \varphi_i \cos \varphi_j}{\pi |r|^2} \, dA_i \, dA_j \tag{2.10}$$

Scenes may contain thousands of patches, consequently producing heavy computation loads. Nevertheless, some artifacts can be introduced, for example, aliasing and shiny surfaces not well synthesized.

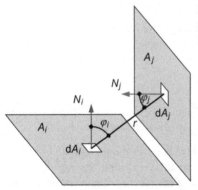

Figure 2.12 The geometric relationship between pairs of patches to determine the value of the form factor F_{ij}.

(A)

(B)

Figure 2.13 A synthetic scene taken from the 3D Art Gallery of Hildur Kolbrun Andresdottir. The realism of (A) profits from all the sophisticated modern techniques. However, (B), a close-up on the rear right of the meeting room, appears less natural due to the exaggerated translucency of the lady.

Figure 2.13 shows an image synthesis with the most recent lighting techniques. In Figure 2.13A, an open space office is adequately rendered, while Figure 2.13 shows artifacts, particularly visible on the human figure (it looks diffused and without relief). Figure 2.14 shows the results obtained for a single scene of the lighting models: (a) flat and unreal, Phong's model; (b) more realistic but incomplete ray tracing; and (c) fully fledged (the corner and the window depth) radiosity.

Conclusion

By looking at the painting by Van Eyck (Figure 2.15), it is easily seen how the models described earlier lack realism. In order to mimic the magic eye of the artist by an automatic procedure, reproducing realistic images of natural subjects may require undesirable computational complexity. Once again, note that photometric laws were not known at the time, and painters can be suspected of producing mere snapshots—in other words, following optical laws even if they ignore them.

In most common situations, artificial systems do not need to understand whether a given object material is closer to a mirror than to some cloth, or where the lighting

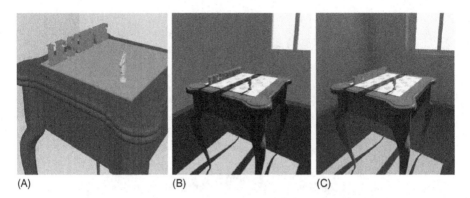

(A)   (B)   (C)

Figure 2.14 Comparative results of scene synthesis by Ledah Casburn: (A) with the Phong model; (B) with the backward ray tracing technique; and (C) with the radiosity technique.

(A)   (C)

Figure 2.15 (A) *The Betrothal of the Arnolfini* by Jan Van Eyck, 1434, National Gallery, London, (B) underlying the perfect rendering of the chandelier, and (C) the realistic image of the mirror content.

of an obstacle comes from. However, for a car to remain on track in a rainy day, it might become crucial to understand reflections (a puddle or black ice on the road). For most flying objects, whatever the weather, understanding the positions of the main light sources will certainly be helpful in keeping to the course and completing the 3D description of the environment (e.g., between sea or snow and sky).

To communicate through images, it is necessary to consider not only the lighting conditions described, but also other more elaborate *features* like morphology, attitude, context, and dynamics.

Chromatic Clues

For almost a century now, we have known that the animal retina is made of neurons that translate light properties into electric signals to the brain. In humans, two types of neurons are present: rods and cones.

- *Rods* number about 100–130 million for each eye, while optic nerve fibers are about 1 million. Note that the further from the retina center (fovea), the stronger the light response due to a cumulative response of a rod cluster.
- *Cones* are about 1–2 million per basic color—red, green, and blue. In the fovea, each cone has a separate connection to the brain; the fovea covers a 1° solid angle and mainly includes cones, which decrease toward the retina periphery. Cones are receptive to given wavelengths; in other words, they act as selective filters (around λ of 0.4 µm, 0.5 µm, and 0.8 µm for blue, green, and red, respectively) (Figure 2.16). They operate above a given intensity threshold (no color in the dark).

Note that two close sets of wavelengths, on each side of the so-called visible domain (which ranges from 0.38 µm to 0.78 µm on average), can influence an accurate response: the infrared and the ultraviolet rays. For instance, a common solid-state camera with a silicon-based sensor perceives farther in the infrared than most human eyes, up to 1.1 µm due to the forbidden gap width. More generally, advances in technology enable visual sensors to cover almost an unlimited range in the electromagnetic wavelength spectrum, from radio waves used for imagery in astronomy (λ about 300 m) to γ-cameras in medical applications (λ around 3×10^{-9} m).

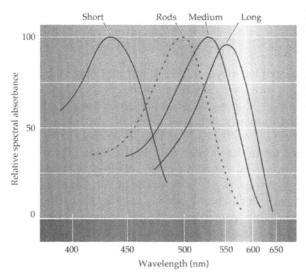

Figure 2.16 Representation of the relative spectrum absorbance as a function of wavelength.
Source: From Neuroscience, Third Edition, © 2004, Sinauer Associates, Inc.

Acoustic images should not be forgotten either, although generated by a different kind of vibration (mechanical). They cover up to the gigahertz in the case of acoustic microscopy, passing through more conventional applications as sonar in water, and ultrasound scans and color ecography in medicine.

In order to improve the image presentation, be it a painting, a photograph, a film, or an image on an electronic screen, it might be useful to fully understand the physiology of human vision. Mimicking animal vision can also help in designing robot vision. For such reasons, mostly economic in the end, the models of color perception are still based on *primary colors*, red, green, blue (RGB). Actually, these colors are primary when considering natural light. But it has been known for a long time that color mixing works differently when considering a camera (receiver) or a TV set (emitter): this leads to the triplet of secondary colors—cyan, magenta, yellow (CMY)—which forms a basis for pigments.

Human perception is basically a multispectral phenomenon, but *color* refers right away to understanding. This is one reason why color adds expressiveness to images, enriching human experience and supporting communication of complex concepts. The machine perception first retains only the underlying physics, that is, the combination of several wavelengths, to the exclusion of any semantics. Along that line, a variety of sensors have been developed to cover the widest frequency range. From the physical point of view, objects in a scene act as filters that absorb wavelengths more or less selectively while re-emitting others that hit sensors or other objects. Black bodies absorb them all, while transparent ones convey them all; a green object, for instance, absorbs red and blue ray components.

The following formulas hold, where the symbol " $+$ " stands for the addition of colors (a linear model is considered here):

$$C = G + B \quad M = B + R \quad Y = R + G$$
$$C + R = M + G = Y + B = \text{White} \tag{2.11}$$

Color Representation

After the above rather anthropomorphic introduction, the first modeling problem is to separate the light intensity (or gray-level variable) from the chromatic ones. The experimentally designed color triangle (Figure 2.17) represents the white color in the center, and the locus of monochromatic colors on the border. It is then natural to use a polar coordinate system, where *Hue* (first chromatic variable) is given by the angle between a color p and the ray connecting the corner 700 nm. The second chromatic variable is *Saturation*, that is, the ratio wp/wp', where p' represents the pure color perceived for that given wavelength. In those conditions, the white center is actually gray, a function of the light intensity during measurements. The gray scale (*Intensity*) cannot be other than perpendicular to the triangle plane. This representation (see Figure 2.18), originated from physiological experiments, gave rise to a simple linear model and formulas to convert the R,G,B framework into the H,S,I one.

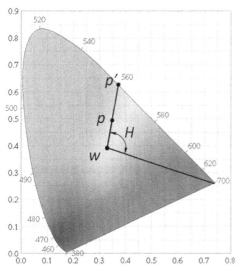

Figure 2.17 The CIE 1931 color space chromaticity diagram. The outer boundary is the locus of monochromatic colors, with wavelengths shown in nanometers. This diagram displays the maximally saturated bright colors that can be produced by a computer monitor or television set. (For interpretation of the references to color in this figure legend, the reader is referred to the web version of this book.)

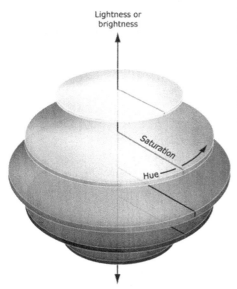

Figure 2.18 A three-dimensional representation of color where the vertical axis corresponds to brightness, the radial axis to saturation, and the longitude axis to hue. (For interpretation of the references to color in this figure legend, the reader is referred to the web version of this book.) *Source*: From Neuroscience, Third Edition, © 2004, Sinauer Associates, Inc.

To normalize the intensity, all variables are first divided by the sum R + G + B, leading to the coordinates r, g, b in a unit cube [e.g., $r = R/(R + G + B)$].

Any color is represented as a point on the maximal triangle ($r + g + b = 1$), and any intensity would be along the diagonal of the cube that links *black* with *white* ($R = G = B$) (Figure 2.19A and B).

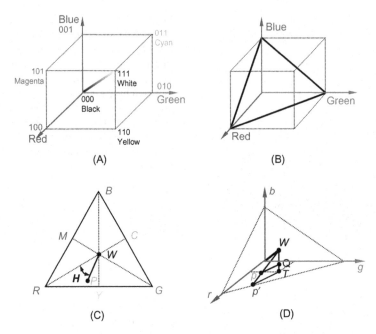

Figure 2.19 (A) The unity color cube and (B) the maximal color triangle. (C) The triangle in its plane maximal color triangle. (D) The triangle in the cube. (For interpretation of the references to color in this figure legend, the reader is referred to the web version of this book.)

The *I*ntensity is measured by the distance to the *black*.
$I = (R + G + B)/3$, possibly normalized for $I_{\max}$ equal to 1.
The *H*ue, which is evaluated by an angle, is given by its cosine (Figure 2.19C):

$$\cos H = \frac{\overrightarrow{WR} \bullet \overrightarrow{WP}}{|\overrightarrow{WR}||\overrightarrow{WP}|} \quad \text{with} \begin{cases} W = \dfrac{1}{3}, \dfrac{1}{3}, \dfrac{1}{3} \\ R = 1, 0, 0 \\ P = r, g, b \end{cases} \tag{2.12}$$

$$\overrightarrow{WR} \bullet \overrightarrow{WP} = \frac{2}{3}\left(r - \frac{1}{3}\right) - \frac{1}{3}\left(g - \frac{1}{3}\right) - \frac{1}{3}\left(b - \frac{1}{3}\right) = \frac{2R - G - B}{3(R + G + B)} \tag{2.13}$$

Working in the plane of the maximal triangle:

$$\cos H = \frac{\frac{1}{2}[(R - G) + (R - B)]}{\sqrt{(R - G)^2 + (R - B)(G - B)}} \tag{2.14}$$

The *Saturation* is obtained by the Thales' theorem (Figure 2.19D):
T: projection of W in the plane (r, g), from which $T = (1/3, 1/3, 0)$
Q: projection of P on WT, from which $Q = (1/3, 1/3, b)$

$$S = \frac{WP}{WP'} = \frac{WQ}{WT} = \frac{WT - QT}{WT} = \frac{1/3 - b}{1/3} \tag{2.15}$$

If we note that such a formulation of the saturation refers to the point of the nearest triangle edge (then corresponding to a maximal ratio), a formula valid in all three cases will put forward the sector of min (R,G,B), leading to:

$$S = 1 - \frac{3 \min(R, G, B)}{R + G + B} \tag{2.16}$$

It appears from the above physical model that color is a property of primitive image features (e.g., morphological), generalizing intensity more than a feature in itself. Because a neuron or pixel population ranges in the millions of individuals where frequencies of occurrence may acquire meanings, first representations are based on statistics.

For machines to achieve color interpretation, some support extra clues are necessary as morphological, spatial, and dynamic ones. Note that the human brain reacts to color and color combinations independently from any prior shape and can even directly trigger actions, as when understanding the time or weather from a reddish or dull sky, serving or adapting to a given dominant color or to a given color couple, and so on.

Intensity Redistribution and Rendering

An image histogram has in the abscissa the pixel gray (or color) value, whereas the ordinate plots the number of occurrences of such value. Such histogram may be manipulated so as to obtain a sharper image, highlight some chromatic distributions, correct over or underexposed images, optimize the contrast distribution, and so forth. The information conveyed by histogram is limited to the first-order statistics, corresponding to the number of pixels having a given gray value, or color component. Working on the histogram, gross level repartitions can be extracted such as dark versus bright parts (Figure 2.20) and dominant levels (e.g., local maxima) up to splitting the histogram into a conjunction of bounded repartitions.

In order to distinguish automatically an object from its background, a typical approach is to first produce the gray-level histogram (obviously, this process applies on the RGB components as well); second, find the best bi-Gaussian fit to the histogram distribution; third, compute the threshold T by minimizing the misplaced pixels (either background pixels in the foreground or vice versa). With a light object in a dark background, the misplaced pixels are represented by the green (levels approximately between 35 and T) and magenta (levels approximately between T and 50) values (for further details see Decision methods section).

Any modification of the gray-level distribution in the histogram provides a different viewer's perception of the image. Moreover, histogram warping can also facilitate the human interpretation, correcting some at acquisition errors or even

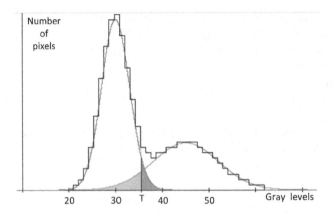

Figure 2.20 An image histogram represented by a black stepwise function, and superimposed by a bimodal best fit to find the optimal threshold separating the foreground from the background.

Figure 2.21 *History of Saint Peter* by Masaccio, around 1427, Church of the Holy Spirit, Florence.

driving the human attention to details that would correspond to specific gray levels. Figure 2.21 displays a gray image (A) with its associated histogram (B).

- To profit from the full gray-level scale (note that very clear and dark pixels are absent), the pixel distribution may be extended by stretching with the following formula:

$$g(i,j) = 255 - \frac{g(i,j) - g_{min}}{g_{max} - g_{min}} \tag{2.17}$$

where g_{max} and g_{min} correspond to the maximum and minimum gray levels, respectively, and $255-0$ is the whole available gray-level scale. In Figure 2.22, the achieved image (A) and its histogram (B) are displayed.

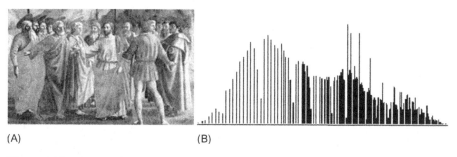

(A)   (B)

Figure 2.22 (A) Extended dynamics of Figure 2.21 and (B) its associated histogram.

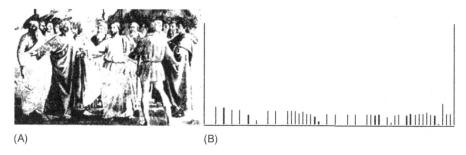

(A)   (B)

Figure 2.23 (A) Contrast enhancement of a gray-level interval and (B) its corresponding histogram.

- To enhance significant details in the image, the whole dynamics can be concentrated on a given interval $[a, b]$ of the gray scale; then a linear transformation inside the interval can be computed by:

$$g(i,j) = \begin{cases} 0 & \text{if } g(i,j) \leq a \\ 255 - \dfrac{g(i,j) - a}{b - a} & \text{if } a \leq g(i,j) \leq b \\ 255 & \text{if } g(i,j) \geq b \end{cases} \tag{2.18}$$

- This process produces the maximal contrast on the interval $[a, b]$ of the gray scale, leading to the image in Figure 2.23 and its associated histogram. Considering this chosen interval, no specific information is particularly enhanced.
- To compensate or even create lighting effects as, for instance, under- or overexposure, a nonlinear transformation of the gray levels can be performed by:

$$g(i,j) = \sqrt{255 g(i,j)} \tag{2.19}$$

$$g(i,j) = \frac{g(i,j)^2}{255} \tag{2.20}$$

- Figures 2.24 and 2.25 display simulated over- and underexposed images obtained by applying the above formulas to our original image.
- To obtain a *uniform distribution* of image contrast, a technique known as *equalization* is employed. This technique consists of making the empiric gray-level distribution as close as possible to a uniform distribution, in an adaptive way. Considering human vision, there is some evidence that limited high-contrast areas attract the attention, disturbing or slowing down the interpretation. On technical grounds, the more uniform a gray-level distribution is, the better contrasted is the associated image—that is, it attains *maximal entropy*. Moreover, as the uniform distribution is unique, wherever it comes from, any given distribution can be accessed from it.

The aimed uniform distribution, equal number K of pixels whatever the gray level, is $p(g) = K$. As a consequence, the probability of a pixel having a gray level g is $P(g) = Kg$. In order to redistribute all pixels to follow this linear function, thereby obtaining the histogram equalization, it is necessary that the cumulative gray-level histogram, $D(g) = \sum_{i=0}^{g-1} h(i)$ where $h(i)$ is the histogram value for the gray level (i), grows linearly with the gray value g. The resulting transformation is given by:

$$g' = g_{max} \frac{D(g)}{D(g_{max})} \tag{2.21}$$

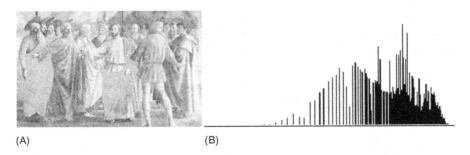

(A)   (B)

Figure 2.24 (A) Simulated overexposure of Figure 2.21 and (B) its corresponding histogram.

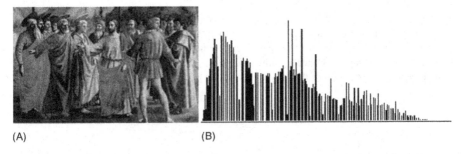

(A)   (B)

Figure 2.25 (A) Simulated underexposure of Figure 2.21 and (B) its corresponding histogram.

where g' is the new gray-level value after equalization; g_{max} is the maximum gray-level value in the original histogram; and $D(g_{max})$ corresponds to the total number of pixels (image size) because g_{max} is the maximum gray level.

Applying the equalization formula, the resulting histogram is as flat as possible, respective to all rounding difficulties. Small classes, corresponding to rare gray levels, will tend to gather with their neighbor classes, whereas large ones remain separated, corresponding to an increased contrast, as in Figure 2.26.

Note that because γ is a gray scale with theoretical distribution θ, the cumulative histogram associated to it is $\Delta(\gamma)$, then $\gamma' = D(g)\ \Delta(\gamma_{max})/D(g_{max})\ \Delta(\gamma)$ is a transformation that transforms the image histogram as close as possible to the distribution θ.

Up to now, histogram transformations refer to natural illumination; in other words, they follow *a passive process.* Nevertheless, other methods are based on artificial guided illumination, that is, with *an active process* enhancing image properties and shape features (Figure 2.27). In practical problems, the facilitated

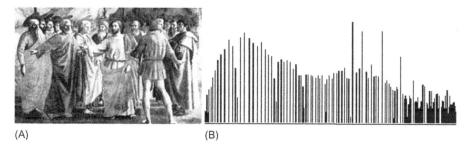

(A)   (B)

Figure 2.26 (A) Equalized image and (B) its corresponding uniform (as much as possible) histogram.

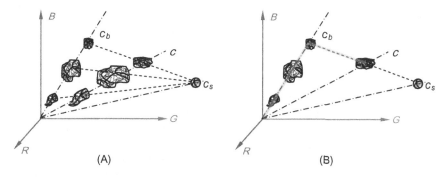

(A)   (B)

Figure 2.27 Dichromatic model: (A) colors of a homogeneous fabric on a $c_b - c_s$ plane; (B) L-shaped corresponding to a specular object with $m_b = m_s = \frac{1}{2}$. (For interpretation of the references to color in this figure legend, the reader is referred to the web version of this book.)

detection of given intensity levels on the image simplifies the location of reference points.

With multispectral images, the histogram becomes a vector of histograms, one per band. In [14] a method was designed to improve a color image on the basis of its content. This method works exactly in the opposite direction of histogram equalization. It is a straight transposition of the pop-out phenomenon; that is, it aims to point out specific features of the image content through the color histogram at a glance.

Given an image, a collection of chromatic histograms (e.g., R,G,B; H,S,V; NTSC standard; and so on) is considered. Provided that the histograms are uncorrelated as much as possible, the method proceeds according to the following steps:

- *Extract the maximum maximorum over all histograms*
- *Mark the corresponding pixels in the image*
- *Remove them from the population*
- *Compute the new histograms and loop*

The method will end on the basis of a preset number of extracted color subsets or when reaching a given size of the remaining classes. Many variations of this approach can be derived, mainly depending on the meaning given to "maximum" with respect to expected noise sources, for example, histogram local features for approximation (e.g., Gaussian).

Note that this process can also be used in a general framework to isolate single image components (*segmentation*), in this case on the basis of their sole color. Here, the balance and mutual control between the representation by color histograms and the picture partition into colored *connected subsets* (potential objects) makes this type of process adaptive in a biologically plausible manner. For instance, pixels belonging to small enough regions can be reinjected into the processed remaining population.

Color Distribution Analysis

The Kubelka—Munk theory [15] allows us to analyze the light diffusion phenomena at a macroscopic scale of the material. It explains the formation of the spectrum reflected by a colored body, by referring to the diffusion and absorption properties of the material. The main assumption made about the material is that the light is diffused isotropically inside it. The dichromatic reflection model proposed in [16] is based on this theory, in other words, that any *inhomogeneous dielectric material*, uniformly colored and dull, reflects light either by surface or by body reflection. In the first case, the reflected beam preserves the spectral features of the incident light to a certain extent; thus the color stimulus is generally assumed to be the same as the illuminant color. The body reflection results from the penetration of light in the material and from its scattering by the pigments of the object. It depends on the wavelength and the physical characteristics of the considered material.

Let P be a point of the scene and p its representation on the image. In general, the object radiance L(λ,P) can be seen as the sum of two radioactive terms, the body reflection L$_b$(λ,P) and the surface radiance L$_s$(λ,P):

$$L(\lambda, P) = L_s(\lambda, P) + L_b(\lambda, P) \tag{2.22}$$

Each one of the terms L$_b$ and L$_s$ is the product of two factors:

$$L(\lambda, P) = I_s(\lambda, P)m_s(P) + I_b(\lambda, P)m_b(P) \tag{2.23}$$

m$_b$ and m$_s$ are two functions which depend only on the scene geometry, whereas l$_b$(λ,P) and l$_s$(λ,P) refer, respectively, to the diffuse radiance and the illuminant spectrum l(λ,P); for conductive materials, the diffusion term vanishes.

Theoretically, the dichromatic reflection model is only valid for the scenes that have only a single illumination source and no recursive reflections. Despite these limitations, it has proved to be appropriate for many materials and many acquisition configurations.

This model is essentially qualitative because the analytic expressions m$_b$(p) and m$_s$(p) are not explicitly defined. By integration of the stimulus on the tri-CCD camera of sensitivities S$_i$(λ), i = R, G, B, it leads to the color component of the diffuse reflection c$_b$(p) = $\left(c_b^R, \ c_b^G, \ c_b^B \right)^T$ and the color vector of the specular reflection c$_s$(p) = $\left(c_s^R, c_s^G, c_s^B \right)$ at pixel p:

$$c_b^i(p) = K_i \int_\lambda S_i(\lambda)/(\lambda, P)R_b(\lambda, P) \, d\lambda$$
$$c_s^i(p) = K_i \int_\lambda S_i(\lambda)/(\lambda, P) \, d\lambda \tag{2.24}$$

The term K$_i$ expresses the gain of the camera in the sensor i.
Thus, the dichromatic model in RGB space becomes:

$$c(p) = m_b(p)c_b(p) + m_s(p)c_s(p) \tag{2.25}$$

According to (2.25), the material colors are distributed in the RGB space on a planar surface defined by $c_s(p)$ and $c_b(p)$, as sketched in Figure 2.27A. According to [15,16,20], the colors of a specular material are located more precisely in an L-shaped cluster. Indeed, in the ideal instance where the object is smooth and uniformly colored, the vertical bar of the L goes from the origin $RGB = (0, 0, 0)$ to the *diffuse color* component c_b, and the horizontal bar of the L goes from c_b to the illuminating color c_s. This case is illustrated in Figure 2.27B. Of course, for faintly saturated images, colors are distributed roughly along the intensity direction. In most cases, objects can be assumed to be Lambertian, so that the illumination contribution is neglected and the term $m_s(p) \, c_s(p)$ vanishes in Eqn (2.25). In other words, an approximation is made here: in changing the location of the illumination color in the RGB space, the shift is the same for all represented diffuse colors. Therefore, colors are supposed to be located around a few dominant directions, an assumption which appears to be true in practice (Figure 2.28).

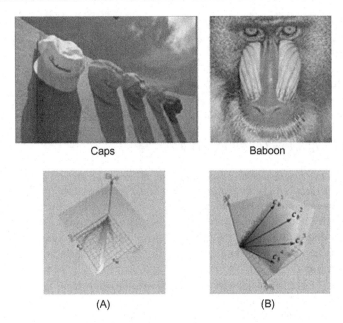

Caps   Baboon

(A)   (B)

Figure 2.28 Natural color images and their color distribution in RGB space (colourSpace Software, available at http://www.couleur.org). The color components are clearly visible in (A) the case of monochromatic items (caps) and less apparent in (B) a fine-grained textured image. (For interpretation of the references to color in this figure legend, the reader is referred to the web version of this book.)

Color components can be extracted accordingly by any clustering method in the 3D color space, or progressively in a sequence of 2D clustering on parallel surfaces that stratify the 3D color space (see, for instance, an application to color-line extraction in the *Shape extraction* section).

The Morphological Track

The drawings in Figure 2.29 show that, unlike photometry, shapes were at all times able to convey rich information beyond their morphological or aesthetic nature. For instance, a bull painted on the cave walls more than 15,000 years ago represents hardly more than the silhouette of the animal; nevertheless, viewers could sense the impressive strength of the animal from the sketched lines on the stone. Moreover, looking at (A), the bulls show their vigor, strength, and vitality, whereas the deer on (B) seem to be scared, weak, and terrified. This elementary sketch describes a complex situation, that is, an ambush, where deer jump everywhere in fear while hunters move franticly despite their skeletal appearance. Transmitting feelings by images will be addressed in Chapter 3 devoted to the role of context. The latter example would indicate that such semantic notion is conveyed by the shape

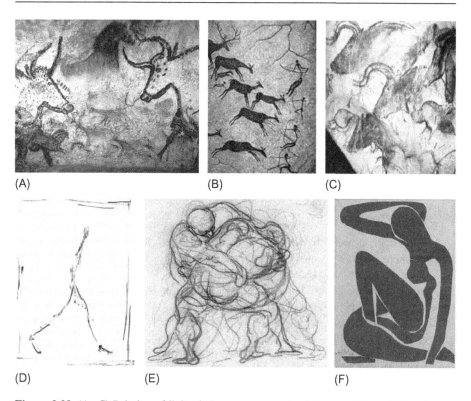

Figure 2.29 (A−C) Painting of living beings on cave walls at Lascaux (about 1500 BC);
(D) *L'homme qui Marche* by Alberto Giacometti, 1948, Nouvelles Images Editor (1976); (E)
Les Lutteurs by Honoré Daumier, 1852, Lyon, Musée des Beaux-Arts; (F) *Nu Bleu II* by Henri
Matisse, 1952, Collections du Musée National d'Art Moderne, Centre Pompidou, Paris.

efficiently, whatever its coding simplicity. It can be checked again in Figure 2.29A
and C, where a mere change in the bulls' relative orientations translates either
aggressiveness or rush. Closer in time, a similar skeleton-like pattern by
Giacometti succeeds in translating the dandy's walk and his slow attitude up to his
hands likely crossed behind his back. Climbing up the scale of suggested abstraction by lines or blobs, Daumier illustrates the burst of energy that is doubly para-
doxical as fighters immobilize one another, and the image is a still one. Likewise,
Matisse makes his character's sensuality burst out of the canvas. Obviously, all the
interpretation process is in the viewer's mind and is triggered by the suggestive
power of a few lines and blobs, evoking original shapes and volumes. In other
words, line/blob images and models—that is, the morphological representation
primitives—should be easier to revert than the single 3D pose from photometrical
methods.

The reflectivity models (coming from the *Photometric track*) are difficult to
revert; they require an extensive additional knowledge or several assumptions to be

further developed along the recognition process: the system geometry has to be known, or predicted, as well as the physical characteristics of objects. In this respect, this technique appears as more complementary, allowing us to filter the knowledge acquired from a scene rather than capturing it. Photometric techniques are basic in image synthesis, for the representation of partial/total results; they do not help much for image understanding by machines. One reason why the photometric techniques might be limited is their low semantic level notwithstanding their high complexity. They are closer indeed to the physics of the image formation than to the description of the involved action, and any additional knowledge or assumption just remains at that level too (low-level vision).

Shape Representation

From the technical point of view, long before translating feelings, lines need to be primarily kept continuous and closed for describing objects so that morphology is exploitable by machines. Indeed, digital images must keep all properties of the acquired natural shapes so that the relationships among single elements—even avoiding a missing pixel—are preserved. For instance, a closed loop like the one of the character O must remain closed in order to be properly recognized by an OCR system. More generally, when digitizing a single object, its image must remain isolated; two objects close to one another should remain disjoint after capture; a straight line should not appear either *convex* or *concave*, whatever the image acquisition limitations.

Typically, a digital scene contains a number of objects that may be analyzed (either sequentially or concurrently). The analysis is based on both *topological* and *geometrical* properties. For this reason, the connectivity between image elements founding the topology must be first ensured during acquisition and then preserved during the computation. Second, peculiar geometrical properties of the objects should also be maintained, for example, in introducing notions like digital *curvature*. When referring again to OCR systems, properties of *openness* and *closure* should be preserved for the automatic reader to distinguish between characters O and C, or properties of *convexity* and *concavity* to distinguish between O and Q.

Contour-Based Representations

A *binary image* is described by a set of 1-elements (*foreground*) and a 0-element set (*background*). Any object, *image segment*, may be fully described by means of: (i) its digital contour as a borderline with the remainder of the image, (ii) its internal blocks that completely cover such segment. In the first case, a well-known code which may fully describe the contour in terms of local slope variations is the Freeman chain code [17] based on the labeling of finite possible slopes of segments joining the contour-pixel centers.

This code is nothing but the discrete version of the intrinsic representation of curves $s = f(\varphi)$, where s is the arc length and φ the tangent angle.

The labels associated to each different contour segment slope are shown in Figure 2.30, respectively, for 4- and 8-connected orientations. The four (respectively, eight) orientation, selected to code lines, actually define the considered pixel neighborhood, that is, the image four (respectively, eight) topology and the corresponding *unit disk*. Two kinds of neighborhoods of a central pixel in a 3×3 window, on a digital plane, are thus defined:

- The so-called 4-neighbors, that is, those sharing a side with the central pixel.
- The so-called 8-neighbors sharing both a side and a vertex with the central pixel.

More generally, the 4-connected (respectively, 8-connected) topology is defined in an equivalent manner after the following distances: $d_1(\mathbf{p_1},\mathbf{p_2}) = |x_1 - x_2| + |y_1 - y_2|$ (respectively, $d_\infty(\mathbf{p_1},\mathbf{p_2}) = \max(|x_1 - x_2|,|y_1 - y_2|)$), also called Manhattan (respectively, Tchebycheff) distance. The Manhattan distance essentially runs only along vertical and horizontal directions, in other words, along roads in downtown New York. The unit disk associated to a topology is simply given in the metric case by $d(\mathbf{o}, \mathbf{p}) \leq 1$.

In Figure 2.31, the black pixels correspond to the object and the red ones to the background; typically this situation is stored via 1-pixel and 0-pixel, respectively.

The notion of a 4-contour of a digital object may now be introduced algorithmically by defining the subset of the object pixels, which have at least one 8-neighbor

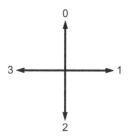
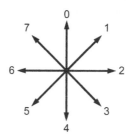

Figure 2.30 Freeman chain codes referred to the 4- and 8-adjacency paths.

Figure 2.31 Digital image with a single connected component of a monk represented with two gray levels, a gray tone for the background, and black for the monk.

belonging to the background. Conversely, an 8-contour of a digital object is given by the object pixels, which have at least one 4-neighbor belonging to the background. As can be seen in Figure 2.32, the 4-contour looks like a staircase (made by just horizontal and vertical segments), whereas the 8-contour shows less pixels because diagonal connections are allowed.

By looking at the left picture in Figure 2.33 (the digital 4-contour of the monk's head), there is a pixel that will be visited twice with a contour following algorithm: such pixels are called brush-past. These pixels may be either single (the path bidirectionally visits the same pixel) or double (the path in one direction brushes-past the same path through an adjacent pixel in the opposite direction). The pixel inside the blue circle is a single brush-past, whereas the one inside the purple circle is a double brush-past pixel. Finally, note that the 4-contour requires more pixels and its path walks only along the four cardinal directions, whereas the 8-contour takes advantage also of diagonal directions.

Figure 2.32 Two contours of the monk digital object, marked with black pixels: a 4-contour on the left, having at least one 8-neighbor on the gray background and an 8-contour on the right, having at least one 4-neighbor in the background.

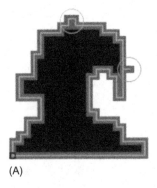 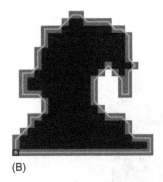

(A)   (B)

Figure 2.33 A monk's head: a 4/8 contour on the left and right, respectively, are indicated by gray pixels with a polygonal white path joining the centers of such pixels.

As defined earlier, the Freeman chain code may be obtained by starting from the marked bottom left contour pixel, going clockwise, until the initial pixel is reached. The strings of chain code labels are, respectively:

$\{F\}_4$ = 001010011000333000110001000111010121111121121222213222 23000303323222221211112122111223333333333333333333 (4 − contour, with 102 code labels)

and

$\{F\}_8$ = 0011021076600021001002211232223234443544460077554443322 34322446666666666666666666 (8 − contour, with 81 code labels).

The length of the contour directly corresponds to the number of pixels, for the 4-contour based on the Manhattan distance. For the 8-contour the perimeter is computed considering diagonal steps to be given a $\sqrt{2}$ coefficient. The following simple formula holds:

$$P_8 = n_{\text{even}} + \sqrt{2}n_{\text{odd}} \tag{2.26}$$

where n_{even} and n_{odd} refer to the number of even/odd code labels.

Other shape features may also be evaluated through Freeman chain codes, such as moments, elongation, and so on. For instance, the area may also be evaluated in terms of the number of pixels for each connected component.

Formulas (2.27) and (2.28) translate the area computation process:

$$y^k = \sum_{i=0}^{k} c_y^i \tag{2.27}$$

$$A = 1 + \sum_{i=0}^{n} c_x^i \sum_{j=0}^{i-1} c_y^j + \frac{1}{2} \sum_{i=0}^{n} \left| c_x^i \right| + \left| c_y^i \right| \tag{2.28}$$

with $c_y^0 = y_0$.

Equation (2.27) computes the ordinate value y^k of the kth pixel of the contour, whereas Eqn (2.28) computes the area. The c components represent the relative increments along the two cardinal directions: c_x for the abscissa will equal 1 when moving eastward (1, 2, 3 orientations) and −1 (5, 6, 7 orientations) when moving westward, while being 0 for both north and south orientations (0, 4). Similarly, c_y for the ordinate component will equal 1 when moving northward (7, 0, 1) and −1 southward (3, 4, 5), again being 0 for both east and west orientations (2, 6). In the above formulas, the superscript i indicates the curvilinear abscissa; i = 0 corresponds to the starting pixel {x_0, y_0}. Note that the third term in Eqn (2.28) adds up all the displacements along each direction that will always be even for closed contours.

Another technique for computing the area shrinks the pattern iteratively (Figure 2.34), using the Freeman's chain codes $\{F\}_{4/8}$ to add up the number of

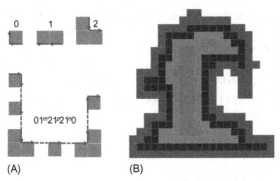

Figure 2.34 A progressively shrunk, 4-contour, of the digital monk's head. (A) Top: graphical D-code representation, and bottom: the generic chain D-coding a concavity; (B) the numbers of codes in the monocolor chains from iterated erosions are summed up for the area computation.

codes in the obtained chains. An algorithm based on *formal grammars*, using code chains, is given here.

A 4-connected example employs the digital version of a derivative, which may be called derivate code D, and is related to the contour curvature defined as follows [18]:

$$D_i = |F_{i-1} - F_i + 5|_{\bmod 4} \tag{2.29}$$

Concavities/convexities correspond to specific sequences of D-codes; for concavities the general corresponding expression is: $01^m21^p21^n0$, where x in yz^x expresses the multiplicity of z; and for convexities it is enough to change 0 for 2 and vice versa.

Global transformations defined by rules of the type in formula (2.30) achieve pattern shrinking or expanding, for instance, in filling concavities up. Pattern shrinking (respectively, expanding) corresponds to the erosion (respectively, dilation) operator, with a unit disk (structural element). Such operators were defined in Mathematical Morphology, by Georges Matheron (1930–2000) and are described in [19].

$$
\begin{aligned}
01^m0 &\rightarrow 1^m02 \\
01^m2 &\rightarrow 01^{m-1}2 \\
21^m0 &\rightarrow 1^{m-1}02
\end{aligned}
\tag{2.30}
$$

Among other significant features of shape, concavities and convexities have always been considered for pattern recognition. Another simple means for extracting such properties uses 3×3 windows iteratively. It is based on the evaluation of the number of background pixels in such windows.

For the successive steps, the evaluation now corresponds to the addition of values of the contour labels within the subarray (including the central pixel label). Figure 2.35 shows the "monk's head" and its labeled contour, with the above technique, after two iterations: the second iteration has only been applied to a fragment of the whole picture and models a wider receptive field equivalent to a 5×5 window. If this process is continued, the higher the number of iterations, the larger the receptive field, the lower the spatial quantization effects, thereby obtaining a more comprehensive description, although at a lower resolution.

A more sophisticated approach to extract the same features is based on the local computation of a Laplacian operator [20] (further defined in the sequel). The method simulates an

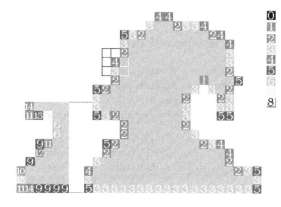

Figure 2.35 A labeled 8-contour displaying convexities and concavities along the boundary of a connected component. The central "monk's head" shows the first iteration of the labeling process with a 3×3 window sketched around label 4, while a particular part of the "head" with the second iteration is on the bottom left. The legend of the labeled pixels is on the top right.

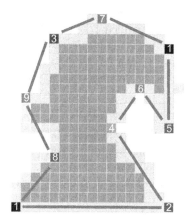

Figure 2.36 A polygonal approximation at fourth step of the monk's head contour. Construction lines (strings and perpendiculars); the starting diameter extremes have labels one.

isotropic diffusion process modeled by the heat propagation equation [21]. Because of the importance of such properties in shape recognition, a wide number of algorithms have been suggested for concavity/convexity detection.

Note that many shape features beyond the area or the curvature (e.g., diameters, symmetry axes, and so on) are important for recognition and can directly be derived from a curvilinear description, thanks to procedures that do not require a transformation back to Cartesian coordinates, and thus compete favorably with more sophisticated ones.

To conclude on contour representations, the *polygonal approximation* will be considered among all such procedures. Its result is of peculiar importance because it addresses the very basic notion of sampling precision, fundamental for the right resolution to perform recognition.

An algorithm schema, freely inspired from related early works [22,23], is given and can be followed in Figure 2.36.

- *Find a diameter d of a closed digital line, or consider the extremity-linking segment els of a nonclosed digital line.*
- *Find the furthest pixel from d or els to the line, and draw both segments joining this pixel to d or els extremities.*
- *For all segments s, find the point p_s of the digital line with maximum distance δ_s to s.*
- *Select the maximum distance δ_{s*} over all segments and draw the two new segments joining the corresponding p_{s*} to extremities of the related segment $s*$.*
- *Stop when δ_{s*} is below a preset threshold (given precision) or at a preset number of segments (storing capacity).*

This version of the algorithm is based on strings (Lagrange's fashion); another version can be equivalently based on tangents (Newton's fashion). In both cases, the convergence depends on the segment management strategy.

Region-Based Representation

The second way to describe a two-dimensional object is by means of a global decomposition, that is, by breaking it down to smaller components that may be easily managed. Two different possible approaches may be considered: (i) planar and (ii) hierarchical. The first one is based on the evaluation of loci of pixels, satisfying a given distance to the border, whereas the second one exploits recursion to subdivide, on a regular *tessellation*, a number of variable-sized subcomponents of the whole object.

The MAT

Two interesting and useful transformations called distance transform (DT) and medial axis transform (MAT) [20] are relevant for detecting specific features and for a perceptual representation of elongated patterns, respectively.

The DT is obtained by labeling all the pixels inside a binary object with their distance to the background; considering the Manhattan distance for labeling the pixels of a binary image like the monk, a picture such as the one shown in Figure 2.37A will be obtained. Every pixel has a color corresponding to its distance label that increases going inward. In practice, this value represents the side of the greatest digital disk having its center on this pixel, which is completely contained in the binary object.

Any pattern can be interpreted as the union of all its *maximal digital disks*. A maximal disk is a disk contained in the object that is not completely overlapped by any other disk. The disk shape is strictly dependent on the chosen distance function. The set of the centers of the maximal disks, with their labels, constitutes the MAT, which is shown in Figure 2.37B. The name of this transform derives from the fact that these centers are located on the medial region of the object in correspondence with its symmetry axis. A procedure to derive the MAT from the DT is based on the comparison of neighboring labels to establish whether a local maximum exists.

This transform is complete in the sense that it is possible to revert it, thereby obtaining the original object back, as shown in Figure 2.37C. This recovery process can be implemented by expanding every pixel belonging to the MAT, using the

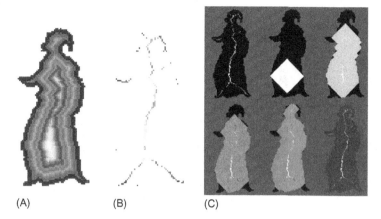

(A)   (B)   (C)

Figure 2.37 (A) Twenty successive differently colored layers showing equidistant contours from the background for a Manhattan distance metric. (B) The corresponding MAT labeled with the same code except for the inmost couple of pixels, which have been framed in black to be discriminated from the background. Note that all the information related to the object is completely contained in this last picture. (C) From left to right and top to bottom, we show a series of six binary objects representing both the monk profile and the progressive approximation of the original shape, obtained by expanding the top 1, top 5, top 10, top 15 levels of maximal discs, using the code corresponding to the smallest size expanded disks. Finally, the last profile presents the full reconstruction of the original object obtained by the set of 20 levels. The subset of MAT pixels that has been included in every monk preserves the label colors corresponding to the distances from the background, as shown in (B). (For interpretation of the references to color in this figure legend, the reader is referred to the web version of this book.)

corresponding maximal disc whose size is given by the pixel label. The logical union of all such discs reconstructs the original object. In Figure 2.37C, the black monk is the original object on a red background, and the disc is a square (Manhattan distance). This figure shows the progressive reconstruction, starting from the set of disks corresponding to the highest level (two white disks, which partially overlap in the second monk's profile), up until the sixth and last monk's profile, where discs, reduced to just one pixel, have been included.

This transform is compact because the full object may be described only by its labeled disk centers. However, the set of disks is not minimal; in fact, they are often heavily overlapped: the minimum set of disks can be derived from the set of maximal discs, as shown in [24].

The picture in Figure 2.37B illustrates how the MAT does not ensure connectivity for a connected object. Also, it is not ultimately thin because different fragments are two pixels wide. For the above reasons, the *skeleton* is introduced. Its computation may be seen as the digital version of a process that models the fire propagation in a windless grass field, where the fire is ignited on the contour of the object. For a circular object, the skeleton coincides with the center having a label equal to its

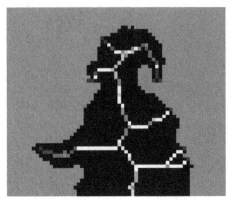

Figure 2.38 White pixels represent linking branches to build the skeleton from the MAT, whereas other pixels are deletable elements that do not change the topology and do not belong to the skeleton.

radius, whereas for a rectangle four bisecting segments will be obtained. Such segments bisect the four square angles and are joined by a segment in the central axis running parallel to the longest side of the rectangle. Unfortunately, in the digital plane these properties are hard to maintain, and therefore only acute angles generate branches, whereas minor curvature variations on the contour may not. Broadly speaking, the skeleton transformation is not reversible in general [25].

Many different algorithms were designed for generating skeletons [26,27].

A simple algorithm starts from the MAT and proceeds in two steps:

- *Find gaps between different branches, and bridge them by joining the extremes along paths with directions dependent on context (white pixels in Figure 2.38).*
- *Thin the obtained branches so as to produce a one-pixel-wide representation (red pixels in Figure 2.38).*

One possible application of the skeleton is contour smoothing, in which by pruning branches with relatively short lengths and then inverting the skeleton transformation, a more regular contour is obtained.

The Convex Hull

The *convex hull*, that is, the minimum *n*-sided convex polygon that completely circumscribes an object, gives another possible description of a binary object [28]. An example is given in Figure 2.39, where an 8-sided polygon has been chosen to coarsely describe the monk silhouette.

To obtain the convex hull, a simple algorithm propagates the object along the eight (more generally, 2n) orientations and then logically OR the opposite propagated segments; and logically AND the four (more generally, n) resulting segments. The contour of the obtained polygon is the convex hull.

The Quadtree Representation

Starting from the full monk object, as shown in Figure 2.40, a four-square splitting process is performed on the full image, and the subdivision process is then applied recursively. This process stops whenever it reaches a homogeneous square (background/foreground). The homogeneous squares are single colored (0/1, respectively, for background/foreground), whereas others require further subdivisions in

Figure 2.39 8-Convex hull of the monk's silhouette.

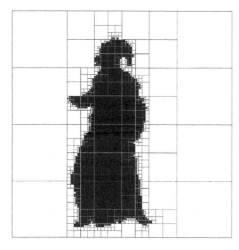

Figure 2.40 A quadtree representation of the monk's image is displayed through a six-level downward recursive subdivision process. As may be easily seen, eight large empty squares can be compactly coded, thereby saving memory space, while the required detail (monk's cap) is preserved if necessary.

order to cater to finer detail. The process ends when no more mixed squares exist. Square sizes are submultiples of the image size. Although the maximum resolution level is not always reached, the transformation is totally reversible [29,30].

Because of the privileged orientation, the obtained blocks may not be the maximal ones included in the object. Moreover, an object translation may result in a different decomposition. Nevertheless, this is an effective hierarchical data structure. In fact, the hierarchy allows selecting an adequate resolution level for the task at end, implementing a version of the focus of attention on salient details of the image. That mechanism facilitates general problem-solving strategies.

Any object may be interpreted as the union of all the foreground (black) squares. A partial reconstruction is obtained by means of a Boolean operation between homogeneous squares of different sizes. The AND-Pyramid and OR-Pyramid representations (e.g., [31]) have been specifically designed to such purpose.

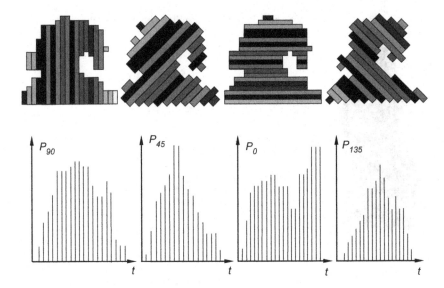

Figure 2.41 Four projections of the monk's head with the four corresponding $P_\theta(t)$s.

Shape Representation by Projections

The same idea of decreasing the dimensionality toward efficient pattern representation is considered here in a completely different way. The intuition leads, as above, to capture the shape in considering that it is roughly homogeneous, such as a binary region, and thus a collection of segments, each one representing its length in a given direction θ and at a given position t (Figure 2.41).

Such pattern coding appears, then, as an intermediate one between contours and regions for shape description. This method should be able to reveal morphological properties (such as elongation, circularity, and so on). Because of its cumulative construction, parts of pixel coordinates are lost, but topological properties could be recovered from a sufficient number of projections.

The thickness of a "quasi"-binary pattern generalizes into the sum of gray levels along the corresponding ray. The sequence of such sums can be gathered into a function $P_\theta(t)$ called the projection of the pattern in the direction θ. The function of two variables $\mathcal{R}(\theta,t)$, defined by the collection of the $P_\theta(t)$s when θ varies from 0 to π, is called the *Radon transform* (Johan Radon, 1887–1956) of the pattern (Figure 2.42).

This type of projection with parallel rays is actually a case of the general projection inspired by physics phenomena (e.g., X- or Γ-rays, and further, tomography) where rays may all originate from a given focus. It is common in machine vision, all the more so as it facilitates hardware implementations.

One major interest of the (parallel) projections, not difficult to prove, is that a pattern can be reconstructed from its projections to a given precision depending on the number of directions and of the digitization fineness, that is, on the sampling

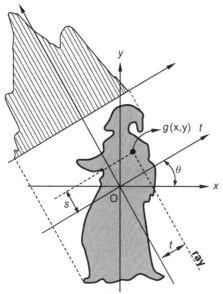

Figure 2.42 The monk's projection with the Radon function parameters.

rate of both θ and t. *A fortiori*, pattern recognition from projections is thus doable, the same as from contours or regions.

More formally, and in a continuous setting, after defining Eqn (2.30), there are two avenues for reconstruction: harmonic or algebraic.

$$P_\theta(t) = \int_{\text{ray}} g(x, y)\, \mathrm{d}s \tag{2.31}$$

Harmonic Techniques for Reconstruction from Projections

Indeed, the Fourier transform $\mathscr{F}$ occurs naturally because all variables are sampled. Let $\pi_\theta(w) = \mathscr{F}[P_\theta(t)]$ and $\gamma(u,v) = \mathscr{F}[g(x,y)]$; then $\pi_\theta(w) = \gamma(u,v)$ when $u = w\cos\theta$ and $v = w\sin\theta$ because along the ray, $t = x\cos\theta + y\sin\theta$. This means (w, θ) are the polar coordinates in the spectrum, and the Fourier transform of the projection is the polar ray of the same angle in this spectrum. Consequently:

$$g(x, y) = \mathscr{F}^{-1}[\gamma(u, v)] = \int_0^{2\pi} \int_0^{+\infty} \pi_\theta(\omega)\, e^{2j\pi\omega(x\cos\theta + y\sin\theta)}\, \omega\mathrm{d}\omega\, \mathrm{d}\theta \tag{2.32}$$

Because of the symmetry of the projection in a rotation by π:

$$g(x, y) = \int_0^\pi \int_0^{+\infty} \pi_\theta(\omega)|\omega|e^{2j\pi\omega t}\, \mathrm{d}\omega\, \mathrm{d}\theta \tag{2.33}$$

Let $h(z)$, the inverse Fourier transform of the filter $|w|$ (its point spread function, that is, its response to the impulse input), be defined in Eqn (2.34):

$$h(n) = \begin{cases} \dfrac{1}{4} & \text{for } n = 0 \\[2mm] 0 & \text{for even } n \\[2mm] \dfrac{-1}{n^2\pi^2} & \text{for odd } n \end{cases} \tag{2.34}$$

$P_\theta(t)$ being given, it is convolved with h to obtain the contribution $Q_\theta(t)$, and then Q is summed between 0 and π. Any approximation of an integral can be used, targeting the best possible approximation of $g(x,y)$. For instance:

$$\tilde{g}(x, y) = \frac{\pi}{N_d} \sum_{i=1}^{N_d} Q_{\theta_i}(x \cos \theta_i + y \sin \theta_i) \tag{2.35}$$

It should be clear that θ_i produces values of t that do not coincide with true pixels in general. Thus, interpolation is necessary, usually in a cordic fashion, that is, a zero-order interpolation, after having computed many more values than theoretically required.

Algebraic Techniques for Reconstruction from Projections

A more physics-related understanding of the reconstruction after projections leads to an algebraic method. Considering that a digitized pattern is actually a collection of small square dots (the pixels), these dots are intercepted by narrow bands (the rays), and the corresponding proportions of the pixel intensities are accumulated accordingly (Figure 2.43). This gives rise to the huge linear system of Eqn (2.36).

$$\left\{ \sum_{j=1}^{\alpha} w_{i,j} x_j = p_i \right\}_{i \in [1,\delta]} \tag{2.36}$$

where δ is the number of projections and α is the number of pixels.

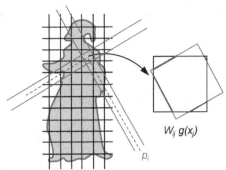

Figure 2.43 A geometric-related projection leading to an algebraic reconstruction.

$W_{ij}\, g(x_j)$

p_i

Interestingly enough, modern resolutions of such large systems are completed by the so-called projection methods! For instance, the iterative scheme designed by Stephan Kaczmarz (1895–1940) is based on the equivalence between finding the intersection of hyperplanes and solving a linear system (Figure 2.44). Its principle is outlined in two dimensions in Figure 2.44; the first variant, Figure 2.44A, leads to the sequence of formulas (2.37).

$$x^j = x^{j-1} - \frac{x^{j-1}w_j - p_j}{\|w_j\|^2} w_j$$

$$w_j = (w_{ji})_{i=1}^{\alpha}$$

$$(2.37)$$

Reconstruction is not always necessary for recognizing patterns in many practical cases. As an example, if there are only the three key patterns represented in Figure 2.45, by using only either their vertical or their horizontal projections (323, 322, 313 and 323, 313, 232, respectively), they can be discriminated. Adding the two characters of Figure 2.46, the five patterns cannot be discriminated, even in the absence of noise. The new vertical and horizontal projections are 232, 313 and 313, 322, respectively. The first character of Figure 2.46A and the second of Figure 2.45 have equal horizontal projection (313), and the third of Figure 2.45 and the second of Figure 2.46A have equal vertical projection (313): both projections jointly are necessary to identify them. The larger the character set, the harder! Ambiguities grow with the number of characters requiring more projections to fight symmetries, such as in the first couple in Figure 2.46B or partial translations, such as in the second couple.

Projections represent a quick and easy coding system to be exploited in many practical recognition cases such as with QR-code matrices, developed in Japan in

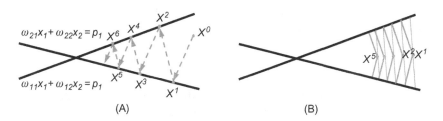

(A)   (B)

Figure 2.44 Two possible schemes for solving linear systems by iterated projections. (A) In projecting alternatively onto both straight lines, their intersection is reached; (B) the same is true in projecting simultaneously and selecting a point of the cord.

   Figure 2.45 Three-by-three matrices for character representation; scanned from left to right, and bottom to top, the characters can be discriminated by either their horizontal projections or their vertical ones.

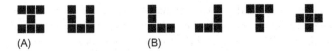

(A)   (B)

Figure 2.46 (A) Two new characters can be discriminated among the five ones only by using both vertical and horizontal projections concurrently; (B) two couples of characters having symmetry and translation, respectively.

1999. Furthermore, by using such projections, both computation time and complexity can be strongly diminished, quickly arriving at practical solutions.

These solutions may save many computations when combined with motion detection, for instance. Indeed, the basic scheme for motion detection relies on matching pixels or pixel sets (ideally the moving patterns) between images in a sequence. Matching homologous projection segments turns out to be enough in many situations. Moreover, such algorithms support balance between the time and angle scales.

Eventually, projections show again at the upper intellectual stages of *intelligent systems*. At this level, configurations of abstract entities referring to tactics/strategy and anticipation are in need of fast understanding. For instance, a robot following a line, or a car on its track (Figure 2.47) should be safe with the first image representation (Figure 2.47B) because the peak of the projection (circled in the picture) indicates the correct direction corresponding to the central line. The second projection (Figure 2.47C) shows that the robot could well use some human intervention. Likewise, in any team game, adversaries forming a line pattern in the orthogonal direction (again a peak in the projection) are less worrisome than when they adopt a surrounding configuration (flatter projection).

The representation by projections is computable upon acquisition; it can serve at various semantic levels along the computer vision process, and reconstruction need not be mandatorily achieved before recognition. However, projections are strongly dependent on the acquisition faithfulness.

Conclusions

In all the above, exhibited patterns were considered. They were assumed to have been already isolated, and then descriptors of such patterns were investigated in an attempt to optimize convenience, simple computations, and perceptive cues. Behind the initial binary representation of these patterns, a wide range of models is understated for patterns to appear homogeneous, and their contours to be continuous, so as to abstract the shape. For instance, before being an obvious line, the contour likely was first an elongated set of pixels with high directional contrast; before being blobs, the pattern parts were connected sets of pixels showing some kind of parameterized uniformity. These models, in turn, may give sense to quadtree hierarchies computing, skeleton pruning, wireframe thinning, and so on. As they are less complex and of a higher-level than lighting models, inverting them establishes

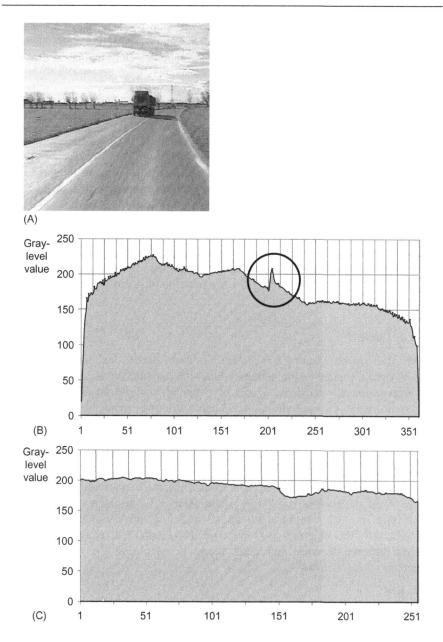

(A)

(B)

(C)

Figure 2.47 Car driving with projections: (A) through windshield view; (B) ideal projection with a 45° angle. The peak of the central line (circled in the figure) shows the correct direction; (C) useless projection—the car receives an unhelpful feedback.

the preliminary step toward shape extraction. This step is called *image segmentation*. It addresses contour analysis, connected regions detection and labeling, motion finding, and so on, targeting the scene semantics and pragmatics. Related basic techniques and associated models are now studied.

Shape Extraction

The hypothesis is that some patterns may pop out from the background directly because of their *shape*, the shape being materialized by its outline. Technically, a line can be extracted by short segments or as a sequence of points. Among the pixels to be chosen as line points, some show peculiar properties that make them salient and support their extraction, independently from being on the line. The corresponding phenomenon in biological vision is the selection of *fixation points* [32] and their chaining along the so-called *scan path* (see *Natural vision* section in Chapter 1). According to [33] "[T]he order of eye fixation points is by no means random, but the salient features of a scene are inspected following a dense and uniform pathway called *feature ring*. . . ." The extraction of points of interest is examined first and then lines.

Points of Interest

The zero-dimensional (*point-wise*) feature was first intended for compression purposes. Modern computer vision systems exploit the same feature for directing attention, because image variations, spatial or temporal, indicate an alteration or an event, respectively. Of such variations, image data can be condensed without significant loss of information. As an example, inside the image, pattern contours linking two consecutive points of interest are simple curves like straight segments. In that, they correspond to *saccades* in the human vision system. Points of interest between images (after motion or stereo) preserve identical features more than others, because they are less sensitive to noise. Thus, the basic model is that of *singular point* of the surface $g = I(i, j)$, where again g is the intensity value (gray level, texture, or color index) and i, j are the spatial coordinates of I, image frame. More generally, this singular point corresponds to a local maximum of a given property. Because of noise and other image perturbations, the model can be declined into three main axes:

1. Statistical
2. Geometrical
3. Both

Statistical Model
First, detectors are based on template matching where a given pattern is compared to the image $g = I(i,j)$ surface. They optimize the split of a pixel neighborhood into a small number of angular sectors, following a given model (Figure 2.48). The model's characteristics obey bounding rules both geometry wise (aperture ratios) and intensity wise (sector uniformity, inter sector contrast, etc.) [34–36].

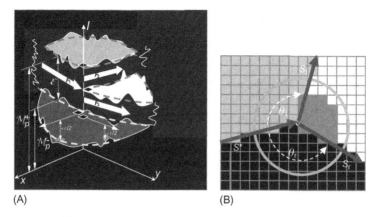

(A)   (B)

Figure 2.48 An example of point of interest based on template matching. (A) The gray-level partition of three sectors in the neighborhood of 2 × 2 pixels: the min−max intersector level variation is ε, the max level variation inside a sector is $\varepsilon/2$; (B) the image of the neighborhood with directional features from the point of interest.

Note that in this contrast-based model, the point of interest lies at the intersection of 2 × 2 actual pixels. Consecutive lines then run along vertices, and by convention they are oriented so that the incoming direction (F_1, then S_* in Figure 2.48) corresponds to the local max intersector variation. Characteristic angles of the point, two in the three-sector case of the example in Figure 2.48, θ_b, and θ_r, are computed from S_*. Orientation and characteristics support reconstructing lines from points when necessary.

The singular points can also be detected through the local variability of the intensity distribution, instead of using the relative order or flatness inside or around objects (regions and edges).

For instance, the historical origin of the feature [37] assumes the interest to refer to a high directional variance around the point. Points of interest are the local maxima of the minimum directional variance over directions. Indeed, if the minimum directional variance of a point is large, so are its variances in all directions, compared to the pixels around.

Geometrical Model

The so-called *gray-level corners* are classically characterized by properties of the first or second partial derivatives (actually their discrete approximation through convolution). Ideally, derivatives are computed in the frame of the surface local *principal axes* (i.e., $(\partial^2 I)/(\partial x\ \partial y) = 0$). Also they follow a *low-pass filtering* (e.g., Gaussian) to set the resolution at which the saliency is looked for. More than points, small regions are actually detected in which a peculiar point is then distinguished. For instance, these regions feature significant change in the *gradient* direction along the locally maximal gradient curve. Figure 2.49A shows an example of derivative configuration of interest, a maximum planar curvature along the steepest gray line.

A variety of singular point detectors were suggested, among others, in [38−41]. For a more compact expression, derivatives can be gathered into a matrix (e.g., the Hessian) to be

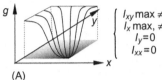
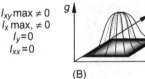

Figure 2.49 (A) Bottom of the gray-level concavity and (B) peak of the gray-level convexity.

(A)   (B)

computed on every pixel at the chosen resolution. The interest then stems from relative amplitudes of the eigen values [42,43]. For instance, the singular point in Figure 2.49B is simply characterized by all first derivatives null and the determinant (product of the eigen values) of the Hessian strictly positive.

Mixed Model

Popular detectors in autonomous vehicles deal commonly with a hybrid of differential and statistical properties.

*The Plessey operator **P** [44] can be viewed as a variant of the Hessian, the fundamental matrix, where the second derivatives are replaced by a statistical metaphor that is the local variance of first derivatives. Then again an interest function is designed, for example, $F = \det \mathbf{P} - k\,(trace\ \mathbf{P})^2$, where k is a parameter to support some adaptation, and trace is classically the invariant sum of the eigen values. Local maxima of F provide the points of interest [45,46].*

Line Extraction

Gray-level images display many *level lines*. Among them, some may stand out due to peculiar global properties such as maximum average contrast, belonging to some class of geometric figures, or bringing to mind a searched given pattern. In the field of machine vision, level lines form the so-called *topographic map* and are the frontiers of level sets, defined by:

$$\text{Lower level sets } X_\lambda = \{x \in R^2, g(x) \le \lambda\}$$
$$\text{Upper level sets } X^\lambda = \{x \in R^2, g(x) \ge \lambda\} \tag{2.38}$$

These lines have various important properties showing a relationship between contrast and line density, and some specific invariances or robustness [47–49]. By construction, level lines never cross, are closed, and can be used for picture reconstruction (inverse topographic mapping) [50].

The extension to color images is not straightforward. In [51] the color space (V,H,S) is totally ordered and lines are constructed according to intensity (V) first, then hue (H), and then saturation (S). In [52] another strategy exploits the physics of lighting under the *Dichromatic Model* [16] (Figure 2.50) and lines correspond to progressive intensity along body colors (Figure 2.51), that is, with respect to the principal axes of the main clusters in the R,G,B histogram.

Given an image, let Γ and C be two different hues showing in it, so-called body colors. They intersect the isointensity spheres Π_λ (see Figure 2.51). The part of the spindle-shaped body color above the intersection represents pixels that constitute

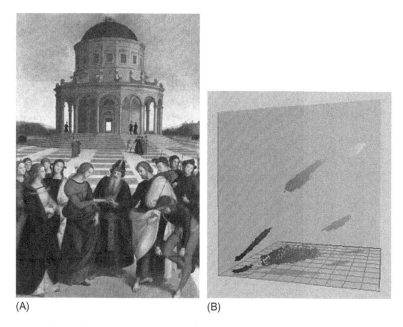

(A)   (B)

Figure 2.50 Two different hues and three brightness levels. (A) Raffaello's painting; (B) the corresponding RGB histogram displayed with the "colorspace" software (http://www.couleur. org/index.php?page = download).

the upper color sets in the image. By definition, the *color lines* are their frontiers. Note that a single body color at level λ (a connected component in the 2D color histogram for level λ) may split into several objects (connected components in the image); thus, the O_is and Ω_js, in general, do not likely correspond to identified patterns. See, for instance, the O_2 subset of Figure 2.48B; it contains obviously many more pixels than the sole red robe of the man labeled O_2 in Figure 2.48A.

Edge Detection

The one-dimensional (*line-wise*) feature is historically the first to have been extensively studied [53–55]. Inspired from the *geodesic lines* in analytic geometry, its basic model is twofold, being designed to grasp both local and global properties:

- P_g: The highest contrast in a single given direction. This property guarantees points on frontiers of objects to be among the selected candidate pixels. In some instances, noise, shadow, blur, and so forth may interfere in this selection. The analytic model is a step function in the direction orthogonal to the likely contour, often with a tilted jump and some combined noise (Figure 2.52).
- P_l: The lowest variations following the likely contour direction (ideally orthogonal to the gray-level gradient). A sequence of such selected pixels constitutes a digital contour line with bounded intensity variation.

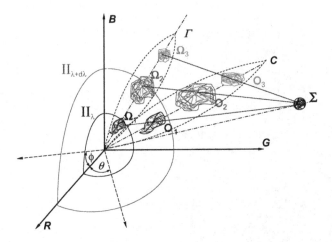

Figure 2.51 Defining color lines: the RGB cumulative space of a given image with light source Σ. Γ and C are two different hues, intersected by the isointensity spheres Π_λ. Body colors are the spindle-shaped body Γ and C, corresponding to two different hues. Following Eqn (2.37), the part of it under the intersection with the isointensity sphere Π_λ (upper level lines) above Π_λ (lower level lines) represents pixels that constitute *color sets* in the image. Their frontiers are the *color lines*. Note that a single body color at level λ (a connected component in the 2D color histogram on the sphere Π_λ) may split into several objects, connected components in the image; thus, the O_is and Ω_js of the 3D histogram do not likely correspond to identified patterns.

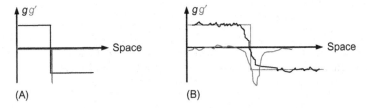

Figure 2.52 (A) Theoretical one-dimensional step edge in black and dotted line its derivative (Dirac signal); (B) corresponding experimental gray-level functions crossing a real edge.

Following these two properties, edge detection algorithms are based on:

- local contrast amplifiers;
- contour line followers.

Note that, only binary images (Figure 2.52A) have a discrete unique contour. As can be seen in Figure 2.52B, the exact location of the border pixel is hard to find in real image.

Local Contrast

A high contrast (i.e., directional intensity variation) is efficiently detected by derivation. It is then followed by the selection of local maxima or by an appropriate *thresholding*. Thanks to suitable convolution properties respective to the derivation and the commutation (images are bounded support distributions), P_g has given rise to an extended set of local operators formulated as *convolution kernels*. All are versions of the gradient (a *high-pass filter*), generalized in some way to account for increased robustness to noise, better conditioned differential operation, more precise direction measuring, and so on. As with points of interest, detectors can be designed, targeting accurate description of the surface $g = I(i, j)$:

- from a *template matching* inspiration, that is, explicitly minimizing a distance to the supposed ideal edge-like image configuration;
- through a more analytic derivative model.

Template Matching Figure 2.53 explains a computing scheme of direct optimization exploited in [56]. The author computes the closest (over all four directions) couple of plane approximations of $g(i,j)$ in every 5×5 neighborhood, to keep the one with maximum angle, provided it is large enough. Yakimovsky [57] designed a more general version, histogram based and without threshold, that was implemented on the rover actually operated on the moon. Similar algorithms are proposed in [58–61].

Mohwinkel and Kurtz [58] identifies $p \times p$ neighborhoods where the response M of a mean operator is the closest to the theoretical one, that is, $M - p^2(m_1^* + m_2^*)/2$ is minimal and small, where m_1^*, m_2^* are the respective estimated means of zones apart from the conjectured edge. Hueckel [59,60] minimize explicitly the distance between the image and the 9-parameter model of a 2D step surface in a circular neighborhood, in projection on the Hankle's (Fourier in polar coordinates) basis. Hummel [61] does the same with the Karhunen-Loeve basis (identical to the principal component analysis (PCA), least correlated orthogonal basis for a corpus of images).

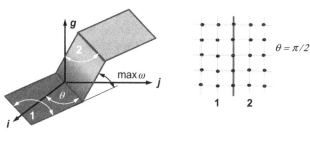

$$a_k, b_k, c_k / d_k = \min \sum_{i,j \in k} \left(g(i,j) - (a_k i + b_k j + c_k) \right)^2 \quad \text{for } k = 1,2$$

Figure 2.53 An edge model of two tilted planes (θ) with different enough relative pan (ϖ). Planes 1 and 2 are identified in 5×5 neighborhoods, to select the couple having maximum pan.

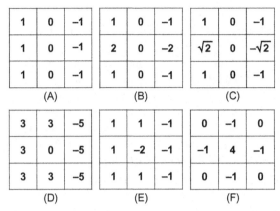

Figure 2.54 Examples of basic and historical convolution kernels: (A) Prewitt's detector, (B) Sobel's, (C) isotropic, (D) Kirsch, (E) compass, and (F) Laplacian.

Analytic Derivative Model Figure 2.54A through D displays four examples of kernels. Figure 2.54A and B are the mere first derivative (i.e., the best theoretical approximation by a plane) combined with a local directional *smoothing* mean and then Gaussian mean: the low-pass filter is parallel to the edge conjectured through the actual derivative direction. Indeed, a high response of the operator for the given gradient direction indicates a potential edge perpendicular to it, and then smoothing along the same potential edge should not disturb the detection. However, it is easy to prove that these coefficients cause a systematic error in further angle computation. That could mislead alignments such as in a Hough transform (cf. *Spatial track—cumulative matching*), the reason why Figure 2.54C filter is proposed notwithstanding its increased complexity. Figure 2.54D filter is not decomposed and interpreted that easily; its only properties are to be a high-pass directional filter with a null response on constant signals, involving eight pixels rather than the six ones of the previous filters: the end effect is an experimentally stated increased robustness to noise. Figure 2.54E is nothing other than the regularized version of the first derivative by the second one in the orthogonal direction, thus involving the complete support of the filter.

In the case of operators stemming from first-order partial derivatives, a maximum response is looked for, either local maximum or over a threshold, whether given or adapted. Note that the second derivative is used too, and among second-order operators the *Laplacian* (Figure 2.54F) is peculiarly popular as being *scalar,* then *isotropic.* There, of course, the *zero-crossing* (inflection) points are looked for [62]. It was shown in [63] that the Laplacian of a Gaussian (LoG) has some optimality, in the least-square sense, under the three following constraints: first, good detection, that is, maximal signal-to-noise ratio; second, accurate edge localization; and third, single-pixel-wide edge response.

Following the Heath Propagation Equation, the LoG is equal to the difference of Gaussian (DoG) with varied standard deviations. This is all the more interesting because it puts forward new efficient computing schemes [64,65]. Similar considerations, but stressing the edge-finding precision, prove a Bessel's function of type K to be optimal. Shen and Castan and Modestino and Fries [66,67] proposed a Wiener's scheme (Norbert Wiener

(1894—1964)) to design the version of LoG best adapted to a corpus of images in a remote-sensing application.

More generally, variational techniques have been helping to model and extract edges since the pioneering work by Geman and Geman [68] that introduces an energy bound to the segmentation (e.g., the cost of setting an edge between two pixels). The stochastic frame they adopt allows defining the potential behind the energy from image cliques according to the Hamersley-Clifford's theorem. Marroquin and others [69—71] designed an energy function very similar to the one in [68], except the frame is functional rather than stochastic. The energy to be minimized sums up the least-square distance from the image g(i,j) to its binary approximation b(i, j); the mean gradient over b (targeting a regular approximation of g); and the length of the contour lines (to balance contour tracing cost and high gradient values). Note that introducing this latter length in the calculus seems to be crucial, but it is not straightforward and was involving, in turn, the Hausdorff's measure. Such techniques allow us to exhibit edges where pixels resemble one another in a loose manner (e.g., fuzzy or semantic [72]).

It is important to note that within the universal optimization framework, the problem of image segmentation amounts to minimizing a distance between the initial and segmented images, explicitly and under constraints. The case of edge segmentation originated a wide set of frontier detections that goes far beyond mere image processing. For example, any clustering is completed by designing the frontiers of classes (generalizing the classical linear separators): methods now referred to as *snakes* exhibit separating lines constructed by balancing between an energy bound to the line elasticity and another bound to the inner cluster attraction.

Line Following

As early as 1972, the line property of the edges highlighted by P_l was motivating detectors of a completely different type. These are automata to find the best successor of an edge point within a given horizon (Figure 2.55). Dimensions and orientation of the horizon can be adapted along the process.

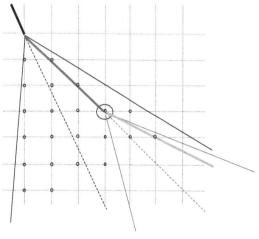

Figure 2.55 An example of a recursive walk over the image, following the contour to be exhibited. The horizon of an edge point is the triangle of depth 5 and basis 6, in the direction of the last found edge segment.

The automaton sketched in Figure 2.55 works (walks!) as follows: starting from an initial pixel and a conjectured edge direction, it searches for the most likely next edge point within the neighborhood. The optimal successor is defined from constraints on the local contrast, the edge direction, the distance between the edge points, and so forth. As the contour grows, the horizon can take into account more pixels on both sides: inner object pixels as opposed to background pixels. Also, more *a priori* information can be considered, such as the object curvature. When the *a priori* information deals with the object nature, the *automaton* becomes part of the subsequent recognition technique. Such automata are usually programmed under the form of a set of rules. They may show quasi-human behavior: the automaton is more or less adventurous, depending on whether the successor is chosen closer or farther, in the case of identical contrast. Also, more or less risk can be taken, such as for early identification of the object.

Because of the recursive modality of the walk, all possible Markovian extensions (Andreï Markov (1856−1922)) have been tried, with transition probabilities identified from a set of training images, for instance [73]. Likewise, advanced decision techniques, based on social or life models, were equally tried, such as ant colonies [74,75] or genetic programming [76−78].

Conclusive remarks on contours:

- Except for variational techniques elaborating closed edges by construction, edge-pixel candidates need to be connected after their detection by the directional contrast amplifiers, for example, Figure 2.54. This is required for the contours to be traced, coded, and manipulated as true lines (e.g., the Freeman's code discussed in *Contour-based representations* section). By the same token, successful pixels are confirmed, belonging to an edge to the exclusion of noise.
- In the same vein, contours can be rebuilt from points of interest in a way more or less adaptive to the image content. Indeed, it should not escape the reader that *corner detectors* are made for exhibiting points that present derivative discontinuities. Therefore, they can be weakened into edge detectors. Linking these sparse points is easily performed thanks to automata like the one in Figure 2.55.
- Conversely and importantly, points of interest can be viewed as informant enough singularities along edges or lines after their detection. Since 1978, Beaudet [79] had conjectured that some operators on convolution kernels had peculiar interesting properties respective to the sensitivity to points or lines.
- *In his study, 60 different kernels had been identified through a least-square approximation of the Taylor's expansion of images. They were then considered as tensors on which scalar reductions would apply: the Laplacian would be more sensitive to lines and isolated singularities, and the determinant would be triggered by corners.*

Whether they are deter inist or stochastic, the contour tracers perform all the better as the initial data are contrasted. Some become trivial in color when running on the hue component, or on textures, if the application makes texture characteristic of objects. This trivial statement, together with the automaton variants designed to include more *a priori* or global information, confirms that asserting contours cannot be fully independent of regions. This is the topic of the next section.

Region Extraction

The two-dimensional (*set-wise*) feature aims at capturing the 2D projections of objects onto the image. Its basic model is that of a *connected set* of pixels, such that regions form a partition of the image: every pixel belongs to one and only one region that is then maximal for inclusion. Indeed p_i being a pixel of image I, R_j a region, and $\mathscr{R}_{\mathscr{I}}$ the set of regions on I, then $p_i \notin R_j \Rightarrow \{p_i \cup R_j\} \notin \mathscr{R}_{\mathscr{I}}$.

Set is considered in its mathematical meaning. That is, all elements share a common characteristic property, the so-called *resemblance criterion*. In the case of region extraction, the property relates to some uniformity of the *intensity* (e.g., constant to a given precision, obeying a given statistic repartition, and so on).

Intensity refers to the straight gray-level or color value, but it can address as well complex indexes of texture or other features such as velocity or range. For still images, *texture* becomes actually a generic variable to be computed from both the intensities and the frequencies around a pixel, thus generalizing gray-level or color notions.

Connected requires a topology to be defined over the image, that is, a unit disk or a radius-one neighborhood. Depending on cameras, usual sensor arrays are hexagonal (then pixels get six immediate neighbors) or squared (then pixels may get 4 (*mod.* $\pi/2$) or 8 (*mod.* $\pi/4$) immediate neighbors, as in Figure 2.30, depending on the chosen truncature of diagonal distances).

After the basic model above, algorithms to find regions need to gather neighbor points resembling one another. Hence, they spend most of their runtime and memory to decide on that. Thus, three main classes of algorithms can be distinguished depending on the relative importance of the decision technique:

- Clustering straight on image data
- Growing regions
- For computing texture-indexes to facilitate decision

Note that, as with the feature, *point of interest* commutes with the feature *edge* in the sense of the two last conclusive remarks on contours; the feature *region* commutes with the others because an edge should be the frontier of a region and, conversely, a region should be the inner part of a closed edge. From an algorithmic point of view, given a topology, it implies that any detector of one ideally serves detecting the other.

Clustering the Image Data

For clustering the image data, all techniques can be used [80–83]. One of the first proposed was a mere *Variance Analysis* on the population of vectors normal to the surface $I(i, j)$ (e.g., *PCA* on gradient directions and amplitudes) [84,85]. The most well spread lately is probably the *C-means algorithm*, and even more so in its *fuzzy* version [86]. Constraints can be introduced in the minimization to involve neighbors or other local phenomena [87–89]. Here again, and unsurprisingly after the remark on feature commutation, the variational formulation brings efficient models

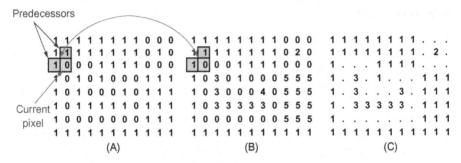

Figure 2.56 Principles of component labeling: (A) image of contours; (B) image of temporary results—the coupled automata scanning these images are figured by their support in gray; (C) final result after equivalence resolution.

out for region extraction. For instance, the *Mumford-Shah's minimization* [71] coupled with levels sets leads to a restoration-oriented segmentation technique, tightly coupling edges and regions.

Growing Regions

Consider now a picture where contours have been found. They are closed lines of 0-valued pixels on a 1-valued background, as in Figure 2.56A.

Such an image does not obey the model of an image of regions. All pixels in the background are 1-valued and are supposed to belong to the same region, as they share this common characteristic property. Yet the background is not connected. The basic algorithm to build an image of regions out of an image of contours is called *connected component labeling*. It is the foundation of region-finding procedures, principles of which are recalled in Figure 2.56.

Two automata run, respectively, on the initial and result image. Their supports, in gray in the figure, are the respective passed neighborhoods of the pixel to label, that is, the set of predecessors respective to the image scan. Given a homogeneity criterion *defining the pixel similarity, if there is no resembling pixel among its predecessors in image (A), the pixel gets a new label in image (B). If all resembling predecessors of the pixel in (A) have the same label in (B), it gets the same label. If it is not the case, a label equivalence between all labels of resembling predecessors is stored in the so-called* equivalence table *to indicate that pixels belong to the same region. The current pixel gets the smallest label. At the end of the first image scan, all equivalent labels in a class are set to the smallest value of that class, and corresponding pixels are revalued accordingly along a second scan.*

Because of its major importance at the articulation between low-level and high-level image processing, the algorithm was optimized in several manners (e.g., dealing with segments rather than with pixels [90]) so as to reach on-the-fly execution for object extraction in real-time vision [91–94].

In varying the criteria of resemblance, and running this connected component labeling on images preprocessed after a histogram or projection analysis (e.g., multi-threshold from a multi-Gaussian approximation, spatial split from a subsampled inverse Radon transform, and so on), one can design as many region segmentation processes. For instance, Ohlander et al. [14] designs the *pop-out* recursive algorithm, already mentioned in the *Chromatic clues* section. It exploits the vector nature of color data. On nine histograms computed from three representations of an image (e.g., RGB, HSV, abc), the maximum mode is extracted and the corresponding pixels are labeled in the image; then they are removed from the population for histograms to be recomputed. Stopping criteria deal with the expected number of regions or their size distribution or the signal-to-noise ratio in remaining histograms.

The drawback of such algorithms is a lack of local adaptation: all decisions on the pixel resemblance are taken globally, on the histogram for instance. Therefore, since the early 1970s, algorithms have been designed where decisions of attributing a pixel to one or another region, and then merging neighboring regions into larger ones, are taken locally and recursively in computing a distance between their characteristics. For instance, in [95] an automata network endeavors to break frontiers between blocks anywhere the contrast is low enough. In [96], histograms of neighbor block-cells and then of neighbor regions are compared for them to merge or not. Too many small uninteresting blocks are considered in the early phases, rending the procedures quite inefficient. This is avoided by a prior rough histogram analysis for coarser initial resolution. However, from the sequential nature, the main drawback of all these so-called *region growing* procedures is dependence on the image scan. Due to the *mutual exclusion* phenomenon (i.e., given (A, B, C) to be clustered, A fits B or C, but B and C cannot match) results ((A, B), C) or ((A, C), B) are bound to the input order or scan.

For this reason, the underlying pyramidal data structure was made explicit in more modern versions. Indeed, regarding action, it could be adequately similar to gather a large number of neighbors at the highest possible resolution or to consider a smaller number of them at lower resolution. The difference relies on the precision of the observation that cannot be other than action driven.

A pyramidal structure (Figure 2.57) is a stack of images I^n with progressively decreasing dimension. I^n(layer of sons) results from I^{n-1}(layer of fathers) thanks to two local mappings υ and $\varkappa$, defining, respectively:

- *the neighborhood of p_{ij}^{n-1} that supports the computation of the intensity attributed to p_{ij}^n;*
- *the operator computing the latter intensity (e.g., mean, Gaussian mean, min, max, modal).*

I^0 stands for the original image (Figure 2.57A).

That hierarchical structure suggests two natural scans: bottom-up, as previously described (initial regions are pixels to be merged up to most extended uniformity), or top-down (initial region is the image to be recursively split up to uniformity). Horowitz and Pavlidis [97] proposed the first version of a recursive split where blocks are separated into four sub-blocks as long as the mean gray level does not remain between given bounds.

Many criteria dealing with the gray-level repartition inside the considered block can be used, but also geometric constraints such as minimal size. Moreover, several criteria can

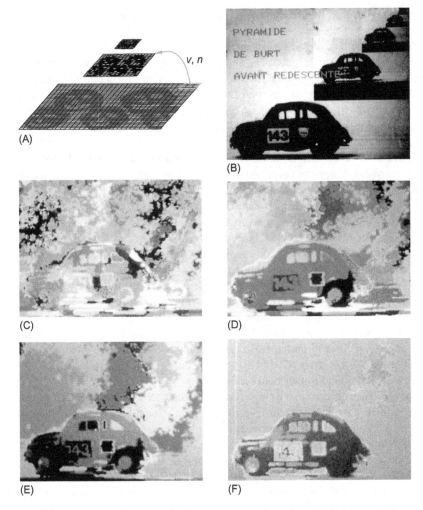

Figure 2.57 An example of a pyramid data structure with an image being processed. (A) Principles of the *v* and *n* mappings; (B) Burt's pyramid; (C–F) bottom-up segmentation results descending from different pyramid layers.

apply with priorities [98]. As usual, the most efficient trade-off consists in oscillating within the pyramid up to stabilization of a given criterion. For instance, Horowitz and Pavlidis [99] consider a merge phase (e.g., between neighbor blocks of different sizes) at the end of every splitting sequence. It may lower the aliasing artifacts from privileged directions (vertical and horizontal) introduced by the block nature of intermediate data. Burt et al. [100] installs bidirectional links between layers: a third mapping a defines among which pixels in $I^{n-1}a$ a son in I^n can choose its father. Intensities are then computed all over the pyramid in an asynchronous manner, as sons move to the closest father, until the process stabilizes (see Figure 2.57B). In the end, considering, for instance, a quad-pyramid, if 2^{2k} regions are searched for,

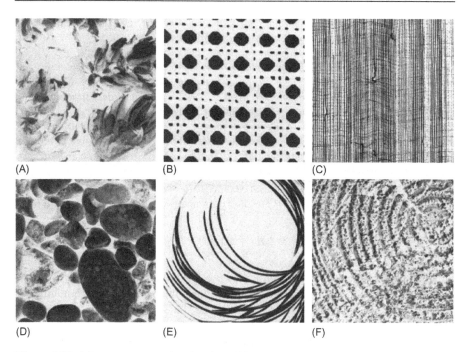

(A)   (B)   (C)

(D)   (E)   (F)

Figure 2.58 A few texture samples showing different structural and statistical distributions from the Brodatz album.

they will be the sets of kin's, in the base (highest definition), of ancestors at the k-layer of the pyramid (Figure 2.57C−F).

Other variants of *split and merge* algorithms come from splitting images in a more adaptive way than just by dichotomy (e.g., with more directions or after quick and dirty evaluation of the greatest global contrast where to cut, and so on). The ultimate variation in that direction consists in making edge and region detection cooperate, as already and more generally introduced after the feature complementarity [101−103].

Texture Indexing

The texture index generalizes the pixel's gray level in relating some neighborhood arrangement. Texture turns out to be tautologically the characteristic of regions when dealing with applications where it gets a physical meaning (manufactured-objects handling, remote sensing, etc.). More specifically, it aims at capturing some intermediate phenomenon participating of both signal intensity and frequency. Then, first operators to measure it belong to global transforms (Fourier, Hadamard, Haar, etc.) of which a sufficient number of carefully selected coefficients are kept. A classification procedure on these coefficients usually achieves texture discrimination. This algorithmic fashion motivated the creation of texture image bases, the oldest of which is the Brodatz album [104] (Figure 2.58).

The Gabor's transform was quasi-designed for texture description [105,106]: it consists of local Fourier by octaves with a Gaussian interpolation. Wavelets are suitable as well. Most textures can be isolated with less than a dozen coefficients.

However, as with edges, the computing complexity still increased by the multidimensional nature leads to operate in the image space rather than in the spectrum. In this space, frequency tuning results from multiresolution, in other words, a pyramidal data structure again. For instance, coefficients of autoregressive filters [107] can be identified to synthesize textured regions out of a white noise. Even more simply, local histograms are used to count directional maxima in a chosen neighborhood or directional variations at a given range.

A special attention has been devoted to the so-called *co-occurrence matrices*, for example, [108,109]: these are bidimensional histograms of the couples of gray-level values at extremities of a chosen vector (*displacement*) being translated over an ROI. Co-occurrence matrices P are thus parameterized by the displacement u_j.

$$P_j = \left[p^j_{m,l} \right] / p^j_{m,l} = P(I(x) = m \wedge I(x + u_j) = l) \tag{2.39}$$

u_j is the displacement with direction j; $(x, x + u_j)$ is the considered couple of pixels both belonging to the ROI; and $I(x)$, $I(x + u_j)$, their intensities; $\mathscr{P}$ is the number of occurrences of a couple of gray levels, that is, the value of its class in the 2D histogram.

To lower the computing burden, neighbors are likely at distance 1, then with 4 or 8 directions considered, whereas multiresolution provides for the distance adaptation. Figure 2.59 gives a toy example.

A double data reduction allows keeping acceptable complexity: the gray scale is adjusted down to three or even two bits, and then a vector of more global variables extracted from these matrices (e.g., energy, moments, entropy, correlation, and so on) summarizes the set of matrices [110]. Note that subsampling the gray scale is physically sensible because the same information contained in the neighborhood is brought up partly through the intensity and partly through the frequency [111]. It is mandatory with respect to computation, as more couple values than pixels in the neighborhood would mean a hollow histogram.

Beyond all the techniques above that rather deal with microtextures [112], the organization of motifs at a more macroscale (see Figure 2.59) is likely achieved with *grammars* to define *placement rules* [113].

It should be understood that, after so big a computing investment to evaluate the texture variable, the decision cost is expected to be comparatively low, ideally a mere threshold, in most cases. Nevertheless, in tricky or ambiguous environment, the texture value would barely replace the gray level in whatever region-finding

$$
I \begin{vmatrix} 0 & 0 & 1 & 1 \\ 0 & 0 & 1 & 1 \\ 0 & 2 & 2 & 2 \\ 2 & 2 & 3 & 3 \end{vmatrix} \qquad
P_0 \begin{vmatrix} 2 & 2 & 1 & 0 \\ 0 & 2 & 0 & 0 \\ 0 & 0 & 3 & 1 \\ 0 & 0 & 0 & 1 \end{vmatrix} \qquad
P_1 \begin{vmatrix} 2 & 1 & 0 & 0 \\ 0 & 1 & 0 & 0 \\ 0 & 2 & 2 & 0 \\ 0 & 0 & 1 & 0 \end{vmatrix} \qquad
P_2 \begin{vmatrix} 3 & 0 & 0 & 0 \\ 0 & 2 & 0 & 0 \\ 2 & 2 & 1 & 0 \\ 0 & 0 & 2 & 0 \end{vmatrix} \qquad
P_3 \begin{vmatrix} 1 & 0 & 0 & 0 \\ 1 & 1 & 0 & 0 \\ 3 & 1 & 0 & 0 \\ 0 & 0 & 2 & 0 \end{vmatrix}
$$

(A)   (B)   (C)   (D)   (E)

Figure 2.59 A small image I, in (A), with its co-occurrence matrices in (B–E); P_i is the matrix relative to the 8-Freman's direction i.

technique that could support vectorization [114,115]. The same remark holds for color extensions.

The Spatial Track

Principles here recalled deal with space sensing from a vector of images, to the exclusion of approaches that may find motion or depth out of a single image, for example, by inverting a blur.

Space Modeling

The human representation of space operates at several semantic levels concurrently. At low level, it benefits mainly from binocular vision for stereo reconstruction or from peripheral vision and retinal persistency for motion sensing. At high level, it takes advantage of: other objects estimated dimensions, relative positions, whether they are static or moving in the scene, and so on. The lighting intensity, its granularity and chromaticity, can be interpreted too, but less frequently, and, in general, less effectively.[1] All static artifacts were exploited by Raffaello (cf. *Photometric track*). The caveman, Giacometti, and Daumier all use the viewers' common-sense knowledge of dynamics' laws (e.g., balance articulation) and of sport patterns or strategies (hunting, wrestling, etc.).

Digital systems instead exploit the lower levels: not requiring any elaborate interpretation, space is sensed through range and motion almost immediately. In this *early* type of vision, models deal mainly with the image acquisition and address the sensor and corresponding scene geometry. Independently from semantics, the multiplicity of images in space (stereo) or time (sequence) allows the desired spatial information to be extracted thanks to an interimage comparison. *Corresponding pixels* are the respective projections of a same physical point figured into several images of the same scene. The apparent *displacement* of the projection between images supports spatial sensing.

As in previous sections, models and representations precede feature extraction and preliminary reconstruction.

Monocular View of 3D Scenes

Human observers, even if unconsciously, are able to reconstruct a three-dimensional scene from a two-dimensional image. This process is known as the *inverse reconstruction problem*, which is an *ill-posed one*, as described in [116].

In order to establish the correspondence between the 3D scene and the image plane, the *pinhole camera* serves as the model. Considering Figure 2.60, f is the focal distance, O is the camera lens position, O is the center of the image plane,

---

[1]For artificial systems such as for some animals, lighting can be controlled in a coherent way, and the warping of resulting patterns can be used for spatial assessment.

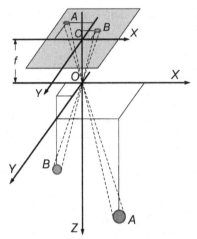

Figure 2.60 Basic geometry of the pinhole camera model.

and A and B are objects in the scene. The spatial three-dimensional coordinates are labeled X, Y, and Z, while X and Y are the corresponding coordinates on the image plane. The fundamental equation of perspective projection is:

$$X = -f\frac{X}{Z}; \quad Y = -f\frac{Y}{Z} \tag{2.40}$$

As may be seen by looking at Figure 2.60, two objects (A and B) are mapped on the image plane by projection through the pinhole O. By knowing only the (X, Y) coordinates on the image plane, it is possible to determine the spatial position in the scene except for a constant factor: an arbitrary image point **I** represents an object point that lies on the straight line containing the segment **IO**.

The placement of an image point in the 3D space may be achieved either by techniques inspired from human processes, such as the ones exploited by Raffaello and explained in the introduction of this chapter, or, generally with a higher accuracy, by means of a multiple view approach. In this last case, two images are usually sufficient, and the problem is the one of finding correspondences between these two images.

Range Acquisition Modeling

In its static mode, the 3D spatial perception addresses recovering the lost Z variable from the planar images. It is mainly based on the *triangulation* process that is now discussed together with related basic difficulties. Reconstruction ambiguities are then highlighted, first through the simplest correlation process.

Binocular Vision

The model of displacement stems from the model of camera. Referring to Figure 2.61, *tie* points can be found on the so-called *epipolar* lines. The general point P, together with the two foci, determines a plane α. Its respective projections,

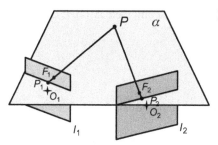

Figure 2.61 Basic geometry of stereo vision.

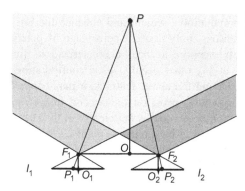

Figure 2.62 Stereovision geometry. The light gray zone corresponds to the image overlapping area of the two viewpoints.

points P_1 and P_2, onto image planes I_1 and I_2 are located at the (epipolar) lines of intersection between the α plane and the image planes.

In practice, a point is selected on one of the two images, and the corresponding tie point will be searched on the epipolar line of the other image. More precisely, assume that P_1 has been selected on I_1, point P is located along the line joining P_1 with F_1 and is projected through $F_2(P_1F_1F_2$ determine $\alpha)$ on the epipolar line obtained by the intersection of I_2 with α.

Finding the Z-Value

To simplify the analysis, two parallel and coplanar images are considered to be taken by cameras having the same focus distance f (Figure 2.62).

Without losing generality, epipolar lines are assumed horizontal in the plane PF_1F_2, so having a common Y-value, with the X-axis along the *baseline* (F_1F_2) and the Z-axis orthogonal to it. Both visual fields of the cameras are sketched in the figure to underline that only the overlapping area can be exploited for the Z-value determination. After Thales, applied in the two triangle pairs: $PF_1O - P_1F_1O_1$ and $PF_2O - P_2F_2O_2$, indicating with B the length of the baseline, and with Δ_1 and Δ_2 the P_1O_1 and O_2P_2 lengths, respectively; the *depth* Z is given by:

$$Z = f \frac{B}{\Delta_1 + \Delta_2} \tag{2.41}$$

The influence of the distance Z on the error of the computed Δ $(\Delta = \Delta_1 + \Delta_2)$ is evidenced by mere derivation:

$$\frac{dZ}{d\Delta} = -\frac{Z}{\Delta} \tag{2.42}$$

Note that the error increases linearly with the depth and is amplified in the case of small Δ values.

Looking for the Tie Point

Some criteria must be followed when choosing the object points for determining the correspondences in order to limit computational weight and enhance the reliability of the determination. For these reasons, only a small percentage of pixels are chosen among those which strongly support a local characterization, for instance, point of interest, edge segment, or any other peculiar local configuration. Nevertheless, although pixels are chosen having the above features, it may happen that some of them do not have a corresponding pixel on the second image, so become useless. For example, in Figure 2.63 three vertices are clearly in the scene but, due to the object opacity, only one is present in both images (point C), whereas the other two are alternatively present (A in image 1 and B in image 2).

After the method presented in the *Shape extraction* section, one of the simplest ways to determine whether a given pixel (p, q) on one image I_1 is a good candidate is to compute the gray-level variance in a limited neighborhood of such pixel. If its value exceeds a given threshold, then a region centered on that pixel, sized $[(2n + 1) \times (2m + 1)]$, is considered and *correlated* with other regions on image I_2. Such regions are centered around pixels of coordinates (i, j) selected on the epipolar line[2]; to compute the correlation between regions of both images, the following formula may be used:

$$C(i,j) = \sum_{r=-n}^{n} \sum_{s=-m}^{m} [I_2(i+r, j+s) - I_1(p+r, q+s)]^2 \tag{2.43}$$

The selected region for correspondence will be the one producing minimum value of $C(i, j)$, if it is below a given threshold. Nevertheless, the location of the corresponding pixel on the second image is still a difficult task. Distortions occur due to the different points of view. To get around these distortions, extracting the homologous pixel P_2 of pixel P_1 exploits gray-level correlation. The physical object orientation may make gray levels of pixels P_1 and P_2 be different even though they are projections of the same material point P, and this is worse on the small region where correlation is computed. See, for instance, Figure 2.64, where

---

[2] The geometry as described in Figure 2.62 assumes parallel cameras at the same height, which allows searching homologous tie points onto horizontal epipolar lines with the same Y coordinate (image row). In practical applications, only a *calibration* phase and *image registration* guarantee such properties.

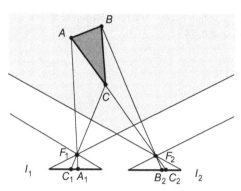

Figure 2.63 An occlusion example: B is occluded in I_1, whereas A is occluded in I_2.

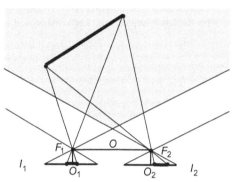

Figure 2.64 Distorted views due to different projections.

the characterizing object points are differently mapped according to the projection slope.

In order to limit computation time, the values of the neighborhood size m, n should be kept low. Due to the distortions mentioned above, small regions turn out to be inadequate. Another way to limit computational cost in many practical applications is to reduce the search interval along the epipolar line. This can be done when a specific range is conjectured *a priori*.

As an example, let us consider the case in which the inspection area has minimum and maximum distance values, like in robotic applications for part handling or in stereo ground-reconstruction using remote-sensing technology. In Figure 2.65, the epipolar line reduces to a segment having $P_{2M}P_{2m}$ for extrema; analytically:

$$\Delta_{2M} = -f\frac{B}{Z_{\max}} + \Delta_1; \quad \Delta_{2m} = f\frac{B}{Z_{\min}} + \Delta_1 \tag{2.44}$$

determining the segment $P_{2M}P_{2m}$.

Another heuristic to lower the computing burden is to exploit constraints as the natural pixel ordering. When inspecting the epipolar segment, we expect pixel ordering to be correct; unfortunately, this is not always true, as may be seen in the

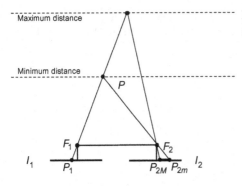

Figure 2.65 The epipolar segment geometry.

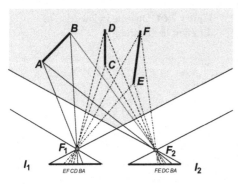

Figure 2.66 The ordering problem as seen by the letter sequence on each image.

example of Figure 2.66 in which the ordered sequence of correspondences is reversed (*DE* on one image and *ED* on the other).

Note that correlation is the simplest matching operator. Gray-level repartition variations can be absorbed by more sophisticated decision techniques, as introduced in the *Shape extraction* section.

Structured Light

A common way to facilitate the solution of the correspondence problem is to play on the lighting conditions. Light can be artificially structured in three possible ways, following dimensions. In the first way, a single object point (zero D) in the scene is highlighted (e.g., with a colored beam), no correspondence problem arises, and triangulation applies directly. In addition, if the beam is laser generated, the time of flight of this coherent light can indicate depth as well. In a second way, a striped illumination pattern (1D) is generated so as to evaluate the object position and shape through the analysis of the stripe distortions. The third option is similar in projecting a grid (2D) illumination.

As an example, Figure 2.67 sketches the effect of striped illumination as seen by a camera placed vertically in front. δp is the distance at a given ordinate value between the line projection of the stripe on the object and the vertical plane. The height h_p of the object at

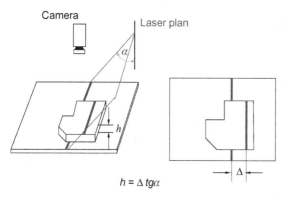

Camera

Laser plan

α

h

Figure 2.67 The use of striped light.

$h = \Delta\, tg\alpha$

Δ

the intersection point may be computed through the tangent of angle α between the horizontal plane and the beam plane, as expressed by the following formula:

$$h_p = \delta p \tan \alpha \qquad (2.45)$$

Motion Modeling

In its dynamic mode, space modeling addresses motion. In many applications, a significant feature of the scene to be analyzed is the movement of some objects during a time interval. Such apparent movements may be either due to the image sensor, as in an airplane photographic campaign (*egomotion*), or due to some scene components, such as cars in a road scenario [117], or both. First, the camera is assumed to remain still; next, egomotion is introduced and compensated for, leading back to the former analysis.

Preliminaries for Motion Analysis

In Figure 2.60, all the segments having extremes on **OA** and **OB** have a common representation in the segment **BA**. If **A** or **B** are moving objects with velocity components V_x, V_y, and V_z in 3D space, the corresponding velocity of the A or B image points, may be computed as follows [Ver96]:

$$V_X = \frac{f}{Z}\left(\frac{X}{Z}V_Z - V_X\right); \quad V_Y = \frac{f}{Z}\left(\frac{Y}{Z}V_Z - V_Y\right) \qquad (2.46)$$

The object speed in the scene is not known *a priori*, so it must be estimated by the detected movement of the object projection on the image. Unfortunately, this problem is ill-posed because it is seldom possible to compute the object speed in space only knowing the planar displacement of its projections.

As an illustrative example, positively using this limitation to attract attention, consider the barber-shop banner usually displayed outdoors, schematically shown in Figure 2.68. Typically, a rotation movement of a three-colored striped pattern on a cylinder perceptually suggests that the whole pattern is translated vertically upward. In some cases, two helices (clockwise and counterclockwise) appear under rotation to clash in the middle of the

Figure 2.68 A traditional barber shop sign.

cylinder. In fact, a rotational movement is the only one really existing, because the cylinder has a fixed size.

Motion Models from Images

Motion models exploit two different invariants. In the first one, peculiar object points are assumed to be recovered from one image to the next; in the second, all visible-point intensities are supposed to be maintained along time. In this connection, two different approaches of motion are distinguished, respectively, named *discrete* or *sparse* and *continuous* or *dense*: first, motion via correspondence [118] and second, motion via local change [119]. In the first case, corresponding points must be found on different successive images. Note that, in stereo vision, to evaluate the position in space, point correspondences must be similarly found from different images. In the second case, a simple local analysis on the whole image must be performed with the limitation that only one motion component may be detected, the one orthogonal to the image contour.

Many authors [120−124] have compared these approaches and evaluated their performance on sets of images, including their impact on computational strategies.

Motion via Correspondence Normally, peculiar points on the first image are located so as to search their corresponding points on the second image. As in the triangulation for stereovision, there is no guarantee that such corresponding points exist, because the camera was shifted and the new point of view may not include such points, moved out of the field of view. The object is first considered as a rigid one and therefore without plastic distortion, and the background is regarded as stationary.

From the implementation point of view, in order to reduce the computational cost, the number of points is limited to the truly characteristic ones. The analysis is restricted to pairs of consecutive images of the sequence. Similarly to the epipolar

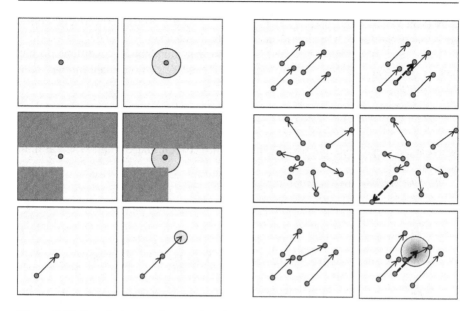

Figure 2.69 Knowledge-based constraints for motion modeling.

segment for stereovision, the corresponding points are searched in a restricted area determined by a few heuristics [125,126] illustrated in Figure 2.69:

- Figure 2.69A shows that a generic central object point can be located in the successive frame within a circle with a radius equal to $V_{max} \Delta t$, where V_{max} is the highest possible velocity of such a point.
- Figure 2.69B shows that the previous circular field is also limited by existing obstacles and physical boundaries contained in the scene.
- Moreover, an extrapolation can enable *tracking* the object point in successive frames, as shown in C. The velocity detected in the two previous frames may be exploited to foresee the future position of the object point (*time filtering*). As before, a displacement will be inside a circle of radius equal to $\frac{1}{2} A_{max} \Delta t^2$, where A_{max} is the maximum acceleration.
- Case D considers that two object points do not likely coalesce into one single point of the following frame, leading to the so-called *consistent matching* criterion. The picture shows four identified points that force the correspondence of the fifth dark one.
- Case E depicts the *common motion* situation: once the motion of the neighbors has been identified, the dark point necessarily maps into a congruent position (the depicted case is an expansion centered in the figure window).
- Case F corresponds to a motion model for a "herd" of points suggesting the most plausible displacement of the dark object point.

Note that as soon as the model gets more complex to include object deformation, such criteria have to be reconsidered.

Motion via Local Change Differently from the previous approach, the computation now is performed with respect to points, evaluating the motion based on the gray-level variations of pixels. Let P_n and P_{n+1} be the pixels, respectively, corresponding to the same 3D point in successive frames n and $n + 1$; under the assumption that this object point remains visible and that illumination conditions do not change, it is assumed that the gray value f of P_n and P_{n+1} is constant (*optical flow constraint*):

$$f(x + \partial x, y + \partial y, t + \partial t) = f(x, y, t) \tag{2.47}$$

where δx, δy represents the pixel displacement between images, and δt is the time interval.

By differentiating, we can write:

$$f_x \frac{\partial x}{\partial t} + f_y \frac{\partial y}{\partial t} = -f_t \tag{2.48}$$

or equivalently, using • for the scalar product, and ∇ for the gradient operator:

$$\nabla f \bullet \overline{V} = -f_t \tag{2.49}$$

Under the hypothesis that $\nabla f \neq 0$, this becomes:

$$\overline{V}_\perp = \frac{-f_t}{\sqrt{f_x^2 + f_y^2}} \tag{2.50}$$

giving the velocity along the gradient direction.

For a more elementary and geometric representation of formula (2.50), gray-level variations due to the movement of the object points are illustrated in Figure 2.70. X corresponds to the location examined along a given spatial coordinate, while four straight lines materialize four potential gray-level variations

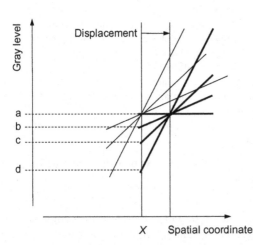

Figure 2.70 Gray-level variations.

(*linearized*) on the object. Bold lines show the gray-level pattern due to the object displacement. If the object point moves along a direction having a constant gray level, no variation can be detected. Conversely, the higher the gradient value, the greater the gray-level variation due to motion, so that the movement along the gradient direction is evaluated easily in accordance through it. Equation (2.50) states that the apparent movement is inversely weighted with the gradient intensity.

The information obtained via this approach only refers to the orthogonal direction with respect to the contour, and through the years a number of algorithms have been given to provide a more detailed movement information [127−131], as will be developed in the *Motion extraction* section.

Spatiotemporal Cues

Although it could serve for analyzing trajectories or movements of scene components, the model here presented aims first at evaluating the shape and position of still components from their apparent motion due to the camera movement (egomotion). Figure 2.71 shows a camera downward shift along the Z-axis.

Thanks to the relativity of perception, it is equivalent to assume that the camera is still and the scene moves in the opposite direction along the Z-axis. In this way, although the **P** point belonging to the *ZX* plane moves vertically down by **dP**, its corresponding image point *P* moves along the *X*-axis by *dP*. Considering the triangle similarity between **PZO** and **POO,** this becomes again:

$$X = f\frac{X}{Z} \tag{2.51}$$

by deriving *X* with respect to *Z*, obtaining:

$$\frac{\mathrm{d}X}{X} = -\frac{\mathrm{d}Z}{Z} \tag{2.52}$$

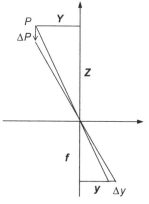

Figure 2.71 Egomotion analysis.

so that the distance Z may be derived by considering that dZ is the known motion of the camera, and (X, dX) is determined from the image.

$$Z = -\frac{dZ}{dX} X \tag{2.53}$$

In this way, the distance with respect to the focal plane can be ideally computed for all the points of the scene.

Points with the same Z coordinate and different X-values get different dX *apparent displacements*. Figure 2.71 illustrates such displacements for a given value k of the Z coordinate. As may be seen, the apparent movements are radial centered on the origin. This origin is called *focus of expansion* (FOE). According to (2.52), a collision time (camera/object) could be estimated: the displacement dX with respect to the FOE has the same relationship as the displacement along the Z-axis with respect to the focal plane.

For a camera having general velocity with components u, v, and w, respectively, along the X-, Y-, and Z-axes, the generic object point X_0, Y_0, Z_0 will be displaced, following (2.54):

$$X = -f\frac{X_O + ut}{Z_O + wt}; \quad Y = -f\frac{Y_O + vt}{Z_O + wt} \tag{2.54}$$

In order to compute the coordinates of the final/original destination of the moving point, we may evaluate (2.54) for $t = \pm\infty$, thereby obtaining:

$$X_{\text{FOE}} = -f\frac{u}{w}; \quad Y_{\text{FOE}} = -f\frac{v}{w} \tag{2.55}$$

Space Extraction

From space modeling, the common framework of 3D (field wise) features extraction is that of the constancy of corresponding pixels over several images. The *field of apparent shifts* from one image to the other, *disparity* in stereo and *velocity* in motion, allows enough original variables to be instantiated for space to be recovered. To complete identification of the interimage transform, it is necessary to follow some well-chosen geometric model (affine, projective) and then cinematic or dynamic. Thus, the so-called *matching process* that exhibits corresponding pixels is the crux of the matter in depth or motion finding, and so they are closely related both technically and functionally.

Matching algorithms and subsequent identification of geometric transforms between images will be the same for motion and depth. In addition, depth helps in finding motion and vice versa: indeed, a displacement can reveal both range and motion through a common notion of *parallax*. The technical analogy and the physical complementarity make them commute even more between them than with points, edges, or regions. However, matching the latter static features lowers the computing burden, as said in the *Space modeling* section, whereas in ambiguous situations (e.g., camouflage) an object might be detectable and its shape be known only after it moves.

Space extraction concentrates on the apparent shifts and focuses on matching processes to exhibit the displacement field. In the sequel, the sole motion is studied for being less constrained *a priori* than depth (see *Motion via correspondence* section). No such constraint, such as epipolar ones, can be imposed except for those coming from knowledge on the original motion (e.g., straight move of the camera in a static environment, transverse mobile trajectory in front of a still camera). For instance, putting together the real movement could benefit from first finding the FOE (Eqn (2.55)). However, 3D image reconstruction or global movement recovery resort already to the interpretation. Again, at the segmentation stage, displacement is the key phenomenon and relies on image matching. As already exploited for modeling, the displacement relativity implies that image changes may be similar whether the camera moves or objects in the scene do. To choose one or the other assumption is yet another interpretation and requires prior hypotheses to be checked from results. It should be understood, however, that the choice may prejudice subsequent methods; for example, trying to identify and subtract the background would be better in static camera situations.

Summarizing, after the basic model of displacement above, algorithms have to exhibit similar points or neighborhoods or regions between images. They can address sparse data, likely significant (e.g., formerly detected points or edge pieces), or they deal with the whole image and aim at computing the *field vector* associated to every pixel. In this latter case of a dense field, the motion-finding operators require a more or less explicit model (trajectory, intensity variation, etc.) and consecutive optimization, as for any other feature. In the sequel, extraction algorithms are studied following this taxonomy.

Sparse Data and Explicit Model

Images to be matched are assumed to have been reduced to a collection of items represented as vectors. These vectors list the *central*-pixel coordinates together with *intensity-related* and *geometry-related* properties.

Central means the pixel itself if it is in isolation, or any distinguished point (center of mass or maximum of a property) if the pixel was associated with a neighborhood like a piece of edge or a small window around. Intensity-related covers all statistical features in the item up to contrast if it is one-dimensional and texture if it is two-dimensional, color if it is available, and so on. Geometry refers to some approximation of the Taylor's type (Tim B. Taylor (1685–1731)) like tangent-orientation (linearization, as in Eqn (2.48)) or curvature, or to projection onto a function basis such as Tchebycheff's (Pafnuty L. Tchebycheff (1821–1894)).

The sets of items can be paired using any technique that minimizes a global set distance computed from individual ones. Once again, the final aim is to identify the parameters of a given model of transform (affine or projective most often) between the images from their match. The number of parameters then depends on the supposed complexity of the displacement: translation, with 2D rotation or with 3D rotation, followed by projections, with scaling or not, and so on.

Correlation-Based Matching

Being the simplest least-square scheme associated with the simplest image preprocessing made correlation extremely popular in industrial systems. Indeed the prior segmentation is aborted and reduced to block cropping. As already explained (*Looking for the tie point* section), blocks $B_{i+r,j+s}$ belonging to a given window ($-n \leq r \leq n$, $-m \leq s \leq m$) in the next image are correlated with $B_{i,j}$ in the current image, for an extremum to be exhibited (minimum for least-square expression, as in Eqn (2.42); maximum for the usual inner product expression). Note that n and m are nothing but translating physical bounds or other *a priori* knowledge on the motion or geometry. Note also that following the above reminders on static segmentation, any distance computed between blocks or between their histograms or their projections, and so forth, can do: maximum correlation is just an efficient (*convolutive*) implementation of the minimal Euclidean distance. Note eventually that the technique suffers a lack of robustness in front of:

- *scaling*, for example, when objects get closer or further from the camera;
- *occlusion*, for example, when objects pass beyond obstacles.

In the case of scaling, linear interpolation among image subparts can compensate to a certain extent (Figure 2.72). In the case of occlusion, secondary picks appearing in the result might jeopardize the process (e.g., for tracking) and must be detected as perturbations. Thus, recursive least squares, quite efficient too, become as popular, but some techniques based on more structural distances profit better from the geometric nature of items.

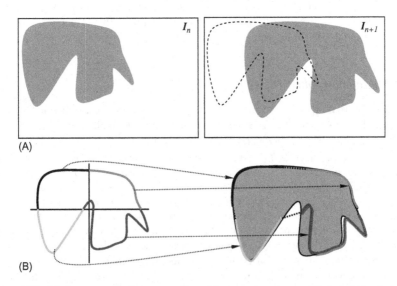

Figure 2.72 (A) Apparent displacement of an object coming closer; (B) correlation between subpatterns to compensate for scaling.

Dynamic programming (Levenstein's distance between chains of characters, as explained in Decision methods section) is known to absorb pattern warping if the data can cluster into sequential subsets such as contours.

As a rule, any constraint from *a priori* interitem link in the image (e.g., being on a same line or region) lowers the *combinatorics* of interimage association.

Cumulative Matching

When a global consensus over couples of homologous items is looked for, a special mention needs to be made of Hough techniques. The Hough transform is originally the exploitation of the *linear algebra*'s duality. For instance, finding alignments of points in a binary image is theoretically equivalent to finding local maxima in the *parameter space*. Indeed, a point (or vector) in a space corresponds to the bundle of linear forms crossing in it and thus is a straight line in the dual (Figure 2.73).

The technique extends to the detection of any parameterized curve and more generally to the identification of any parameterized phenomenon. This is further detailed in *Structural track* section in Chapter 3. As for space extraction, the Hough transform has been applied as a voting process by couples being tentatively matched. Couples are scanned in a random or exhaustive manner, to exhibit the most likely parameters of the transform translating the apparent motion. The number of parameters to identify implies the number of exploited components in the items: for example, a translation needs two parameters from which a pixel is enough; translation plus 2D planar rotation amounts to five parameters, then two rigidly linked segments; and so forth.

Bipartite Graph Matching

When the population under decision is not considered as the set of possible couples, but the stress is put on the distinction between images, then the underlying structure of bipartite graph is put forward in the optimization problem. Decision models are more of the social type, such as in the *stable marriage* [132] or the *college admission* problem, and they are among the popular ones in modern combinatorics [133−136].

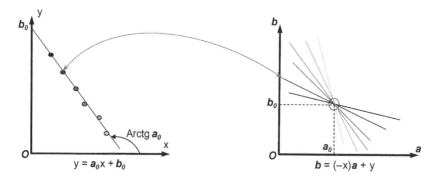

Figure 2.73 The Hough transform duality between edge points and straight-line parameters.

$$\odot(m_i / f_j) =$$

m_1	m_2	m_3	m_4	m_5
f_2	f_1	f_2	f_1	f_5
f_5	f_2	f_3	f_3	f_3
f_1	f_3	f_5	f_2	f_2
f_3	f_4	f_4	f_4	f_1
f_4	f_5	f_1	f_5	f_4

$$\odot(f_i / m_j) =$$

f_1	f_2	f_3	f_4	f_5
m_5	m_4	m_1	m_3	m_4
m_1	m_5	m_4	m_2	m_2
m_4	m_2	m_2	m_4	m_3
m_2	m_1	m_3	m_1	m_5
m_3	m_3	m_5	m_5	m_1

Figure 2.74 An example of preference lists in the case of a 5 × 5 population.

m_1
f_2

m_1	m_2
f_2	f_1

m_1	m_2	m_1
f_2	f_1	f_2
		f_3

m_1	m_2	m_3	m_4
f_2	f_1	f_2	f_1
f_5	f_2	f_3	

m_1	m_2	m_3	m_4	m_5
f_2	f_1	f_2	f_1	f_5
f_5	f_2	f_3	f_3	f_3
f_1	f_3	f_5		f_2
f_4				

Figure 2.75 The five steps of the men-first marrying process on the population of Figure 2.74.

Each element of two respective populations (finite subsets with cardinal n), say *Women* (or *Image q*) and *Men* (or *Image q + 1*), has sorted the members of the other subset (opposite sex or other image) into its preference list (Figure 2.74). A matching $\mathcal{M}$ being a one-to-one correspondence between men and women, if (m, w) is a matched pair in $\mathcal{M}$, we note $\mathcal{M}(m) = w$ and $\mathcal{M}(w) = m$. Man μ and woman ω form a *blocking pair* if (μ,ω) is not in $\mathcal{M}$, but μ prefers ω to $\mathcal{M}(\mu)$, and ω prefers μ to $\mathcal{M}(\omega)$. If $\ell_x(y)$ is the rank of y in the list of x, (μ,ω) is blocking if:

$$\ell_\mu(\omega) \prec \ell_\mu(\mathcal{M}(\mu)); \quad \ell_\omega(\mu) \prec \ell_\omega(\mathcal{M}(\omega)) \tag{2.56}$$

If there is no blocking pair, then the marriage $\mathcal{M}$ is stable.

In [132], an algorithm is designed with complexity $O(n^2)$ to guarantee stability. Elements x of one subset are asked to select their preferred mate y. In the case of conflict, two x wanting the same y, the given y chooses and the neglected x tries further in its list (Figure 2.75). The algorithm is unfair to one-half the population and it may make every couple unhappy: indeed, men get their best possible choice and women their worst, or vice versa.

Note that the "women first" process would bring $\mathcal{M} = (f_1,m_5)$, (f_3,m_1), (f_4,m_3), (f_5,m_2), (f_2,m_4).

Zavidovique and Suvonvorn [137,138] designed new solutions based on the so-called marriage table (Figure 2.76), where couples are framed by the mutual ranks of partners. Adapted scans of the table allow adding constraints such as minimal global satisfaction $(\min \sum_{x,y \in M} \ell_x(y) + \ell_y(x))$ *and maximum fairness* $(\min \sum_{x,y \in M} |\ell_x(y) - \ell_y(x)|)$.

Added constraints do not allow to favor *Image q* or *Image q + 1* against the other (passed against future), and to balance the locality of the stability with a global quality of the matching. The resulting matching processes prove more suitable to motion detection while still keeping an acceptable complexity.

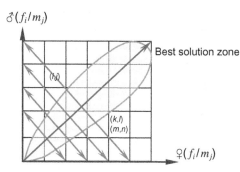

$\male\,(f_i / m_j)$

Best solution zone

(i,j)

(k,l)
(m,n)

$\female\,(f_i / m_j)$

Figure 2.76 The marriage table where abscissa are female preferences and ordinate male ones (in couple (i,j) i is the fourth choice of j and j the second of I; in couples (k,l) and (m,n), it is the other way around).

Relaxation Matching Schemes

The preference lists translate an *a priori* based on the similar appearance of items and on their homologous topologic situations. As with region, growing could likely rely on automata network deciding step after step; matching for motion or stereo could benefit from an opportunistic and stepwise consensus. The corresponding paradigm is called *relaxation* and is based on a function $\mathscr{R}(x, y, x', y')$ ranging between -1 *(forbiddance)* and 1 *(agreement)*, where 0 values the *don't care* situation. $\mathscr{R}$ can be *discrete* (e.g., $-1,0,1$) or *continuous* (e.g., *sigmoid* function); it can operate in a *deterministic* or *stochastic* manner. In all cases, it measures the compatibility between the two events: x matches y, while x' matches y'. Starting from an initial statement, the likelihoods of couples are decremented in the case of disagreements with influential neighbors or incremented if supported by other evidence. Based on this fundamental scheme, many algorithms were tried: most of them suffer from a high complexity and sensitivity to initial conditions and neighbor definition. The relaxation scheme has been used for modeling and normalizing shapes too [139,140].

Dense Data

Dense Data and Explicit Model

As already introduced in the *Motion via local change* section, the model here is strictly in the invariance of the local configuration of the surface $g = I(i, j)$. In other words, the paradigm is that any variation of the gray-level value is a consequence of the sole displacement. That translates into: $I(i, j) = $ constant, and thus, in the ideal world of derivable functions, into the optical-flow constraint. Note that the lapidary presentation hides many difficulties bound to the physics of the phenomena.

To begin with, under the optical-flow paradigm, the intensity remains constant along the trajectory t of a material point. Making image I appear in equations assumes that the acquisition device C is derivable too, and that the composed derivation formula applies. If $\circ$ is the map product, the composition of functions t and C produces the image sequence and then the desired expression $\nabla(C \circ t) = [\nabla(C) \circ t]\nabla t$, appearing in (2.49). Note that derivability is not granted under the involved transformations including projections, and trajectories are the unknowns!

However, the model turns out to be fruitful in many cases, and the class of derived techniques to compute the apparent velocity is referred to as the *differential optical flow*. Space extraction under that model consists thereafter in solving a linear system adequately built from the data. That raises classically two problems:

1. The theoretical number of equations, equal to the number of unknowns, is not correct in practice due to noise and singularities.
2. The system becomes ill-conditioned when a derivative is small.

Then, first, least squares serve again involving more pixels, all the more naturally as partial derivatives are computed through surface approximation and convolution (see points of interest and edges detection in the *Shape extraction* section), both performed over a neighborhood already. Second, adding constraints (*regularization*) is necessary.

The surface smoothness expressed through the second derivative is popular [121]. Another type of constraint was proposed by Millour [141] that is more bound to the physics of phenomena and resulting signals. They start from the fact that, at regular points, odd and even derivatives are null when the other is extreme. So by derivation and linear combination, the formal result of Eqns (2.57) is obtained:

$$I_x u + I_t = 0 \quad \Rightarrow \quad \left(\lambda^2 I_x^2 + I_{xx}^2\right)u + \lambda^2 I_x I_t + I_{xx} I_{xt} = 0 \qquad (2.57)$$

It is interesting in several manners:

- $\left(\lambda^2 I_x^2 + I_{xx}^2\right)$ *is not null in ordinary points.*
- *It depends only on the amplitude and frequency of a sinusoidal input.*
- *It maintains its order of magnitude under a variation by an octave.*

The latter properties lead to a computing scheme in multiresolution that aims at solving (2.57) on progressively filtered versions of the image (separately in the horizontal and vertical directions), giving access to varied motion ranges by the same token.

Dense Data and Implicit Model

The model in this last track is almost a mere transposition of the edge phenomenon from the space-to-time domain. The same naive idea prevails first: "for motion to be perceived, gray levels have to change," as for edges to be perceived there had to be a high enough contrast. The main technique is then to compute image differences. After the reminder on edge detection (*Shape extraction* section), it should be understood that:

- *Image* has to be taken in a broader meaning: the difference is computed between homologous pixels (with same i, j coordinates) or between small neighborhoods characterized by some texture or color index.
- *Difference* itself stands for any time differential operator mixing image approximation with high and low-pass filtering.

Primary edge detectors (Figure 2.54) output candidate contour pixels confirmed when some neighbors constitute a line together. Likewise, image differences output candidate moving-object pixels to be confirmed thanks to neighbors forming a

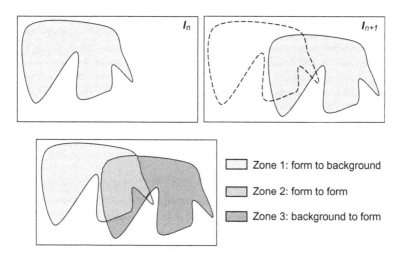

Figure 2.77 Two consecutive images of the same object and the resulting three regions corresponding to parts that were revealed, maintained, or hidden along motion.

region with homogeneous motion characteristics. The difficulty then comes from the ambiguities bound to the approach. In the case of a fixed camera, the result of the image difference is a binary image (or an image with a small dynamics per pixel) displaying three regions per object instead of the ideal one region (Figure 2.77).

After region growing and the interpretation of such triplets, motion characteristics can be inferred in terms of translation and rapprochement, for instance. However, further interpretation such as for the history of the movement (starting and ending conditions, trajectory) may remain tedious.

Along the *time-filtering* line, Sethi and Nagel [142] designed a cumulative process that consists in summing the differences between the current image and a reference (original) image over time. The analysis of monotonous sequences in the accumulator gives access to the initial and final object positions, whereas the constant sequences are indicative of the trajectory, provided the target moved more than its own dimension (zone 2 of Figure 2.77 disappeared).

The technique reminds of the $\Sigma\Delta$ modulation, well known in signal processing. Actually, this one too is explicitly used under several variants of the motion update [143–145]. It is known to be efficient after having been proven a natural binarizing process in analogical vision devices called retinas [146, 147]. It consists in estimating the mean M_n and variance V_n of the image sequence: they are incremented or decremented depending on their comparison, respectively, with the current image I_n and the temporal difference $|I_n - I_{n-1}|$. Every pixel where the difference is less than the variance is considered belonging to the background, and else to a moving object.

An ultimately sophisticated version of such temporal filtering, for background subtraction to exhibit moving regions, consists in coupling a Markovian model of evolution with relaxation schemes. That achieves concurrently noise removal (images are locally more homogeneous) and background management (along iterations, homogeneous zones in the image of differences, that is, static in the image, can be progressively filled up). First models of energy proposed in [148] were monoresolution, with a limited spatiotemporal neighborhood. Today's versions are in multiresolution and based on cliques of order two. Here again the aim is a better estimation of the binary image of motion, based on the preceding estimation and the current difference, and following a model of energy. As already mentioned, relaxation is greedy and converges slowly, from which come suboptimal versions as the iterative conditional modes. Moreover, relaxation depends crucially on the initial state, which is here a binary (threshold-driven) version of the image of differences.

Space Extraction from Egomotion

In the case of a mobile camera, space sensing and reconstruction by stereo or motion are even more closely related, whether conceptually or technically. Indeed, both features can make the camera displacement to arouse interest in given parameterized surfaces such as planes. An extended research was completed these last 20 years on 3D motion or structure-from-motion estimation [149−154] to quote among the precursors. Irani et al. [154] exemplifies methods exploiting the above-mentioned parallax generated by motion (*motion parallax, affine motion parallax, plane,* and *parallax*).

They mostly exploit the fact that depth discontinuities make it doable to separate camera rotation from translation. For instance, in approaches such as plane and parallax, knowing the 2D motion of an image region where variations in depth are not significant permits us to eliminate the effects of camera rotation. Using the obtained residual motion parallax, the translation is exhibited.

A single example is now detailed to illustrate the peculiar duality between volume and dynamics sensed from egomotion. In [155], motion vectors of given lengths and directions are proved to lie on the image at particular loci. The location and form of these loci depend solely on the 3D motion parameters. Considering an optical-flow velocity field, equal vectors lie on *conic sections*. This result is valid for stereo disparity too. In [156], it is proven that the disparity is constant along a line of a stereo pair of *rectified images* and varies linearly over a horizontal plane in function of the depth. Then, in the 2D histogram "disparity values versus line index," the so-called *v-disparity* frame, a straight line of modes translates a road or building or obstacle plane. The computation was later generalized to the other image coordinate and vertical planes, using the *u-disparity*. Note that both studies [155,156], foster *isovalue curves*, velocity, or disparity. The second one promotes an extraction procedure in a novel projection space built on a set of line disparity histograms. Bouchafa and Zavidovique [157] defends that such process is general, because any move of a camera results into an apparent shift of pixels among images, disparity for a stereo pair, and velocity for an image sequence. They transpose the *v-disparity* to motion in designing the so-called *c-velocity* frame. This frame leads to voting schemes as well [158], which additionally rends detection robust against optical flow imprecision.

The camera model is the classical pinhole one again. The case considered is that of an onboard sensor moving on a smooth road (avoiding rapid bumps that shift the FOE).

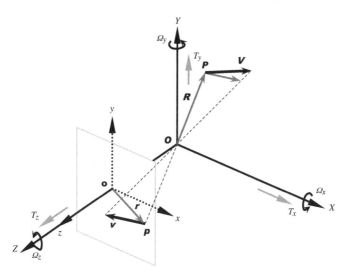

Figure 2.78 Camera and motion models.

*The egomotion verifies the same motion model for all still objects (Figure 2.78), defined by three translations **T** and three rotations **Ω**. Conversely, mobile obstacles pop out as not resorting to the former dominating model.*

Under such assumptions, the following classical equations hold (e.g., [159]):

$$u_t = \frac{-fT_X + xT_Z}{Z}, \quad u_r = \frac{-xy}{f}\Omega_X - \left(\frac{-x^2}{f} + 1\right)\Omega_Y + y\Omega_Z$$

$$ \tag{2.58}$$

$$v_t = \frac{-fT_Y + yT_Z}{Z}, \quad v_r = \frac{-xy}{f}\Omega_Y - \left(\frac{-y^2}{f} + 1\right)\Omega_X + x\Omega_Z$$

where $w = [u, v]^T = [u_t + u_r, v_t + v_r]$ stands for the 2D velocity vector of the pixel $p(x,y)$ under the focal length f.

*With no loss in the generality of computations, assume a translational straight move **T** = $[0, 0, T_z]^T$ of the camera in the Z direction; $[u, v]^T$ becomes:*

$$u = \frac{T_Z}{Z}x, \quad v = \frac{T_Z}{Z}y \tag{2.59}$$

Suppose now the camera is observing a planar surface of equation:

$$n^T P = d \tag{2.60}$$

Table 2.1 Four Moving Planes of Interest

Horizontal (road)	$n = [0,1,0]^T$	$T = [0,0,T_z]^T$	dist. d
Lateral (buildings)	$n = [1,0,0]^T$	$T = [0,0,T_z]^T$	dist. d''
Frontal$_1$ (fleeing obstacle)	$n = [0,0,1]^T$	$T = [0,0,T_z']^T$	dist. d'
Frontal$_2$ (crossing obstacle)	$n = [0,0,1]^T$	$T = [T_X,0,0]^T$	dist. d'

with $n = [n_x, n_y, n_z]^T$ the unit vector normal to the plane and d the distance from the plane to the origin. According to notations of Figure 2.78, the corresponding motion field is given by:

$$u = \frac{1}{fd}\left(a_1 x^2 + a_2 xy + a_3 fx + a_4 fy + a_5 f^2\right)$$
$$v = \frac{1}{fd}\left(a_1 xy + a_2 y^2 + a_6 fy + a_7 fx + a_8 f^2\right) \tag{2.61}$$

where:

$$a_1 = -d\omega_y + T_z n_x, \quad a_2 = d\omega_x + T_z n_y, \quad a_3 = T_z n_z - T_x n_x, \quad a_4 = d\omega_z - T_x n_y$$
$$a_5 = -d\omega_y - T_x n_z, \quad a_6 = T_Z n_z - T_y n_y, \quad a_7 = -d\omega_z - T_y n_x, \quad a_8 = d\omega_x - T_y n_z \tag{2.62}$$

In an urban environment, for instance, four pertaining cases of a moving plane (see Table 2.1) can be considered toward scene reconstruction: obstacles, road, and building. The corresponding motion fields, after (2.61), are:

$$(a)\begin{cases} u = \dfrac{T_z}{fd}xy \\[2mm] v = \dfrac{T_z}{fd}y^2 \end{cases} (b)\begin{cases} u = \dfrac{T_z}{fd'}x^2 \\[2mm] v = \dfrac{T_z}{fd'}xy \end{cases} (c)\begin{cases} u = \dfrac{T_z'}{d'}x \\[2mm] v = \dfrac{T_z'}{d'}y \end{cases} (d)\begin{cases} u = -\dfrac{T_x}{d'} \\[2mm] v = 0 \end{cases} \tag{2.63}$$

Let w_o, w_r, and w_b be, respectively, the module of the apparent velocity of an obstacle point, a road point, and a building point. It becomes:

$$|w_r| = \left|\frac{T_z}{fd_r}\right|\sqrt{y^4 + x^2 y^2}, \quad |w_b| = \left|\frac{T_z}{fd_b}\right|\sqrt{x^4 + x^2 y^2},$$
$$|w_0| = \left|\frac{T_x}{d_o}\right| \quad or \quad |w_0| = \left|\frac{T_z'}{d_o}\right|\sqrt{x^2 + y^2} \tag{2.64}$$

Each type of w leads to the corresponding expression of c and the related isovelocity curve. For instance, in the case of the road plane:

$$c = \left|\frac{w}{K}\right| = \sqrt{y^2(y^2 + x^2)} \quad where \quad K = \left|\frac{T_z}{fd}\right| \tag{2.65}$$

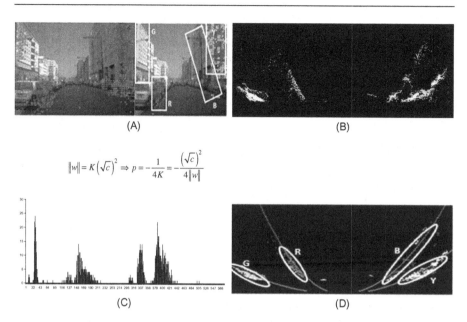

$$\|w\| = K\left(\sqrt{c}\right)^2 \Rightarrow p = -\frac{1}{4K} = -\frac{\left(\sqrt{c}\right)^2}{4\|w\|}$$

Figure 2.79 Results obtained from a database of the French project "Love" (Logiciel d'Observation des Vulnérables). (A) Left: optical flow. Right: resulting vertical plane detection. Planes get a label according to K-mean clustering, and the same color as that of the corresponding parabola. (B) Resulting c-velocity for the building model. Each vote is normalized by the number of points in each c-curve. (C) Example of a 1D Hough transform on the c-velocity space for detecting parabolas. For each (c,w) cell, a P-value is cumulated. Classes of the histogram split by K-mean or any other clustering. (D) Results of parabolas extraction using the 1D Hough transform followed by a K-mean clustering (four classes). In white, the discarded points: they probably belong to another plane model. (For interpretation of the references to color in this figure legend, the reader is referred to the web version of this book.)

The final formula above proves that c, constant along isovelocity curves by definition, is proportional to w there, just as the disparity is proportional to the line value v. The image of a plane can thus be extracted as a set of pixels verifying this property, abstracted into the constancy of K. To that aim, a first cumulative process in the c-velocity frame (c,w) exhibits the straight lines (or equivalently, the parabolas in the $(\sqrt{c},w)$ frame used for both homogeneity and computation complexity reasons), and a second one extracts automatically K. See Figure 2.79 for examples of results. The reader can refer to [160] for an analysis of perturbations and uncertainty computations bound to this process.

Decision Methods

Exploiting shape and space models for feature extraction confirms the prime importance of decision (*optimization*) in the processing schemes, whether it is for straight matching or for solving differential equations. The most abstract mathematical representation of the decision is a binary function from the option space into $\{0,1\}$: valid choices or interesting elements give 1 and others give 0. Examples from the above set of image processing operators are:

- selecting points where the response of a filter is over a given threshold;
- aggregating neighbors of a pixel that show similar enough characteristics;
- retaining parameters of a displacement model that gather enough consensus from enough pixels.

Due to the physics of involved phenomena, interesting elements of the decision space are meant to gather into compact subsets, so that a decision amounts to a comparison with a threshold. The above-mentioned binary function turns into a step function that, in turn, generalizes trivially into:

- multithreshold in the case of multiple intervals;
- subset separation that founds most clustering processes in more than one dimension.

It generalizes less trivially into *stochastic*, *possibilistic*, or *fuzzy* versions in the case of intermediate values between 1, or *kept* (interesting, conform to model, etc.), and 0, or *discarded* (uninteresting, too far from the model, etc.).

It should be underlined that, binary or not, thresholding may easily be made an adaptive process, if not even, an intelligent one. For instance, the choice can be conditioned to the one of neighbors (according to a given topology of the data to cluster) or to past choices (according to a total order (scan) of the same data), and can be performed in a *deterministic* or a *stochastic* (e.g., *Markovian*) manner.

An interesting example of local adaptation is the hysteretic threshold where two values $t+$ *and* $t-$ *support the following type of decision rule:*

- *If* $x < t-$ *then* $x: = 0$
- *If* $x > t+$ *then* $x: = 1$
- *If* $t- < x < t+$ *then* *"see_neighbors"*

where see_neighbors is a procedure that assigns 0 or 1 to the result, depending on the neighbors' choices (e.g., a majority or minority process, or similar to the life game, and so on) among neighbors which could come to a decision already.

Again, because of the physics of phenomena, so crisp a decision as a mere threshold is likely to remain theoretical. Indeed, assigning a given value to a function does not make sense if it were only for noise. Then a mathematical expression as $f(x) = 0$ is weakened more realistically into $min \ \|f(x)\|$ where $\| \ \|$ is a *norm* (thus positive) and *min* is taken in the same conditions as the previous threshold.

Beyond this Heaviside's representation (Oliver Heaviside 1850–1925) of the decision in general, in the peculiar case of image processing, pattern recognition, and scene analysis, decision techniques are fruitfully sorted by the semantics of the underlying model: statistics, structural, and then semantic.

Statistical Decision

The corresponding techniques fit well cases where knowledge, specific to elements under decision, does not exist or matter. Decision models stem from a universal data representation usually bound to mechanics. The paradigm here is that elements are considered instances of some more general production. They do not have any other importance than through the *class* they belong to. The class makes the frequency of the corresponding instance. Elements are reduced to a limited set of variables (their *characters*), and the classes are composed of elements showing the same values of their characters. A clustering process then deals with grouping classes in a coherent way, following some predetermined criteria. Most computing addresses the histogram (the empiric version of the probability distribution), which gets as many dimensions as the number of characters. For a well-posed problem, clusters are usually asked to offer the minimal internal variance, whereas the inter-cluster variance is maximal.

As variables are too many from the very stage of acquisition, a PCA can reduce their cardinality in securing maximal decorrelation. PCA is a perfect example of exploiting generic models, here the inertia, to separate among data. It consists in diagonalizing the autocorrelation matrix of the characters to keep only the desired number of eigen vectors corresponding to the larger eigen values. Note that the process is a mere rotation of the decision space followed by truncature and that separation has to be further completed. Note also that new variables, which are linear combinations of the initial characters, could not be interpretable any more. For instance, applying the PCA straight on the population of pixels of a satellite image often outputs the intensity as the first new character, but others refer to chromaticity and are not so easy to qualify.

Another class of techniques to separate the histogram uses predefined distributions, among which the *Gaussian* is the most popular as corresponding to a conjunction of enough independent phenomena. These *parametric techniques* aim at, first, prior identifying the correct distributions of the targeted type from the moments of the histogram; and second, separating this histogram by specific surfaces (threshold generalization) to minimize the *misclassification error* (i.e., attributing type A elements to class B and vice versa; see Figure 2.20). The misclassification error is the measure of the corresponding residuals or overlapping parts of the identified distributions. Note that region growing is an illustration of the risk taken from missing variables, here topological ones. Indeed, separating Gaussians in the histogram of the image (see *Color distribution analysis* section), does not give any information about the actual regions. For these image regions, as developed in the *Shape extraction* section, topology is crucial and here totally absent from the process; hence the necessity of further labeling components.

Structural Decision

Here, the paradigm is fully abstracted into a single informatics object: the *chain of characters*. Indeed, the structure of a scene is meant to translate only relations between distinguished generic objects. The relations are supposed explicit, for example, bound to space or time, and objects are coded with alphanumeric symbols. They may be complicated, showing their own structure (e.g., tree), and they may be associated with some measure or *likelihood*.

The chain coding has induced specific distances and associated minimization processes. The type of decision, in the scene recognition case, deals more systematically with rules that relations and objects must verify for the structure to be recognized. Keeping nonexplicit a distance between objects can be considered the mechanism of abstraction that renders the grammatical decision process closer to intelligence.

Among distances between chains, beyond counting the number of varying elements (Hamming distance, Richard W. Hamming 1915−1998), the Levenstein's distance was made popular for pattern recognition, first in the speech recognition area, where words are naturally sequences of phonemes (or formants, depending on the acquisition space). It is a transformational distance based on the cost of three elementary operators on chains (a_i) and (b_j) to be compared:

- *Elision: $a_i \rightarrow \varnothing$;*
- *Insertion: $\varnothing \rightarrow b_j$*
     where $\varnothing$ represents the empty element or chain;
- *Substitution: $a_i \rightarrow b_j$*

$d_{\mathscr{L}}\ [(a_i),(b_j)]$ is defined as the minimum cumulated cost of operations to transform (a_i) into (b_j) or, conversely, with the additional constraint (triangle rule) for $d_{\mathscr{L}}$ to obey the distance definition:

$$\text{cost (substitution } (x, z)) + \text{cost (substitution } (z, y)) \geq \text{cost (substitution } (x, y))$$

$$(2.66)$$

In considering peculiar transforms, named traces, that are increasing in the following sense:

$$\text{if } a_i \text{ is substituted for } b_j \text{ and } a_k \text{ is substituted for } b_l, \text{ then } k > i \Rightarrow l > j \quad (2.67)$$

Wagner and Fisher [161] proposed a recurrence formula. Indeed, for a given subset of b_js involved in the transformation, a trace gets a minimal cost because any intermediate operation would increase the cost, and on traces the transforms can proceed from left to right. Then:

$$D_{\mathscr{L}}(i,j) = \min\{D_{\mathscr{L}}(i-1, j-1) + \text{cost (substitution } (a_i, b_j)), D_{\mathscr{L}}(i-1, j)$$
$$+ \text{cost (elision}(a_i)), D_{\mathscr{L}}(i, j-1) + \text{cost (insertion } (b_j))\}$$

$$(2.68)$$

The Wagner's recurrence sends us back to dynamic programming as formalized by Bellman (Richard Bellman, 1920−1984) and, more specifically, to the [162] algorithmic scheme.

On top of its common use in isolated word recognition, the algorithmic vein outlined here now serves in any case where warping can be considered the variation process in a cluster. Consequently, many modern applications for object recognition from their edges or regions were designed, as well as in motion finding or stereo, where the change of point of view results trivially into a deformation of tracked structures.

The process of describing objects, thanks to more elementary ones in accordance with association rules, has been completely formalized within the frame of the Grammar theory. By definition a grammar G is a quadruplet (V_N, V_T, PR, S) where:

- V_N is the nonterminal vocabulary, that is a set of chains of symbols that serve to complete an analysis and describe patterns but are not specific to the patterns. They constitute the variables of the description process.
- V_T is the terminal vocabulary, the constants of the process, that is, a set of elementary chains of symbols that belong to the objects upon which decision is made and which gather into final descriptions.
- PR is a set of production rules; that is, they can be written under the form $a \rightarrow b$, with a and b two chains of elements from V_N and V_T. $\rightarrow$ means "can be rewritten as."
- S is a generic symbol meaning *pattern*, *sentence*, and so on, and more generally the object of the decision or recognition. So it is the starting point of every analysis.

The whole decision process then amounts to rewriting an unknown incoming pattern or situation in terms of V_T, starting from S, and in using the sole rules of PR. Eventually, a pattern will be recognized as obeying a given grammar G supposed to describe all objects of class O, the same as a compiler recognizes correctly written instructions without guaranteeing any result of the programmed algorithm. Note that grammars can serve as well an analysis process or a generation process (e.g., *drawing grammars*). In the analysis, the different tries of rules to be applied for completing the rewriting can be embedded in a decision tree: each node is the application of a rule, and edges point to consecutive rules applying on the part of the chain that was not yet translated.

To be recognized as belonging to a given class, it is enough that the pattern or situation be described in terms of a given vocabulary and according to given composition rules. It suggests that the difficulty then is not so much to apply rules. Of course, in realistic cases where rules can reach several thousands in number, cleverly optimized *parsers* sorting and caching adequate rules at each step can help. However, the real geniality in such technique is:

- to design a dense enough vocabulary, mainly V_T, considering the noise, tolerance to distortions, and admissible ambiguities;
- to extract rules from a finite number of examples for them to apply to a continuum of cases.

Indeed, a given pattern may have an infinity of instances among which a small number establishes the grammar, from which comes potential abusive generalization. Conversely, a given pattern is recognized by an infinity of grammars, starting with the universal grammar which recognizes everything. Nevertheless, grammatical inference provides a continuous description (grammar) from discrete ones (examples) making well an abstraction process.

Note that Noam Chomsky invented a classification of grammars with respect to the context inside rules. The last and more specific type, called regular, was shown to be equivalent to finite state automatons. Therefore, they can be defined in another way when assimilating them to their productions:

$\mathscr{A}$ being an alphabet (set of symbols), three operations are defined on chains: first, concatenation $[(x, y) \mapsto xy]$; second, union [in the classical set theory meaning]; and third, power for iteration $[x^+ = \{x, x^2, \ldots x^n \ldots\}]$. The class of regular grammars is the smallest set closed for these operations (i.e., if G_1 and G_2 are two regular grammars, concatenation, union, and repetition of productions of G_1 and G_2 produce a new regular grammar). Such a representation by productions and the equivalence with automata open doors to efficient implementations whenever they are valid.

Grammars are commonly used for the recognition of objects and static scenes where relations are topological dependencies (relative position, inclusion, intersection, distance contiguity, continuance, etc.). For a less trivial example, the 3D reconstruction of polyhedral patterns from their silhouette, as proposed in [163], then extended to cylindrical-like objects [164] is grammatical. It relies upon a classification of junctions in "V," "W," "Y," and "T" types according to their possible occurrence, with respect to the convex or concave nature, along a scan of the outline (see also The linguistic/syntactic tracksection in Chapter 3).

Semantic Decision

Although *intelligence* in general is not addressed here—only *intelligent decision* is—the concept is still difficult to circumscribe. Intelligent decision could refer to some *expertise*, then dealing with the most flexible *data retrieval* from a database. In that case, intelligence could amount to a mere least-square approximation of the processing result by prestored solutions. It can address the adaptability too, up to learning. In that case, capturing behaviors and coding them as rules including *free variables* would be the question. This can even lead to automatic generation of controllers [165,166]. As already mentioned, the primary difficulty will be the representation of the data. Eventually, semantics covers practically all stages that cannot be addressed by statistics or structure, and thus models will be searched for in every sector of social or living realms.

Theoretically, semantic decision can be defined in a technical and incremental manner through the notion of *tree scan*. In connection with grammars, the tree generalizes both the previous chain (i.e., the description, object of recognition, or decision) and the decision tree stemming from the analysis. They merge into a single complicated informatics object that will remain implicit most often. Its nodes are subparts of various natures, and edges are valued (unlike at the grammatical stage).

Then both nodes and edges are given some attributes that can be, in turn, evaluated; that is, they are not assigned a fixed value during the decision process (free variable). For instance, one mandatory attribute translates the local importance of the path toward the decision to make, one reason why it is not always statically preset. Within that frame, the intelligent decision results from scanning the tree that describes the object (or scene, situation, etc.), whereas upper-bounding the decisional worth of branches likely not to be visited. The tree-scan model underlines the importance of the a priori knowledge and its coding: bounding branches to be abandoned is logically done in a predictive manner and cannot be justified else than at the end with the resulting decision viability. Note that using random phenomena to control the choices rather than static bounds is nothing but introducing statistic decision back into recognition, that is, gambling. Random control of choices can be implemented as a random search of the next visited node. It can be as complex as randomly neglecting paths in the decision, possibly under the external control by a cooling variable, as in the simulated annealing model.

Note that a more structural instance is etymologically the already mentioned relaxation (see Relaxation matching schemes section) that is declined in as many models as imagination can deliver. Then it can mix as well with stochastic processes (e.g., genetic models).

Eventually, more than the valuated-tree structure underlying an intelligent decision, what matters is the physics, social, or biological model driving both the scan of the decision space and the measure of priority. Note that, in programming and parameterizing the decision, the tree structure again remains implicit most often.

Conclusion

The kernel of image processing techniques, summarized in the previous sections, underlines the linguistic stage reached by the field. It appears as a structured set of operators in need of rules to combine them to the service of image analysis toward scene interpretation. The vocabulary of basic objects and functions to interpret the image content is constituted by features and decisions. Features are themselves declined into operators to extract them out of the data. Decisions first deal with the choices of operator-parameters, and then they are taken on the results of these operators, targeting recognition at progressively more abstract level.

For seeds of generic combination rules, it was already underlined that:

• *Features commute in the following sense*: *Points of interest* are salient points of contours and, conversely, contours are smooth curves linking points of interest. *Contours* are frontiers of regions, whereas regions are inner parts of contours. Any static feature (*region*, edge, or point) may be perceivable only because it shows consistent spatial characteristics (motion or depth) and, conversely, *motion* or *depth* is that of regions, edges, or points. All these features can be extracted in a gray level, color, or texture space, depending on which one is available.

Consequently, procedures to find a feature can always be made to find another. From a system point of view, combining several features cannot result in other than a more robust recognition, against ambiguities for instance.

• *Feature extraction and decision commute*: What is addressed here is that the computing complexity can be shared adaptively over them. The bigger the computing power devoted to segmentation, the simpler the decision. For instance, it was already mentioned that projecting a gray-scale image into a texture space should ideally make region finding feasible by a mere threshold or by some histogram separation at most. Having found significant objects in every image makes motion finding a mere correlation, and so forth. Consequently, segmentation can combine processing and local decision to anticipate more global decision toward image analysis and further action.

Nevertheless, it has to be clear that part of Raphael's capture of basic physics laws (see Figure 2.1) and subsequent image analysis cannot be completed by computers, at the current stage, without additional knowledge on top of these laws. For a machine to find that a human being is in front of another, not only corresponding regions of the image had to be correctly exhibited and gathered, but also the incomplete perception of the occluded human needs to trigger hypotheses. Such hypotheses prompt some model matching that ought to rely on an abstract representation of human beings. Logically, this human being had to be synthesized back in some manner. The commonsense knowledge that generalizes basic physics laws can still be considered precompiled. Beyond it, appears the notion of a *dynamic knowledge*, contingent to the scene that is called *context*. This is the subject of the next chapter.

References

[1] B.T. Phong, Illumination for computer generated images, Commun. ACM 18 (6) (1975) 311–317.

[2] R.L. Cook, K.E. Torrance, Reflectance model for computer graphics, Comput. Graph. 15 (3) (1981) 307–316.

[3] B.K.T. Horn, Understanding image intensity, Artif. Intell. 8 (1977) 201–231.

[4] B.K.T. Horn, R.W. Sjoberg, Calculating the reflectance map, Appl. Opt. 18 (11) (1979) 1770–1779.

[5] R.J. Woodham, Photometric method for determining surface orientation from multiple images, Opt. Eng. 19 (1) (1980) 139–144.

[6] W.E.L. Grimson, Binocular Shading and Visual Surface Reconstruction, MIT AI Memo, No. 697, 1982.

[7] K. Ikeuchi, Determining surface orientation of specular surfaces by using the photometric stereo method, IEEE Trans. PAMI 3 (6) (1981) 661–669.

[8] T. Poggio, V. Torre, C. Koch, Computational vision and regularization theory, Nature 317 (1985) 314–319.

[9] A.P. Pentland, Local shading analysis, IEEE Trans. PAMI 6 (2) (1984) 170–187.

[10] B.K.T. Horn, M.J. Brooks, The variational approach to shape-from-shading, Comput. Vis. Graph. Image Process. 33 (1986) 174–208.

[11] A. Appel, Some techniques for shading machine renderings of solids, in: AFIPS 1968 Spring Joint Computer Conference, 1968, pp. 37–45.

[12] T. Whitted, An improved illumination model for shaded display, CACM 23 (6) (1980) 343–349.

[13] C.M. Goral, K.E. Torrance, D.P. Greenberg, B. Battaille, Modeling the interaction of light between diffuse surfaces, Comput. Graph. 18 (3) (1984) 213–222.

[14] R. Ohlander, K. Price, D.R. Reddy, Picture segmentation using a recursive region splitting method, Comput. Graph. Image Process. 8 (3) (1978) 313–333.

[15] P. Kubelka, F. Munk, Ein Beitrag zur Optik der Farbanstriche, Physik 12 (1931) 593–601.

[16] S.A. Shafer, Using colour to separate reflection components, Colour Res. Appl. 10 (4) (1985) 210–218.

[17] H. Freeman, Computer processing of line-drawing images, J. ACM Comput. Surv. 6 (1) (1974) 57–97.

[18] J.P. Gambotto, B. Zavidovique, Algorithms for region expansion and shrinking based on chain-codes transformations, in: Proceedings of Sixth ICPR, Munich, FRG, 1982, pp. 343–346.

[19] J. Serra, Image Analysis and Mathematical Morphology, vol. 1, Academic Press, London, 1982.

[20] A. Rosenfeld, A.C. Kak, Digital Picture Processing, Academic Press, Orlando, FL, 1976.

[21] V. Cantoni, S. Levialdi, Contour labeling by pyramidal processing, in: M.J.B. Duff (Ed.), Intermediate-Level Image Processing, Academic Press, London, UK, 1986, pp. 181–192.

[22] T. Pavlidis, Polygonal approximations by Newton's method, IEEE Trans. Comput. C-26 (1977) 800–807.

[23] J. Sklansky, V. Gonzalez, Fast polygonal approximation of digitized curves, Pattern Recognit. 12 (5) (1980) 327–331.

[24] I. Ragnemalm, G. Borgefors, Toward a minimal shape representation using maximal discs, in: I. Ragnemalm (Ed.), The Euclidean Distance Transform, Dissertation No. 304, Linköping University, Sweden, 1994, p. 245.

[25] C. Arcelli, M. Frucci, Reversible skeletonisation by (5, 7, 11)-erosion, in: C. Arcelli, L. Cordella, G. Sanniti di Baja (Eds.), Visual Form Analysis and Recognition, Plenum Press, New York, NY, 1992, pp. 21–28.

[26] F. Leymarie, M.D. Levine, Simulating the grassfire transform using an active contour model, IEEE Trans. PAMI 14 (1) (1992) 56–75.

[27] C. Arcelli, L.P. Cordella, S. Levialdi, From local maxima to connected skeletons, IEEE Trans. PAMI 3 (1981) 134–143.

[28] S.G. Aki, G.T. Tousaint, Efficient convex hull algorithms for pattern recognition applications, in: Proceedings IV ICPR, Kyoto, Japan, 1978, pp. 483–487.

[29] H. Samet, The Design of Analysis of Spatial Data Structures, Addison-Wesley, Reading, MA, 1989.

[30] H. Samet, Applications of Spatial Data Structures, Addison-Wesley, Reading, MA, 1990.

[31] H. Samet, Foundations of Multidimensional and Metric Data Structures, Morgan Kaufmann, San Francisco, CA, 2006.

[32] A.L. Yarbus, Eyes Movements and Vision, Plenum Press, New York, NY, 1967.

[33] B. Julesz, Visual pattern discrimination, IRE Trans. Inf. Theory 8 (1962) 84–92.

[34] M. Girard, Digital Target Tracking, NATO Group, Aalbörg, Denmark, 1980.

[35] S.M. Smith, J.M. Brady, Susan, a new approach to low level image processing, Int. J. Comput. Vis. 23 (1) (1997) 45–78.

[36] N. Suvonvorn, B. Zavidovique, EFLAM: a model to levelline junction extraction, in: Proceedings of International Conference on Computer Vision Theory and Applications, Setubal, Portugal, 2006.

[37] H.P. Moravec, Visual mapping by a robot rover, in: International Joint Conference on Artificial Intelligence, 1979, pp. 598–600.

[38] H.H. Nagel, On the estimation of optical flow: relations between different approaches and some new results, Artif. Intell. 33 (3) (1987) 298–324.

[39] L. Kitchen, A. Rosenfeld, Gray-level corner detection, Pattern Recognit. Lett. 1 (1982) 95–102.

[40] O.A. Zuniga, R. Haralick, Corner detection using the facet model, in: IEEE CVPR Conference, Washington, DC, 1983, pp. 30–37.

[41] K. Rangarajan, M. Shah, D.V. Brackle, Optimal corner detector, Comput. Vis. Graph. Image Process. 48 (1989) 230−245.

[42] F. Rouge, G. Stamon, B. Zavidovique, Détection de Points d'Intérêts et Approximation Polynomale de Surfaces, RFIA 94, Paris, France, 1994.

[43] R.M. Haralick, Digital step edges from zero crossing of second directional derivatives, IEEE Trans. PAMI 6 (1) (1984) 58−68.

[44] C.G. Harris, M. Stephens, A combined corner and edge detector, in: Fourth Alvey Vision Conference, Manchester, UK, 1988, pp. 147−151.

[45] J. Shi, C. Tomasi, Good features to track, in: Ninth IEEE Conference on Computer Vision and Pattern Recognition, Xi'an, China, 1994, pp. 214−225.

[46] C. Tomasi, T. Kanade, Detection and Tracking of Point Features, Carnegie Mellon University Technical Report CMU-CS-91-132, Pittsburgh, PA, 1991.

[47] P. Monasse, F. Guichard, Fast computation of a contrast-invariant image representation, IEEE Trans. Image Process. 9 (5) (2000) 860−872.

[48] L.D. Stefano, S. Mattoccia, F. Tombari, ZNCC-based template matching using bounded partial correlation, Pattern Recognit. Lett. 26 (14) (2005) 2129−2134.

[49] S. Masnou, Disocclusion: a variational approach using level lines, IEEE Trans. Image Process. 11 (2) (2002) 68−76.

[50] V. Caselles, B. Coll, J.M. Morel, Topographics maps and local contrast invariance in natural images, Int. J. Comput. Vis. 33 (1) (1999) 5−27.

[51] B. Coll, J. Froment, Topographic maps of color images, in: XV ICPR, 3, Barcelona, Spain, 2000, pp. 609−612.

[52] M. Gouiffes, B. Zavidovique, A color topographic map based on the dichromatic reflectance model, EURASIP J. Image Video Process, 2008, Article ID 824195, 14 pp.

[53] S. Levialdi, Finding the edge, in: J.C. Simon, R.M. Haralick (Eds.), Digital Image Processing, NATO ASI, D. Reidel, Dordrecht, 1981, pp. 105−148.

[54] B. Zavidovique, G. Stamon, Considération sur les méthodes de détection de contour en traitement d'image, in: Proc. IASTED−DAVOS, 1981.

[55] V. Cantoni, I. De Lotto, M. Ferretti, A template matching operator for edge-points detection in digitized pictures, Signal Process. 4 (1982) 349−360.

[56] E. Persoon, A new edge detection algorithm and its application in picture processing, Comput. Graph. Image Process. 5 (4) (1976) 425−446.

[57] Y. Yakimovsky, Boundary and object detection in real world images, J. ACM 23 (4) (1976) 599−618.

[58] C. Mohwinkel, L. Kurtz, Computer picture processing and enhancement by localized operations, Comput. Graph. Image Process. 76 (5) (1976) 401−424.

[59] M.H. Hueckel, Operator which locates edges in digital pictures, J. ACM 18 (1) (1971) 113−125.

[60] M.H. Hueckel, A local visual operator which recognizes edges and lines, J. Assoc. Comput. Mach. 20 (4) (1973) 634−647.

[61] R.A. Hummel, Edge detection using basis functions, Comput. Graph. Image Process. 9 (10) (1979) 40−55.

[62] E.C. Hildreth, The detection of intensity changes by computer and biological vision systems, Comput. Vis. Graph. Image Process. 22 (1) (1983) 1−27.

[63] J.F. Canny, Finding Edges and Lines in Images, M.S. Thesis, MIT Press, Cambridge, MA, 1983.

[64] R. Deriche, Using Canny's criteria to derive a recursively implemented optimal edge detector, Int. J. Comput. Vis. 1 (1987) 167−187.

[65] J.F. Canny, A computational approach to edge detection, IEEE Trans. PAMI 8 (6) (1986) 679–698.

[66] J. Shen, S. Castan, An optimal linear operator for edge detection, in: Conference on Vision and Pattern Recognition, Miami, FL, 1986, pp. 109–114.

[67] J.W. Modestino, R.W. Fries, Edge detection in noisy images using recursive digital filtering, Comput. Graph. Image Process. 6 (1977) 409–433.

[68] D. Geman, S. Geman, Stochastic relaxation, Gibbs distributions and the Bayesian restoration of images, IEEE Trans. PAMI 6 (1984) 721–741.

[69] J.L. Marroquin, Surface Reconstruction Preserving Discontinuities, Research Report LIDS-P-1402, 1984.

[70] J.L. Marroquin, S. Mitter, T. Poggio, Probabilistic solution of ill-posed problems in computational vision, J. Am. Stat. Assoc. 82 (397) (1987) 76–89.

[71] D. Mumford, J. Shah, Optimal approximation by piecewise smooth functions and associated variational problem, Commun. Pure Appl. Math. 42 (1989) 577–685.

[72] T.F. Chan, L. Vese, Active contours without edges, IEEE Trans. Image. Process. 10 (2) (2001) 266–277.

[73] A. Martelli, Edge detection using heuristic search methods, Comput. Graph. Image Process. 1 (1972) 169–182.

[74] V. Di Gesù, Artificial vision and soft computing, Fundam. Inf. 37 (1–2) (1999) 101–119.

[75] S. Cagnoni, É. Lutton, G. Olague (Eds.), Genetic and Evolutionary Computation in Image Analysis and Signal Processing, EURASIP Book Series on Signal Processing and Communications, vol. 7, Academic Press, 2008.

[76] V. Di Gesù, G. Lo Bosco, Image segmentation based on genetic algorithms combination, in: Proceedings of Image Analysis and Processing, Cagliari, Italy, 2005, pp. 352–359.

[77] S.M. Bhandarkar, Z. Yiqing, W.D. Potter, An edge detection technique using genetic algorithm-based optimization, Pattern Recognit. 27 (9) (2005) 1159–1180.

[78] C. Harris, B. Buxton, Evolving edge detectors with genetic programming, in: Proceedings of First Annual Conference on Genetic Programming, Stanford, CA, 1996, pp. 309–314.

[79] P.R. Beaudet, Rotational invariant image operators, in: Proceedings of International Joint Conference on Pattern Recognition, Kyoto, Japan, 1978, pp. 579–583.

[80] J.C. Dunn, A fuzzy relative of the ISODATA process and its use in detecting compact, well separated clusters, J. Cybern. 3 (1974) 32–57.

[81] R.N. Davé, R. Krishnapuran, Robust clustering methods: a unified view, IEEE Trans. Fuzzy Syst. 5 (1997) 270–293.

[82] A.K. Jain, M.N. Murty, P.J. Flynn, Data clustering: a review, ACM Comput. Surveys 31 (3) (1999) 264–323.

[83] M. Haldiki, Y. Batistakis, M. Vazirgiannis, On clustering validation techniques, J. Intell. Inf. Syst. 17 (2–3) (2001) 107–145.

[84] T.C. Pong, L.G. Shapiro, R.M. Haralick, A facet model region growing algorithm, in: Proceedings of PRIP81, 1981, pp. 279–284.

[85] T.C. Pong, L.G. Shapiro, L.T. Watson, R.M. Haralick, Experiments in segmentation using a facet model region grower, Comput. Vis. Graph. Image Process. 25 (1) (1984) 1–23.

[86] J.C. Bezdek, Pattern Recognition with Fuzzy Objective Function Algorithms, Plenum Press, New York, NY, 1981.

[87] Y.A. Tolias, S.M. Panas, On applying spatial constraints in fuzzy image segmentation using a fuzzy rule-based system, IEEE Signal Process. Lett. 5 (10) (1998) 245–248.

[88] Y.A. Tolias, S.M. Panas, Image segmentation by a fuzzy clustering algorithm using adaptive spatially constrained membership functions, IEEE Trans. Syst. Man Cybern. A Syst. Hum. 28 (3) (1998) 359–369.

[89] A. Hafiane, S. Chaudhuri, G. Seetharaman, B. Zavidovique, Region-based CBIR in GIS with local space filling curves to spatial representation, Pattern Recognit. Lett. 27 (4) (2006) 259–267.

[90] J. Bajon, M. Cattoen, S.D. Kim, A concavity characterization method for digital objects, Signal Process. 9 (3) (1985) 151–161.

[91] P. Adam, B. Burg, B. Zavidovique, Dynamic programming for region based pattern recognition, in: Proc. ICASSP, 1986, pp. 2075–2078.

[92] K. Suzuki, I. Horiba, N. Sugie, Linear-time connected component labeling based on sequential local operations, Comput. Vis. Image Underst. 89 (1) (2003) 1–23.

[93] K. Wu, E. Otoo, A. Shoshani, Optimizing connected component labeling algorithms, Pattern Anal. Appl. 11 (2008) 749–756.

[94] L. Lacassagne, B. Zavidovique, Light speed labelling: efficient connected component labelling on RISC architectures, in: Proc. IEEE IICIP, Cairo, 2009, pp. 3245–3248.

[95] C.R. Brice, C.L. Fennema, Scene analysis using regions, Artif. Intell. 1 (3) (1970) 205–226.

[96] J.L. Muerle, D.C. Allen, Experimental evaluation of techniques for automatic segmentation of objects in a complex scene, in: G.C. Cheng (Ed.), Pictorial Pattern Recognition, Thompson Book Co., Washington, DC, 1968.

[97] S.L. Horowitz, T. Pavlidis, Picture segmentation by a directed split and merge procedure, in: Proc. ICPR, Copenhagen, Denmark, 1974, pp. 424–433.

[98] A. Gagalowicz, O. Monga, A new approach to image segmentation, in: Proc. ICPR86, Paris, France, 1986, pp. 265–267.

[99] S.L. Horowitz, T. Pavlidis, Picture segmentation by a tree traversal algorithm, J. ACM 23 (2) (1976) 368–388.

[100] P.J. Burt, T.H. Hong, A. Rosenfeld, Segmentation and estimation of image region properties through cooperative hierarchical computation, IEEE Trans. Syst. Man Cybern. SMC-11 (12) (1981) 802–809.

[101] P. Lemkin, An approach to region splitting, Comput. Graph. Image Process. 10 (3) (1979) 281–288.

[102] D.L. Milgram, Region extraction using convergent evidence, Comput. Graph. Image Process. 11 (1) (1979) 1–12.

[103] T. Pavlidis, Y.T. Liow, Integrating region growing and edge detection, IEEE Trans. PAMI 12 (3) (1990) 225–233.

[104] Available from: http://www.ux.uis.no/ ~ tranden/brodatz.html

[105] M.R. Turner, Texture discrimination by Gabor functions, Biol. Cybern. 55 (1986) 71–82.

[106] M. Clark, A.C. Bovik, Texture segmentation using Gabor modulation/demodulation, Pattern Recognit. Lett. 6 (4) (1987) 261–267.

[107] M. Comer, E. Delp, Segmentation of textured images using a multiresolution Gaussian autoregressive model, IEEE Trans. Image Process. 8 (3) (1999) 408–420.

[108] L.S. Davis, M. Clearman, J.K. Aggarwal, An empirical evaluation of generalized cooccurrence matrices, IEEE Trans. PAMI 3 (2) (1981) 214–221.

[109] C.C. Gotlieb, H.E. Kreyszig, Texture descriptors based on cooccurrence matrices, Comput. Vis. Graph. Image Process. 51 (1) (1990) 70–86.

[110] R.M. Haralick, Statistical and structural approaches to texture, Proc. IEEE 67 (5) (1979) 786–804.

[111] S.W. Zucker, Toward a model of texture, Comput. Graph. Image Process. 5 (1976) 190–202.

[112] M. Tuceryan, A.K. Jain, Texture analysis, in: C.H. Chen, L.F. Pau, P.S.P. Wang (Eds.) World Scientific Publishing Co., Handbook of Pattern Recognition and Computer Vision, World Scientific Publishing Co., Singapore (1993) 235–276.

[113] J. Rushing, H. Ranganath, T. Hinke, S. Graves, Using association rules as texture features, IEEE Trans. PAMI 23 (8) (2001) 845–858.

[114] D. Blostein, N. Ahuja, Shape from texture: integrating texture element extraction and surface estimation, IEEE Trans. PAMI 11 (12) (1989) 1233–1251.

[115] N. Jhanwar, S. Chaudhuri, G. Seetharaman, B. Zavidovique, Content based image retrieval using motif cooccurence matrix, Image Vis. Comput. 22 (14) (2004) 1211–1220.

[116] J.L. Mundy, A. Zisserman (Eds.), Geometric Invariants in Computer Vision, MIT Press, Cambridge, MA, 1992.

[117] H.H. Nagel, From digital picture processing to image analysis, in: Proc. ICIAP, Pavia, Italy, 1980, pp. 27–40.

[118] J.K. Aggarwal, L.S. Davies, W.N. Martin, Correspondence processes in dynamical scene analysis, Proc. IEEE 69 (5) (1981) 562–571.

[119] B.K. Horn, B.G. Schunk, Determining optical flow, Artif. Intell. 17 (1981) 185–204.

[120] T.S. Huang, R.Y. Tzai, Image Sequence Analysis: Motion Estimation, Springer-Verlag, Heidelberg, 1981.

[121] J.K. Aggarwal, N. Nandhakumar, On the computation of motion from sequences of images—a review, Proc. IEEE 76 (8) (1988) 917–935.

[122] P. Thevenaz, Motion analysis in pattern recognition, in: R.A. Vaugham (Ed.), Image Processing in Physics, Adam Hilger, Bristol, 1990, pp. 129–166.

[123] V. Cappellini, A. Del Bimbo, A. Mecocci, Motion analysis and representation in computer vision, J. Circ. Syst. Comput. 3 (3) (1993) 1–35.

[124] A. Del Bimbo, S. Santini, Motion analysis, in: V. Cantoni (Ed.), Human and Machine Vision, Plenum Press, New York, NY, 1994, pp. 199–221.

[125] J.M. Prager, Segmentation of Static and Dynamic Scenes, COINS-Technical Report 79-7, Computer and Information Science, University of Massachusetts, MA, 1979.

[126] D.H. Ballard, C.M. Brown, Computer Vision, Prentice Hall, Englewood Cliffs, NJ, 1984.

[127] B.G. Schunk, The motion constraint equation for optical flow, in: Proceedings of Seventh International Conference of Pattern Recognition, Montreal, 1984, pp. 20–22.

[128] E.C. Hildreth, Computations underlying the measurement of visual motion, Artif. Intell. 23 (1984) 309–354.

[129] H.H. Nagel, On a constraint for the estimation of displacement rate in image sequences, IEEE Trans. PAMI 11 (1) (1989) 490–498.

[130] A. Verri, F. Girosi, V. Torre, Differential techniques for optical flow, J. Opt. Soc. Am. 7 (5) (1990) 912–922.

[131] Y. Aloimonos, Z. Duric, Estimating the heading direction using the normal flow, Int. J. Comput. Vis. 13 (1994) 33–56.

[132] D. Gale, L. Shapley, College admissions and the stability of marriage, Am. Math. Mon. 69 (1962) 9–15.

[133] C. Teo, J. Sethuraman, W. Tan, Gale-shapley stable marriage problem revisited: strategic issues and applications, in: Proc. IPCO'99, Springer-Verlag, Berlin/Heidelberg, 1999, pp. 429–438.

[134] D. Bianco, S. Hartke, A. Larimer, Stable matchings in the couples problem, Morehead Electron. J. Appl. Math. 2 (2001) 1–12.

[135] D. Manlove, Stable Marriage with Ties and Unacceptable Partners, Technical Report TR-1999-29, Computing Science Department of Glasgow University, UK, 1999.

[136] T. Kavitha, K. Mehlhorn, D. Michail, K. Paluch, Strongly stable matching in time O(nm) and extension to the hospitals-residents problem, in: STACS, 2004, pp. 222–233.

[137] B. Zavidovique, N. Suvonvorn, G.S. Seetharaman, A novel representation and algorithms for (quasi) stable marriages, in: Proc. ICINCO'05, Barcelona, Spain, 2005, pp. 63–70.

[138] N. Suvonvorn, B. Zavidovique, Globally satisfying and equitable stable marriages and their complexity, Int. J. Pure Appl. Math. 52 (3) (2009) 439–468.

[139] S.W. Zucker, R.A. Hummel, A. Rosenfeld, An application of relaxation labeling to line and curve enhancement, IEEE Trans. Comput. 26 (4) (1977) 394–403.

[140] S.W. Zucker, R.A. Hummel, A. Rosenfeld, Correction to "An application of relaxation labeling to line and curve enhancement," IEEE Trans. Comput. 26 (9) (1977) 922–929.

[141] C. Millour, Contribution à la Vision Dynamique: Une Approche Multi-résolution et Multi-traitement, Ph.D. Thesis, Université de Paris Sud (Paris XI), Paris, France, 1989.

[142] I.K. Sethi, H.H. Nagel, On the analysis of accumulative difference pictures from image sequences of real world scenes, IEEE Trans. PAMI 1 (2) (1979) 206–214.

[143] A. Manzanera, J. Richefeu, Robust and computationally efficient motion detection based on sigma-delta background estimation, in: Proc. IEEE ICVGIP, Kolkata, India, 2004, pp. 46–51.

[144] A. Manzanera, J. Richefeu, A new motion detection algorithm based on sigma-delta background estimation, Pattern Recognit. Lett. 28 (2) (2007) 320–328.

[145] M. Vargas, S.L. Toral, F. Barrero, An enhanced background estimation algorithm for vehicle detection in urban traffic video, in: Proc. IEEE Conference on Intelligent Transportation Systems, Beijing, China, 2008, pp. 784–790.

[146] T. Bernard, B. Zavidovique, F. Devos, A programmable artificial retina, IEEE J. Solid-State Circuits 28 (7) (1993) 789–798.

[147] T. Bernard, B. Zavidovique, Silicon vision: elementary functions to be implemented on electronic retinas, in: Eleventh IAPR International Conference, The Hague, The Netherlands, 1992, pp. D1–D10.

[148] F. Heitz, P. Bouthemy, Multimodal estimation of discontinuous optical flow using Markov random fields, IEEE Trans. PAMI 15 (12) (1993) 1217–1232.

[149] Q.T. Luong, O.D. Faugeras, Camera calibration, scene motion and structure recovery from point correspondences and fundamental matrices, Int. J. Comput. Vis. 22 (3) (1997) 261–289.

[150] R.I. Hartley, In defense of the 8-point algorithm, in: Proceedings of IEEE International Conference on Computer Vision, Cambridge, MA, 1995, pp. 1064–1070.

[151] W.J. MacLean, A.D. Jepson, R.C. Frecker, Recovery of egomotion and segmentation of independent object motion using the em algorithm, in: Proceedings of the Fifth British Machine Vision Conference, York, UK, 1994, pp. 13–16.

[152] E.C. Hildreth, Recovering heading for visually-guided navigation, Vis. Res. 32 (6) (1992) 1177–1192.

[153] G.P. Stein, O. Mano, A. Shashua, A robust method for computing vehicle ego-motion, in: IEEE Intelligent Vehicles Symposium (IV2000), Dearborn, MI, 2000, pp. 362–368.

[154] M. Irani, B. Rousso, S. Peleg, Recovery of ego-motion using region alignment, IEEE Trans. PAMI 19 (3) (1997) 268–272.

[155] C. Fermuller, Y. Aloimonos, Global rigidity constraints in image displacement fields, in: Proceedings of Fifth International Conference on Computer Vision, Zurich, Switzerland, 1995, pp. 245–250.

[156] R. Labayrade, D. Aubert, J.P. Tarel, Real time obstacle detection on non flat road geometry through V-disparity representation, in: IEEE Intelligent Vehicles Symposium, Versailles, 2002, pp. 646–651.

[157] S. Bouchafa, B. Zavidovique, C-velocity: a cumulative frame to segment objects from egomotion, Pattern Recognit. Image Anal. 19 (4) (2009) 583–590.

[158] S. Bouchafa, B. Zavidovique, Efficient cumulative matching for image registration, Image Vis. Comput. 24 (1) (2006) 70–79.

[159] H.C. Longuet-Higgins, K. Prazdny, The interpretation of a moving retinal image, Proc. R. Soc. Lond. B 208 (1980) 385–439.

[160] S. Bouchafa, B. Zavidovique, Error analysis of C-velocity detections, in: Proceedings of Pattern Recognition and Image Analysis, St. Petersburg, Russia, 2010, pp. 177–180.

[161] R.A. Wagner, M.J. Fisher, The string-to-string correction problem, J. ACM 21 (1) (1974) 168–173.

[162] A. Viterbi, Error bounds for convolutional codes and an asymptotically optimum decoding algorithm, IEEE Trans. Inf. Theory IT-13 (2) (1967) 260–269.

[163] D. Waltz, Understanding line drawings of scenes with shadows, in: P.H. Winston (Ed.), The Psychology of Computer Vision, McGraw-Hill, New York, NY, 1975, pp. 19–91.

[164] J. Malik, Interpretation of Line Drawings of Curved Objects, Ph.D. Thesis, Department of Computer Science, Stanford University, Stanford, CA, 1985.

[165] L. Foulloy, B. Zavidovique, Towards symbolic process control, Automatica 30 (3) (1994) 379–390.

[166] D. Luzeaux, B. Zavidovique, Process control and machine learning: rule based incremental control, IEEE Trans. Autom. Control 39 (6) (1994) 1166–1171 and 3, 40, 562.

3 The Role of Contexts

Contexts According to Artists

Context in image interpretation can be defined as some external information exploited to fully understand an image: different meanings are achieved on the basis of other images, circumstances, or more generally, cultural knowledge. Image retrieval from databases can be considered the genuine application where context is decisive.

Chapter 2 mentioned that "for image contents, natural forms are too complex." Likewise, for image contexts *interrelations* of natural forms are too complex to be dealt with directly as a whole. Each single subpart must be processed in an organized manner (e.g., hierarchically, in isolation, top-down or goal driven, and bottom-up or data driven). Subparts may emerge from:

- the image topology, for example, foreground/background, at a precise location in the picture;
- their very nature, for example, pattern or color;
- temporal or circumstantial instances, for example, by filtering or tracking.

The common interesting feature of all these examples is the necessary external information; the sole information extracted from the image is not enough to fully understand it. In the former example of the *Holy Marriage* (see Figure 2.1), all information is included in the picture, and its interpretation relies on the knowledge of elementary laws of physics that artists in the Renaissance period were experimentally discovering. In the nineteenth century, artists began freeing themselves from such laws, to enrich the conveyed information. For instance, Impressionists favored color or texture over drawing (e.g., shapes were still preserved by Georges Pierre Seurat and most *Dottists*, whereas the apparent borderlines are broken down). Along times, the perspective laws are abandoned for an "extended sensing," suggesting, for example, feelings to be triggered.

An interesting example of the intensive use of context, free from any either practical or physics' rule, is the painting *Guernica* by Pablo Picasso (Figure 3.1). This painting, created immediately after the event, and very likely under an emotional shock, refers to the extermination of a little Spanish town, bombed by the German air force allied to the right-wing nationalists, and it became a symbol of war atrocity. Many clues of this picture, providing the feeling of atrocity, were created by the painter and are technically analyzed here, listed by their correspondence to abstraction levels of image retrieval.

3C Vision. DOI: 10.1016/B978-0-12-385220-5.00003-6

Figure 3.1 *Guernica* by Pablo Picasso, 1937, Museo Reina Sofia, Madrid.

Direct Retrieval

Whenever a new painting is considered, the viewer is enabled to interpret the painting, performing the inverse link by him- or herself, provided that he or she has enough global knowledge on the facts and objects pertaining to the painting. Such items include external information, dates, names, and so on. Natural ways of providing this knowledge are:

- *Metadata*: For instance the title of the painting or the name of the artist, evocative in themselves of the horror of the represented subject, by knowing its history. More generally, any key word can help if some relationship between the intended goal of the retriever and the painting is known.
- *Explicit cues*: The war situation or the Spanish political framework can be recovered through the weapons (spear, sword) and the bull, respectively, represented in the painting. This implies only common knowledge, such as the use of weapons in a war or the bullfight practice in the Spanish tradition.

Recognition-Based Retrieval

At this level, the reference knowledge is more remote (e.g., a story, another painting, a custom symbol), likely cultural. The viewer does not have an explicit depiction of all features leading to the painting context and to its represented drama.

Literature motif: A text related to a similar history, generally known by the observer, can be depicted and recalled by the picture producing the same emotional effects. Likewise, a part of the picture relating to a known character suffices to evoke atrocity: the woman holding her child refers to "courage mother"[1] or "Cecilia's mother."[2] Note that the observer will blend picture components with his or her own broad knowledge: there is not a simple, direct search of a woman, a child, or even a "mother with her child." These components could well refer to a Madonna; in this case, the painter would imply a different meaning. Here the child's head is bent toward the ground, suggesting he is dead. The mother's head is bent toward the sky, signifying desperation, imploration, or imprecation. The observer's interpretation is obviously connected to his or her knowledge of the Spanish war situation.

Image motif: The W pattern of the raised arms around the stretched head refers to *Tres de Mayo,* a reference masterpiece that portrays the dramatic execution of heroes anchored to the Spanish tradition, by Francisco Goya, an icon himself of the universal culture.

Extended motif: A variety of interpretation paths can be exploited: for instance, the spear in the horse's chest recalls the Calvary of Christ or, in general, a martyr, on the basis of the Christian symbolism (*religious motif*). Another possible path is supported by the horse being a symbol of goodwill,[3] as also transmitted through most children's tales (*popular motif*).

Search-Based Retrieval

At this level, the viewer may not have in mind explicit motifs from which to retrieve the painting semantics. The artist has created his own motifs to illustrate the "message" (here transcending the war atrocity) to be interpreted by the viewer. The reference knowledge is even more implicit and hidden because it is likely to reside in the blending of motifs rather than in the motifs themselves. Inspection strategies and data-driven scans will become favored tools toward semantics.

[1] *Mother Courage and Her Children*, Berthold Brecht (1939).

[2] *I promessi sposi*, Alessandro Manzoni (1840–1841).

[3] *Animal Farm*, George Orwell, 1945.

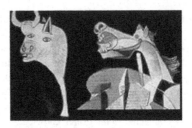

Form contrast: Knowing the Spanish traditions and war context, the quiet bull, looking afar, and close to a terrified horse, delivers a message of total indifference by contrast between the two different animal attitudes: the bull's flat stillness and the abnormally twisted attitude of the horse. The perception of suffering is based on common knowledge. The organization of the subject surrounding the horizontal bull's body—desperate women, frantic horse, and strange bird, all three with some verticality—completes the information on who is friend or foe, despite the absence of any weapon around.

Juxtaposed components: The broken sword together with the delicate flower is small in size but crucial in meaning. It primarily refers to death, where flowers are used to express pain and love for the departed. Nevertheless, due to its size compared to the dead body nearby, and to its position at the very central bottom of the picture, it implies that there is always hope, even if the situation is far from the light. This interpretation, based on well-agreed-upon references about death, or relative sizes and orientations, is also confirmed by the symbolic verticality of a tiny blossoming flower.

Paradox and surprisal: Why would an electric bulb shining like the sun, central and at the top of the frame as expected for a sun, need to be supplemented? A surprising soft and humble oil lamp is adjoined. The competition between the efficient electric light source and the derisory primitive one indicates the infatuation of technology. The light rays from the electric lamp look like razor edges, whereas the oil lamp does not produce any tangible illumination. This addition reminds concurrently that technology may cause damage and is not dependable, whereas the older oil lamp is robust and reliable, even if backward. On the other hand, another dimension in the symbolic interpretation is bound to the eye shape of the ceiling light: it unveils the cruelty, whereas the other lamp struggles in vain to do it.

General set up: The general information conveyed by the overall painting composition still follows some rules known since the drawings on the cave walls and extensively exploited by painters during all times. The (meta) juxtaposition of group components (see also the earlier points on *Form contrast* and *Juxtaposed components* for the interpretation of this peculiar quadruplet: woman−bull−bird−horse) evokes in itself a highly conflicting situation. Note that one of the most important vectors for that devastation is the absence of color on this monochromatic masterpiece.

The analysis and interpretation of a painting is strongly based on the use of context knowledge in different ways:

- by a model-driven strategy, using the observer's knowledge;
- by blending the information coming from the painting and the one of the observer (a mixed model and data-driven strategy);
- by the creation of new metaphors from the artist or attributed to him (solely data driven).

Context in Natural and Artificial Vision

Definitions of context have appeared under multiple forms in past years, and consequently a number of context-related problems have been highlighted. Paolo Lombardi, in his PhD thesis,[4] carried out background work and proposed a classification that constitutes a significant part of the section.

In some works, context refers to the image morphology in the neighborhood of a pixel, both spatial and temporal [1]. Although acknowledging this kind of contextual information, it will be assumed that individual modules, if optimized, exploit it independently. Following many other authors, we assign to context a high-level meaning.

---

[4]Co-tutorship of Virginio Cantoni and Bertrand Zavidovique.

For [2], a context is a set of scene attributes either general (e.g., day/night) or local (e.g., scene region classification). They include light generation and propagation conditions, and all interpretative models necessary to provide a semantic explanation of the scene. Motion model switching, as one of the simplest context handling process, has been applied in contour tracking [3]. The same concept of optimal model selection is found in a face-detection system [4], where context adaptation consists in choosing the best color model for skin detection.

In [5], operator selection strategies when only one operator can be activated at a given time are considered. Strategies must be optimized in the sense of maximizing information acquisition in the shortest temporal horizon.

In a Bayesian framework, this consists in selecting the most informative sensor probability distribution p(z|x), where x is the state vector *and z is the* observation vector.

In [6], advocates for a perceptive control that covers the gap between operator intrinsic characteristics and extrinsic parameters measured in the image under analysis are described. An operator is never good or bad, but simply more or less adapted to a situation. A context change causes a modification of the relative importance and reliability of operator/feature measurements in a classification task.

Thus, a context-related problem consists in identifying an optimal decision strategy for object classification (e.g., decision tree and associated decision thresholds).

In [7,8], an operator context is defined by some (*Bayesian*) evidence that operator results are reliable. The key concept is to apply a vision module only in the specific case when it is known to work satisfactorily.

In [9], three types of contexts have been discussed:

1. *Physical context*, involving information on scene geometry, photometry or radiometry, illumination, weather, and geography as well as the appearance of scene features in previously interpreted images.
2. *Photogrammetric context*, related to the acquisition conditions of the image or sequence under study (e.g., look angle, focal length, date and time of day, image size, resolution, camera model).
3. *Computational context*, that is, all information about the internal state of processing and its control, including the type of task, task planning strategies, acceptable processing time, and the hardware.

In [10], three context-related problems are defined:

1. Each vision operator has context-dependent assumptions that limit its applicability scope (*candidate generation*).
2. Contextual dependence of the metrics is used for operator performance evaluation (*candidate evaluation*).
3. Consistency of scene interpretation depends on the presence or absence of certain objects or features (*consistency determination*).

In [11], context is considered as an environmental specialization of individual algorithms. Implicit assumptions on perceptive algorithms lead to great improvements in performance, but also imply restrictions to the application domain. Implicit assumptions are in fact partial *theories* about the environment. Theories must be tested. This implies providing sufficient information to support such theories (i.e., context analysis).

In [12], context is regarded to change with tasks, original image quality measures, and the quality of intermediate processing results. This approach comes from the multiple vision system (MVS) hypothesis, which follows theories explaining human vision not as monolithic but as composed of multiple pathways, each serving a unique visual task. According to MVS, a machine vision system should include them all. Thus, a visual context is determined by active pathways, their tasks, and parameters.

In [13], context is a knowledge base containing information like user specifications and types of sensors used, as well as a taxonomy to describe some measurable image parameters in human-like language (e.g., objects: small (0−15 pixels), large (15 pixels or more)).

In [14], context includes cues used for object representation, previous stable interpretations of images in a sequence, motion behavior of objects, and prior knowledge on scene evolution.

A list of information types forming a context is provided in [15]:

- *World knowledge*, that is, physical knowledge independent of the sensors and specific observed site.
- *Site knowledge*, that is, current set of beliefs about the site, reconstructed geometry, and so on.
- *Other contextual information*, including acquisition conditions, available computation resources, and image-understanding algorithm requirements.

Essentially, these elements are a union of prior external world knowledge and of system self-knowledge.

An Operative Definition of Context and Events

Despite their variety, all the earlier definitions contain the common concept of *context* as an interpretation framework that provides the consequences of perceptive inputs, on the basis of perception theory.

Probably a definition of *context* in computer vision, yet rather a nonoperative one, could be given by dividing a perceptive system into an *invariant part* and a *variable part*.

The *invariant part* includes structure, behaviors, and evolutions that are inherent to the system itself and that are not subject to a possible change, substitution, or control. Examples may be the system hardware, sensors, and fixed connections between them; basic aspects like survival, endemic breakdowns, mobility constraints, and so on.

The *variable part* includes all system parameters, ambient behaviors, and relationships among components, which can be controlled. By means of these parts, the system may work depending on the outer world and situation, with the purpose of better interacting with other agents and objects. According to this view, *context* is what induces changes to the *variable part* of a system.

Context becomes a particular configuration of internal parameters when mapped into the system, through its variable parts.

Similarly, the following definition provides the meaning of a *context change* in computer vision. *Context change*, from the point of view of an automatic perceptive system, is a loss of validity of any *a priori* setting currently used for scene interpretation. In other words, a *context* is changed whenever the system is working in a configuration that is no more valid and then turns to another valid configuration.

A *context* is *valid* if the automatic interpretations in the current scenario correspond to an acceptable extent to the intentions of the system programmer.

In the previous section, many kinds of prior knowledge and interpretative schemes were attributed to *context*. Some are related to hardware aspects (e.g., camera calibration, resolution, and acquisition noise), others to scene knowledge (e.g., geometrical or topological relations), and others again to system perceptive cues (e.g., observed inputs, processing parameters like thresholds tuning).

Hereafter, a plausible inventory of *variable parts* is provided in order to specify the context concept into a more technical and usable definition. In perceptive systems, elements that can be parameterized and thus controlled are *a priori* models of external objects, models of system components, and the relationship among them.

In computer vision, *context Q* can be defined as a triplet:

$$Q \equiv (A, O, I) \tag{3.1}$$

where *A* is the *model set* of object classes in the environment; *O* is the *operator set*, that is, the set of visual algorithmic modules used in the observation process; and *I* is the *decision policy* to distinguish which object belongs to which class.

The *model set A* gathers all the *a priori* knowledge about the outer scene, while the *operator set O* builds the *a priori* knowledge of the perceptive system. The *decision policy I* uses the *a priori* assumptions to perform interclass separation and intraclass characterization. Note that all knowledge acquired from previous frames may count as *a priori* knowledge for image understanding of a new frame. This knowledge accumulation can lead to a worse scene interpretation if the acquired knowledge is incorrect.

A change in any instance of one among the triplet (*A, O, I*) marks a context change (elsewhere called an event).

The real world contains, in general, high variability and variety levels—too high for mathematical and statistical models to describe it completely. The components outside such descriptions are commonly termed noise. An automatic system—and maybe the human mind itself—is necessarily endowed with models to interpret reality—for which the so-called context is a part. These models, by definition, logically ignore noise. In the present framework, the computer vision noise is distributed over multiple elements: some noise is inherent to the scene; some is passed onto its description via object models (i.e., transferred to *A*); some is added by acquisition devices and computer implementation (i.e., transferred to *O*); and some is also present in the approximations made through classification (i.e., transferred to *I*).

The Perception and Action Framework

Today one emerging issue of research on sensor systems and data analysis is that of distributed sensor networks. In this matter the context appears crucial in two different ways: first, the external parameters necessary to situation interpretation by the network must be identified; second, for a circumstantial sensor subset, the supplementary subnetwork delivers contextual information, including some internal to the whole network (e.g., its own configuration and dynamic changes). Wireless technology has recently made it possible to connect light and cheap cameras together, opening projects like MIT Media Lab "Eye Society" [16] in which a "society" of intelligent cameras solves calibration and scene-modeling problems through data exchange. Each single camera can independently pan and tilt and move along an overhead lighting track. Each camera is in constant communication with its fellow robot cameras and is independently capable of analyzing its own data and sharing information on what it sees. Each one of these cameras can be considered the advanced implementation of *active* visual sensors [17], as they were named in these last decades, supporting an effective implementation of the *perception and action* framework of biological systems [18] (for a detailed description, see the *Cooperative data analysis* section).

The Biological Solution

The quoted new equipments supported the development of new areas of research such as the *exploratory vision*, a term introduced in [19], in which the (external) context is actively identified through a controllable camera.

Explorations are analogous to the corresponding investigations of human vision obtained through eye/head/body movements. These movements support the context assessment, and interestingly they may be either slow (e.g., head or body muscles) or extremely rapid (certain eye muscles), indicating different context modalities. In biological vision, particularly in human vision, the eye movements include very fast inspection capabilities given by the *saccades*. In fact, the *scan-paths* recorded by Yarbus [20] are well known. In his work, sequences of observer's eye fixation points (looking at paintings and other artifacts or at particular scenes of ordinary life) were analyzed. The order of the fixation points is not at all random, but the salient features of the visual field are inspected following a pathway with dense areas around the "critical points." The mean time between two fixation points is around 250 ms, which can be considered the average time to build the local retinal context.

At the higher level of the control hierarchy, with more subtle and detailed scans, an element-by-element scrutiny is achieved by a fast-moving aperture of a *searchlight of attention* (with steps lasting 15÷50 ms each). In this case, no eye "mechanical" movements are required [21]; eyes are directed to some "gross center of gravity" [22] of points of interest, and then step-by-step a search-light scrutinizes each single point of interest (among 10 in average).

The level of data abstraction becomes higher going from the retinal neurons to the central cortical ones, whereas pattern location precision decreases: there is a semantic shift from "where" toward "what" in the scene [23−25]. In fact, as information passes through the visual pathway, the increasing receptive field size of neurons produces translation invariance. The large receptive fields of neurons at late stages lead to the mislocalization and the potential resulting miscombination of features. Moreover, the simultaneous presence of multiple objects increases the difficulties in determining which features belong to which objects. This difficulty has been termed *binding problem* [26]. The solution to the binding problem, an example of context loss, is provided by an *attention mechanism* that only allows the information from a selected spatial location; an example of context recovery, acting at the higher brain stages [27−29].

The Multiresolution Artificial Approach

Among the different proposals of artificial visual systems that directly address the context problem at the image level, the most promising are based on the *logmap transformations* of the spatial domain [30,31], and on *multiresolution processing* [32−35]. Both approaches consist of analyzing the images through a data structure that supplies the scene content at variable resolution (see *Region growing* section in Chapter 2), so allowing the exploitation of the most appropriate data details for the operation, the task, and the image at hand.

As a general strategy, large components can be analyzed at low resolution, whereas small components are tackled at full resolution. The emulation of the *focus of attention* typical of biological systems can be easily implemented by a multiresolution representation.

In this connection, as already mentioned in Chapter 1, in the *Hypothesis testing* section, three different representations have been suggested:

1. *Pattern tree* [36], where the subpatterns are represented as nodes of a tree; each descendant node corresponds to a detail of the subpattern of the parent node.
2. *Models feature graph* [34] based on an acyclic graph; also in this representation, nodes correspond to subpatterns or features with a hierarchical organization. The difference with respect to the pattern tree is that nodes may be reached via different paths from other nodes.
3. *Refinements grammar* [37], in which a linguistic approach is followed to describe 2D objects at different resolution levels by means of a context-sensitive grammar. Production rules codify the image variations from a coarser to a finer level.

These representations allow us to guide the focus of attention mechanisms. An object recognition process may be considered as a node-to-node sequence of partial matches. At each stage, the successive step is determined according to the partial results. This strategy is composed of two basic steps:

1. The selection of a low-level scale to hypothesize the presence of what is being looked for.
2. The zooming on the exact position at a higher scale to achieve evidence of the presence/ absence of the target.

The selection of the optimum level from which the search has to start is a particularly critical task that depends on the characteristics of the object target at hand. In general, for reasonable constraints (like the original spatial resolution, the maximum shift allowed to the target in the search space, etc.) the number of used levels turns out to be less than or equal to 3 or 4. These cases correspond to data reduction factors 64–256.

The second step of the strategy is generally called the "refinement" and is effectively implemented by progressing top-down through iterative rearrangements. More precisely, starting from the results of the first screening (ROI), the refinement is accomplished step-by-step at every intermediate level, until maximum resolution is reached; at each level the confidence in the selection is verified, and the spatial position of scrutiny is refined by checking (e.g., by thresholding a suitable figure of merit) the near neighbors at the next level.

Such processes are obviously fully contextual in all possible ways.

A Common Paradigm for Biological and Artificial Vision

As quoted, in both the biological and the artificial scene interpretation, a key constraint consists in a trade-off between resolution and spatial range: the same channel can be activated to attend to a large visual area with low resolution, or to a small visual area with fine resolution [24]. Such a trade-off is needed because of the limited amount of information that the high-level (attention) process can manipulate. This bottleneck involves appropriate level selection and commutation, referring back to the switch representation cited in the introductory bibliography of section *Context in natural and artificial vision*. Given a peculiar pattern to be recognized, the observer's judgment decides (contextually) on the fineness of the analysis, and different judgments likely lead to different spatial resolutions. A neuroanatomical model of such a process, called *dynamic routing*, was elaborated by Anderson et al. [21].

In [38], it was suggested that the human visual system is composed of both a pyramidal analyzer and an iconic visual memory: without activation of the icons into the memory, visual perception cannot exist. The visual field is analyzed in parallel at different levels with a variety of resolution degrees. The memory contains a set of icons linked by associative connections. Each icon corresponds to a very small amount of information and, because of the limited attention bandwidth, the pyramidal resolution of the segment to be compared cannot exceed the icon size: hence there is again a bottleneck between the pyramidal analyzer and an iconic visual memory.

A quite similar approach has been proposed, for artificial vision [39]; the planned approach integrates attention and recognition systems, using active (where and what to sense) and selective (how to control the stream of computation) perception. The three main characteristics of this system are scale-space representation using pyramidal descriptors; hierarchical, localized, and robust indexing and classification of the feature models using a distributed associative memory; and adaptive saccade and zoom strategies guided by saliency to locate and identify target objects.

In searching for a target that is defined as the odd element among distractors (thanks to a distinctive feature), two mechanisms can direct the analysis process (referred to as *visual attention*):

1. *A top-down mechanism*, which is exploited when the target is known.
2. *A bottom-up mechanism*, activated when the target is unknown and the search is driven by some patterns.

These two processing modes are known in the community of vision psychologists, as *feature search* mode and *singleton detection* mode, respectively. Note that, when the target distinctive feature is known, both these strategies may be employed. When the distinctive feature is not explicitly known, only the latter strategy can exhibit the "odd" target.

From the performance point of view, two factors turn out to be determinant for the search: the resolution required to make the judgment and the *a priori* knowledge about the target. Reference [40] contains experiments with both these factors utilizing stimuli containing an odd element. The authors compared different search tasks that required different resolutions. For instance, if the oddness stems from a significant difference in color, the detection or identification can be done at low resolution. In such cases, the *response time* (RT) is not affected by the number of distractors in the scene (*flat search function*). Here, the target knowledge has no effect because the detection can be achieved without attention focusing (*pop-out* phenomenon).

On the contrary, for a detailed discrimination a small aperture of attention is necessary. A critical factor then becomes the *a priori* knowledge of the target's distinctive feature. In fact, this knowledge allows us to direct attention, thanks to a top-down mechanism, toward the location of highest response (activity) for that feature. The effectiveness of this mechanism is still independent from the number of distractors (*flat search function*).

Directing attention in a bottom-up manner is needed when the distinctive target feature is unknown. In this case, the element density increases with the number of distractors, thereby obtaining a stronger contrast against the odd target (*lateral inhibition mechanism*). This is the reason why increasing the number of distractors decreases the RTs (*negative search functions*) [40].

Note that in the case described in [27] mentioned earlier, the discrimination factors are made by a feature combination. Then a *serial search* through all items is required. A *positive search* function ensues, discriminating between target and distractors, which, in this case, share some features (Figure 3.2).

The multiresolution approach has been widely investigated by the computer vision community. Among the proposed multiresolution systems, different precursors are presented in a survey of the family of pyramidal implemented architectures [35]; the multiresolution constructor module [23], and the foveated artificial retinas, Cortex I [41], and FOVIA [42] are mentioned for their simplicity or explicit biological inspiration.

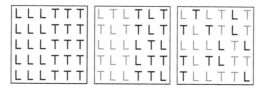

Figure 3.2 Three regions composed by two different textures are shown. In the left region, the first three columns contain a letter L, and the other three columns on the right contain the letter T. The middle region contains letters L and T distributed randomly, but the left three columns have a lower gray level than the three right ones. Finally, the right region contains letters L and T randomly distributed; both letters can be black or with an intermediate gray level: in the left three columns, Ts are black and Ls are brighter; on the right three ones, the opposite is true. The partition of the couple of textures is quite evident in the two left and middle regions, but not detectable in the right one: shape and gray level produce pop out, but their conjunctions do not!

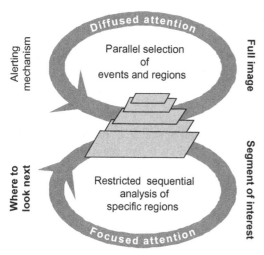

Figure 3.3 The 8-cycle of biological and artificial attention systems.

A common framework for both biological and artificial solutions is sketched in Figure 3.3. A multiresolution scheme based on the pyramid-processing theory is exploited in [43].

A model of "peripheral-like" vision aiming to select the relevant areas complements the latter attention mechanisms above. It consists of a parallel implementation of simple operators, so the complete field of view can be analyzed at a low resolution. This preattentive phase in artificial vision likely fosters specialized or parallel hardware again.

The full capabilities of the complete system, at the highest level of detail, are still required to analyze selected image segments in sequence to interpret the scene semantics. The *a priori* knowledge on the scene guides the interpretation phase, and, when no result is achieved, a new region of interest is analyzed. It is worthwhile stressing how multiresolution hardware systems can noticeably raise the process performance by supplying features at different scales at low cost. This design favors locality measures and correlation along the scales in both coarse-to-fine and fine-to-coarse modalities. Additionally, it facilitates the implementation of a sequence of hypothesis-testing steps for the recognition of complex objects in the presence of similar "distractors."

The trade-off between resolution and range appears to be an elementary metaphor of context implementation both in biological and in computer vision. Generalizing the distinctive feature of an odd item while keeping the multiresolution mechanism, sends us straight back to definition (3.1) by analogy, with A the feature, O the image-processing operators within the pyramid, and I the scanning strategy. Within this generalization process, the scanning broadens toward image content retrieval. Simultaneously, the context is brought forth, analogously for human and machine, following the same abstraction levels adopted by the artist.

Direct Retrieval

The *a priori* knowledge regarding scene and object appearances is contained in the *model set A*. Three groups of knowledge can be explicitly listed inside A:

$$A \equiv (\{d\}, P_{\{d\}}, V_{\{d\}}) \tag{3.2}$$

where $\{d\}$ is the *object knowledge* describing their appearance (the former distinctive feature); $P_{\{d\}}$ is the occurrence prior probability in the scenario; $V_{\{d\}}$ is the *evolution functions* describing the dynamics.

The *object knowledge* or *object description d* indicates the set of features and/or attributes characterizing an object type. The set of all object descriptions $\{d\}$ is the total scene-interpretation capability of the system, namely the set of all available *a priori* models of object classes that the system can recognize from raw data. It involves also interrelational models to evaluate scene consistency. This notation may include a class *unknown*. This class leaves room for the detection of odd items on the sole information that they do not resort to any listed model (e.g., *pop-out mechanism*); also, the system is able to learn/build online its own object models. Moreover, the image itself can be thought of as an object, thus $\{d\}$ may include a description of global scene properties.

After [44], the terms *object knowledge* and *object description* are preferred to be the more common *object model* because the latter often refers to a template or to a shape model. Conversely, object knowledge is willingly more general, including distinctive features such as color, specific motion, and grouping of other objects (e.g., a crowd is a group of persons). Object descriptions are the first interface between a higher level planning system and symbol grounding strategies. They act as identifiers for objects.

The probability vector $P_{\{d\}}$ is the vector of *prior probability of object occurrence* in a scene; in other words, P_d is the prior probability that object d is present in the scene. Experimentally, it can be estimated by counting the frequency of object presence in the scene over a sufficiently large and representative set of training sequences.

P_d is distinguished from *object knowledge d* because object descriptions are inherently attached to an object, whereas its probability of occurrence sometimes depends also and sometimes more on external causes to objects. Thus, it is a methodological choice to separate d and P_d instead of making P_d just another attribute of d. This helps in isolating different types of context changes [5].

Evolution functions $V_{\{d\}}$ indicate the set of temporal evolution descriptions of an object state parameters, that is, their motion models. They can be linear (matrix) or nonlinear, although the linear case is by far the most common in computer vision for the sake of low computational complexity. Examples are the camera self-motion matrix and an object evolution matrix.

$$x_d(t+1) \equiv V_d(x_d(t), x_d(t-1), x_d(0)) \tag{3.3}$$

Although V_d could be included among the attributes of d, by separating it, some adaptive systems in literature can be considered. In this way, different motion models [2,3] can be distinguished. Moreover, context change is in essence dynamic; that is, time plays a special role not to be mistaken for other dynamic phenomena. Note, in fact, that two distinct timescales coexist here: a fine timescale t related to object state $x(t)$, and a coarse timescale n related to evolution models $V_d(n)$.

Note that motion is a peculiar case of "change," and models, which remain trajectories in a well-selected space, address the spatiotemporal evolution in its wider sense, for example, a growing population, an aging metallic structure (growing rusty parts), an aging face (increasing wrinkles density), a complicating network (growing number of vertices), and so on.

The case considered in this section, the direct goal-driven retrieval, corresponds to an object-target feature not belonging to the other objects, as modeled in set A (i.e., admitted by the scenario at hand). Different model-driven strategies can be applied to implement the visual search; its effectiveness essentially depends on the capability to select the appropriate features for recognition or interpretation.

The Biological Visual Search

The paradigm of visual search was conceived primarily with a set of *early-vision* primitives following the *reconstructionist approach* [45]. Early vision, according to Marr, is a *data-driven* process in which sets of *intrinsic images* are derived from the visual scene to support a 3D reconstruction of the scene. *Early processing* is organized into a hierarchy of increasingly complex feature detectors [46]. The set of preattentive primitives is potentially wide and can vary substantially with the context. They usually include again geometrical and physical entities such as color, morphology, and motion.

In Figure 3.4, a theoretical framework suggested by Treisman and Gormican [47] is shown. Various components are singled out:

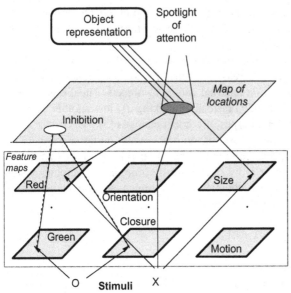

Figure 3.4 The framework proposed by the feature integration theory. The red X stimulus is analyzed in parallel through its primitive features, each one corresponding to an individual feature map. The spotlight of attention acts on a locations map, binding together the features within the focused area. This binding constitutes the current object representation. A feedback inhibition improves effectiveness by discarding *a priori* locations containing a different attribute. (For interpretation of the references to color in this figure legend, the reader is referred to the web version of this book.)

- A set of *feature maps*, each gathered in parallel, each corresponding to a different primitive feature like a color component, a particular orientation, and so on.
- The master *map of locations* that specifies *where* items are on the scene, but not *what* they are (without knowing which features occupy what locations). The master map is linked to all the specialized feature maps.
- The *attention window*, a restrained area within the master map set so that the activity is limited to the features currently in the attended location (they are then bound all together), temporally excluding others from further processing.
- The *temporary object representation*, an item representation currently provided by the binding of features. By means of a *recognition network*, the temporary object representation is compared with the object descriptions collected in the long-term memory (LTM).

Activation is pooled for each feature map within the attention window. It results in an average measure of the degree to which each feature is present. Thus, *attentive processing* would vary continuously, from completely divided attention spread over the scene as a whole, to sharply focused attention on one item at a time [47]. Between these two extremes, the attention spotlight can be set at variable intermediate sizes. The finer the scan grain, the more precise the location and, as a consequence, the more accurately conjoined the features present in the different maps. The size of the attention window is likely adjusted to establish an appropriate *signal-to-noise ratio* for the target features that are currently revealed [48].

Within fast presentations, during which attention may not be focused quickly enough [49], or when different objects with similar features are too close together [50], the target features may be misplaced or wrongly conjoined. This is the case of illusory conjunctions, which, however, are controversial for some authors [51].

Four general principles are suggested by Duncan and Humpheys [52] to governing searches:

1. Search efficiency varies continuously across tasks and conditions; there is no clear implication of a dichotomy between serial and parallel search modes.
2. Search efficiency decreases with increasing target–distractors similarity.
3. Search efficiency decreases with decreasing distractor–distractor similarity.
4. The preceding two factors interact to scale one another's effects.

Target–distractor and distractor–distractor similarities may be combined producing the following effects: increasing target–distractor similarity produces a relatively small effect when distractor–distractor similarity is high; decreasing distractor–distractor similarity produces small effect if target–distractor similarity is low. Alterations in search efficiency can be understood by considering both these variables together. Note that the relative importance of different stimulus attributes depends on the psychological context.

Following [52], the human visual system is assumed to apply three basic stages:

1. The perceptual process produces a structured representation of the visual field at several levels of spatial scale. The whole description is derived in parallel; it is hierarchical, but does not produce immediate behavioral control except for reflex ones. This description is phenomenologically outside awareness: it is preattentive.
2. The selection process accesses the visual short-term memory (VSTM) on the basis of the matching between perceived descriptions and an internal template of the information required for current behavior.
3. The selected information contained in the VSTM consciously controls current behavior.

According to Cave and Wolfe [53], each location holds an activation value for each feature map (e.g., one activation for color and another for orientation). Each activation value is actually a couple of variables, respectively, for bottom-up and top-down activation:

• The bottom-up component does not depend on the expected target and remains the same even when nothing is known about the target features. It depends on the mismatch between the value in that location and the values for the entire visual field (cf. the class *unknown* of model (3.2)). For a color homogeneous visual field, with a zero gradient, the bottom-up component for color activation has a low value everywhere. This component contributes to singleton search (see Figure 3.2), but its most important effect is produced in conjunction searches.
• The top-down component is simply given by the knowledge of the target features. More precisely, it depends on the similarity between the feature value at that location and the corresponding target feature value. For example, if the target is vertical, then each location with a vertical element has a high activation in the orientation map.

Both the top-down and the bottom-up components are summed together for each location of the single feature map. In turn, the activation values for each feature map at each location of the visual field are summed up to produce a single overall *activation map*, which represents the parallel contribution to stimulus-target matching.

The subsequent serial analysis operates over a limited area, one at a time, and is constituted by a collection of complex processing mechanisms. The areas are ordered by the activation level and then sequentially analyzed. In the case of target absence, the serial stage does not require every item to be processed: the analysis ends when the activation of all the unprocessed items goes below a certain threshold.

On the basis of the described experimental results, in [54] the feature integration model was updated in introducing a feedback between the feature maps and the location map. In fact, this top-down mechanism inhibits locations containing unlikely features; that is, they exclude from search those items having strong mismatch with the target features.

The Artificial Visual Search

Instantiating Q

Considering the case in which an unknown input image segment and the basic properties (template) of the object target are given, the problem is to determine whether the segment belongs to the target class.

In an artificial perceptive system, the self-knowledge is contained in O (see the definition for "operative context"), the operator set, which obviously includes all operators introduced in Chapter 2. In practice, O contains also all information about the observation parameters: extracted features, noise connected to observation procedures, working assumptions of the operators, operation cost, confidence measure, and so on. In the sequel, the set of all the available operators is broadly indicated by O.

Let us assume, for simplicity, that the input image segment has been extracted by an ideal operator (e.g., a generic contour follower cf) without introducing error and noise and that the templates are properly represented in their raw-data form (rdf).

Some difficulties can arise when large variations and distortions are expected in this segment; in many cases, either a flexible template matching or a "rubber mask" can solve the difficulty.

The decision policy I is usually based on a preselected matching criterion or a similarity measure (e.g., a correlation function like the minimum square error E). The context in this simple case can be defined as:

$$Q \equiv (\{p\}, O, E) \tag{3.4}$$

The Direct Matching Track: An Example

The goal is to recognize a complete, isolated, rigid shape on the plane, knowing that it can be an instance of a given prototype (or template) shape, eventually corrupted by noise, arbitrarily translated, rotated, and scaled. Given a feature extractor yielding shape descriptions in the form of sets of points on the plane $\{q\}$, each point corresponds to the estimated location of a shape feature. Moreover, it will be assumed that the feature extractor neither omits good feature points nor introduces spurious ones (so that the prototype $P = \{p\}$ and the instance $U = \{u\}$ points sets have the same cardinality).

Having $Q \equiv (rdf, cf, E)$, and working on a 2D plane, the matching problem can be set as [55]:

GIVEN	a pair of set points P and U
FIND	a total matching M and a registration R
MINIMIZING	the error E

the matching M is a one-to-one mapping from P into U (*bijection*). The registration R is a one-to-one mapping of the image plane into itself, consisting of a composition of translation (t_x, t_y), rotation (θ), and positive (nonzero) scale (s).

For each $p = \,<x,y>\, \in I$ (image plane):

$$R = s \begin{bmatrix} \cos\theta & \sin\theta \\ -\sin\theta & \cos\theta \end{bmatrix} \begin{bmatrix} x \\ y \end{bmatrix} + \begin{bmatrix} t_x \\ t_y \end{bmatrix} \tag{3.5}$$

the error E of a matching M and a registration R for the point sets P and U can be defined, for example, as the sum of squares of location errors between the matched pairs of points P and $R(U)$:

$$E = \sum_{p_i \in P} \left\| R(M(p_i)) - p_i \right\|^2 \tag{3.6}$$

The object is recognized (i.e., belongs to the template class) if $E_{\min} < \varepsilon$ where ε is given and derived from the accuracy in the template definition and depends on the context.

To reduce the computing time, a few prior constraints can be introduced:

- Constrained translation: A straightforward and general method of constrained translation would prior match the centroids of P and U:

$$\overline{p} = \frac{1}{n} \sum_{i=1}^{n} p_i, \quad \overline{q} = \frac{1}{n} \sum_{i=1}^{n} q_i \tag{3.7}$$

- Constrained scale: In many cases, scale s is constant or, if variable, can be bounded fixing, for example, the maximum distance of objects from the camera. In any case $\hat{s}$ can be estimated by:

$$\hat{s} \cong \frac{\displaystyle\sum_{i=1}^{n} \left\| p_i - \overline{p} \right\|}{\displaystyle\sum_{i=1}^{n} \left\| q_i - \overline{q} \right\|} \tag{3.8}$$

- Constrained rotation: Given P and U, deriving intrinsic constraints on rotation does not seem complicated. However, the feature extractor may have to provide an estimated orientation for some, or all, feature points with worst case for this estimation.

Recognition-Based Retrieval

When the search is not restricted to just one target, but the goal is to recognize the presence of possible different instances belonging to a set of classes of different objects (appearing anywhere in the field of view), the recognition and classification problem still addresses the three components of Q:

1. The definition of the model set A: that is for each class of objects to be recognized, the *a priori* knowledge should be explicitly defined. Note that, this definition relies on the object goal and *situational knowledge* (set of parameterized situations made of objects, their orientations, relative positions, and evolutions). As an example, in many practical tasks, it is necessary to recognize an item belonging to a class under the assumption of rigid motion, independently from the orientation. Karyotyping is an example of such case. In other cases, orientation is used for discrimination: for example, in character recognition for the classes N and Z. Common data structures for the model representations are image raw data, feature arrays, strings, trees, tables, semantic graphs, and so on.
2. The detection of the regions of interest (segment of image) to be analyzed by the operating set O. The segmentation process is performed exploiting tracks of Chapter 2, looking for homogeneity on the basis of photometric, morphologic, or spatial features. In practice, all image content analysis operators can be applied.
3. The definition of the decision policy I: that is, the discriminating strategy applied to the output provided by the operator set O. It obviously includes all thresholds and decision parameters necessary to distinguish among objects. The definition is clearly related to the object knowledge A and to the perceptive operators O. Commonly used functions are based on correlation, similarity measures, minimum distance, maximum likelihood, minimum risk, statistical parameters, and so on.

A set of templates or prototypes, one for each class, must be defined before solving the three-quoted subproblems. An unknown image segment is then matched or compared with the template of each class, and then classified via a preselected matching criterion or similarity measurement. The disadvantage of this approach is that it is sometimes difficult to select a good template for each class, define an appropriate matching criterion, and detect all possible regions of interest (ROIs). These difficulties are especially remarkable when large variations and distortions are expected in the segment under study.

The Biological Visual Classification

Context in Attention Focusing

As already stated, research work conducted on both human and machine vision led to the reconstructionism framework, based on a systematic representation of physical properties, independent from any image content and purpose. This supports quantitative features (such as slant, tilt, reflectance, depth, and motion) as a primal step for successive analysis and actions. The most common paradigms in psychology, building on a set of such quantitative features, are the pop-out theory and the selective phase introduced by Pylyshyn [56]. In the latter theory, a small number of salient items in the visual field are indexed and thereby made readily accessible for the following visual tasks. *Interrupt theories* [51] justify how the observers can detect salient sites by a *difference signal* arising from a discontinuity. Discontinuity automatically draws attention to the location of substantial differences, without identifying the corresponding features. These processes can still be classified as data driven, triggered by a discontinuity in space or in time:

• *Discontinuity in space*: According to Julesz [57], the visual scene is preattentively represented as a map of differences in textons. That is, local areas substantially differing on certain features from their neighbors are detected. Their feature identities are not recognized: the preattentive system knows where a texton gradient occurs but is unaware of what kind of discontinuity has been detected. Note that target detection requires, for comparison, at least one different neighboring element to form a feature gradient.

• *Discontinuity in time*: The selective attention is model driven; nevertheless, when the attention is captured by bottom-up stimuli, data driven and irrelevant to the current task that triggers involuntary spatial attention (e.g., web-page advertisement with short sentences coded in flash language, i.e., banners). A new event, like the abrupt appearance of an object in the visual field, draws the attention to the ex-novo object. Yantis and Jonides [58] suggested the existence of an attention capture mechanism tuned to abrupt onset and directing visual attention to the onset location, resulting in the efficient identification of the newcomer at that location.

The mechanism directing the analysis to a particular ROI is referred to as *spatial attention*. Orientation is usually defined in terms of foveation toward a stimulus (*overt orientation*). Stimulus foveation should improve the efficiency of target processing through increasing acuity. This process can be voluntary (model driven) or involuntary; in this last case, it is *data driven* and involves a discontinuity. When attention focusing is model driven, the set of models participates naturally of the context at this level. The abrupt appearance of a cue, free of any context except for the sudden variation, produces the automatic orientation of the *focus of attention* to the cue location (*stimulus driven* [59]). Nevertheless, voluntary and automatic attention orientations are not independent. It has been demonstrated [59] that when context is more entailed, for instance, the location of the target is exactly known, the subject can override the attention capture produced by abrupt onsets toward other locations.

Most studies on spatial attention have used a cost−benefit paradigm [60] in which the validity of the cue is evaluated. Different models have been discussed:

• *Spotlight model [61], in which attention is conceived as a light beam.*
• *Zoom-lens model [62], in which the focus of attention can be differently sized; the narrower the focus, the greater the benefit in processing.*
• *Gradient model [63], in which attention translates into a distribution of resources over the scene; the shape and dispersion of the distribution depend on to the direction of attention.*

Whether it is spotlight or zoom-lens models, the beam is moved from one location to another corresponding to the attention shift, whereas in the gradient model the attention is not moved per se, but rather resource gathering emerges at the cued location. Note that when attention is moved elsewhere, following an exogenous cue, the processing of stimuli at the previously cued location is inhibited. This important behavior is called inhibition of return and helps context handling to remain naturally Markovian. On the other hand, no inhibition occurs following an endogenous cue. The inhibition of return is particularly important in avoiding further exploration of locations and items that have already been inspected. The eye movements, which take a long execution time and are followed by a refractory period, require particular control-effective mechanisms.

Context in Pattern Handling

Object recognition and scene understanding are quite complex processes, in which many objects, with different positions and lighting conditions, and with different perspectives, are gathered simultaneously. The combinatorial explosion of the possible instances of the same object prevent a discrete interpretation like the *grandmother cell* concept, in which for each possible instance there is a referent neuron [64]. While flowing through the visual system, the scene information is coded by scene points in the retina; it is represented by simple pattern primitives in the striate cortex [46] and gathers into more and more complex structures in the extrastriate areas of the brain. Objects at the highest levels are encoded as *patterns of activation* in a complex network of information-transform neurons that are feature sensitive [65,66].

The visual system of primates is organized into a hierarchy of cortical areas, as shown in Figure 3.5. The visual information input goes from the retina to the striate cortex (V1) via the lateral geniculate nucleus of the thalamus (LGN). Within the retina, at the optic nerve connection, there are two main classes of cells: the magnocellular (M) and the parvocellular (P) ganglion cells. The properties of these two ganglion cells are different, although partly overlapping: the M cells are more sensitive to low spatial and high temporal frequencies, whereas the P cells are more sensitive to high spatial and low temporal frequencies [67]. From V1, the visual information is analyzed in the extrastriate areas specialized for different features of the visual signal. Two major processing streams originate in V1 [68]: the ventral stream that originates from the P layers, involves areas V2 (thin stripes and interstripes), V4, and IT, and deals with the analysis of shape, color, texture, and object recognition; and the dorsal stream, which originates from the M layers of V1, includes areas V2 (thick stripes), V3, V5, and PP, and is specialized in visual movement analysis and space allocation also used (in frontal areas) for environment orientation and object grasping. A substantial

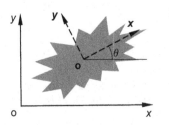

Figure 3.5 Central moments.

crosstalk occurs at many levels of the hierarchy (between peripheral and central levels) of the two streams [67], specifically between IT and PP areas [69].

The receptive field size increases passing from V1 to IT cells; these last cells respond maximally to complex foveal stimuli; their selectivity is relatively invariant over size, inversion, and color transformations. This suggests that they reflect object identity rather than local features [70]. Object identity in turn involves higher level context, that is, closer to action. For instance, Ungerleider and Mishkin [71] suggested that the P and M ganglion cells subdivision would have functional value: the P stream would carry over information about "what" an object is (main part of A in the Q model) and the M stream about "where" it is (part of O in the Q model). Milner and Goodale [72] suggested that neuropsychological and neurophysiological data accounts for the dichotomy between visual perception versus visually directed action (introducing I of the Q model). Visual perception, regarding the "what" stream concerns the meanings and significance of objects and events and tends to be objectcentered. It is connected to the features of invariant representations (i.e., size, shape, and color) and relationships among them.

The visually directed action stream provides the visual-motor mechanisms that support actions such as manual grasping. In this case, the underlying visual-motor transformations are viewer centered. Moreover, given that the position and local orientation of a target object, in the action space of the observer, is rarely constant, computations must take place de novo every time an action occurs (see the definition of "context change" leading to formula (3.1)).

In [66], it is suggested that the architecture of the visual system is organized according to the principles of modularity and computational flexibility. The adoption of separate, specialized modules for different subtasks allows neuronal architecture to be optimized for various particular types of computation. The feedback connections from the higher centers allow the brain to reorganize its computational structure adaptively. Similar considerations were leading to the competition between image operators adopted as an architectural model in [73].

The Computer Vision Solution

According to its active mode, which extensively profits from the foveation, biological vision mixes ROI detection and pattern interpretation. Machine vision is not related to an acquisition control in such a systematic manner. Attention driving is more likely a selection of a model after independent ROI finding, possibly conditioned by preset scale and feature detections. Any adoption of the resolution level or preprocessing strategy would then be the result of some feedback, introducing a different type of context.

Instantiating Q

The model set A constituted by a set of templates, or prototypes $T = \{t\}$, one for each class, is supposed to be known. The input segment, with unknown classification, is matched or compared with the template of each class, and the classification is based on a preselected matching criterion or similarity measure SM (minimum distance, maximum likelihood, and minimum risk). The disadvantage of this approach is that it is sometimes difficult to limit the number of classes (the

M cardinality of *A*), to select a good template *t* for each class and to define an appropriate matching criterion *SM*.

Assuming we have a limited number of classes *M*, each one representing a distinct target, two standard approaches can be defined: a statistical theoretic one based on a limited set of predefined features or a linguistic (or syntactic) structural one.

The statistical theoretic track. This approach establishes *M* parameterized *decision functions* $D \equiv d_1(x),\ d_2(x).\ \ldots,\ d_M(x)$, with the property that if a pattern *x* belongs to the object class ω_I, then:

$$d_i(x) < d_j(x) \text{ for } j = 1, 2, ..., M \text{ and } i \neq j \tag{3.9}$$

where *M* is the number of classes.

This decision theoretic approach requires the parameters of the discriminant functions to be previously estimated. Algorithms to perform the estimation exploit allegedly representative sample patterns within a training process.

A typical example of this approach adopts a truncated moments set *CMS*, introduced below, for the model set *A*. In this case, $Q \equiv (CMS, Os, E)$.

The Moments Theory for Segment Classification

The conventional definition of the 2D moment of order (p + q) of a binary function f(x,y) is [74,75]:

$$M_{p,q} = \iint_R x^p y^q f(x,y)\, dx\, dy \quad p,q = 1,2,\ldots \tag{3.10}$$

The double moment sequence $\{M_{p,q}\}$ is uniquely determined by f(x,y); and, conversely, f(x,y) is uniquely determined by $\{M_{p,q}\}$.

A truncated set of moments may offer a more convenient and economical representation of the essential shape characteristics of an image silhouette than a pixel-based representation.

A complete moment set (CMS) of order n is defined as the set of all moments of order n and lower ones. The operations that correspond to translation, rotation, and scaling are closed with respect to CMS of f(x,y), which represents a convenient model set for a classification process.

Let the CMS of order n be:

$$
\begin{matrix}
M_{0,0} & M_{0,1} & M_{0,2} & M_{0,3} & \cdots & M_{0,n} \\
M_{1,0} & M_{1,1} & M_{1,2} & \cdots & M_{1,n-1} \\
M_{2,0} & M_{2,1} & \cdots & M_{2,n-2} \\
M_{3,0} & \cdots & M_{3,n-3} \\
\cdots & \cdots \\
M_{n,0}
\end{matrix}
$$

Conventional Moments' Transforms

Transforms of conventional moments useful for a normalization process are:

- *Scale change* λ

$$M'_{p,q} = \iint_R x^p y^q f\left(\frac{x}{\lambda}, \frac{y}{\lambda}\right) dx\,dy = \lambda^{2+p+q} M_{p,q} \tag{3.11}$$

- *Translation (a,b)*

$$M'_{p,q} = \iint_R (x+a)^p (y+b)^q f(x,y)\,dx\,dy = \sum_{r=0}^{p}\sum_{s=0}^{q} \binom{p}{r}\binom{q}{s} a^{p-r} b^{q-s} M_{r,s} \tag{3.12}$$

- *Reflection (y-axis)*

$$M'_{p,q} = \iint_R x^p y^q f(x,-y)\,dx\,dy = (-1)^q M_{p,q} \tag{3.13}$$

- *Rotation* θ

$$M'_{p,q} = \iint_R (x\cos\theta + y\sin\theta)^p (y\cos\theta - x\sin\theta)^q f(x,y)\,dx\,dy$$
$$= \sum_{r=0}^{p}\sum_{s=0}^{q} \binom{p}{r}\binom{q}{s}(-1)^{q-s}\cos\theta^{p-r+s}\sin\theta^{q+r-s} M_{p+q-r-s,r+s} \tag{3.14}$$

Definition of the Standard Moment Set (SMS)

- *Scale normalization*

    A normalization can be achieved by scaling $M_{0,0}$ to 1, which corresponds to standardizing the segment area. The resulting λ value is given by:

$$\lambda_n = \frac{1}{\sqrt{M_{0,0}}} \tag{3.15}$$

- *Translation normalization*

    A translation normalization is achieved by adopting the central moments $\{\mu\}$, that is, by putting the axis origin in the segment center of mass (in this case, $\mu_{1,0} = \mu_{0,1} = 0$; Figure 3.6). The correspondent translation is given by:

$$\bar{x} = \frac{M_{1,0}}{M_{0,0}}; \quad \bar{y} = \frac{M_{0,1}}{M_{0,0}} \tag{3.16}$$

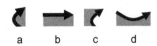

Figure 3.6 Terminal symbols V_T used to describe the chromosome contours.

a   b   c   d

- *Rotation normalization*

    A rotation normalization is achieved by rotating the axis so that the x-axis coincides with the principal inertia axis (in this case, $\mu_{1,1} = 0$, $\mu_{2,0} \geq \mu_{0,2}$, $\mu_{3,0} \geq 0$). The rotation θ is given by:

$$\tan 2\theta = \frac{2\mu_{1,1}}{\mu_{2,0} - \mu_{0,2}} \tag{3.17}$$

With the above normalizations, the SMS becomes:

$$
\begin{array}{cccccc}
1 & 0 & \mu_{0,2} & \mu_{0,3} & \cdots & \mu_{0,n} \\
0 & 0 & \mu_{1,2} & \cdots & \mu_{1,n-1} & \\
\mu_{2,0} & \mu_{2,1} & \cdots & \mu_{2,n-2} & & \\
\mu_{3,0} & \cdots & \mu_{3,n-3} & & & \\
\cdots & \cdots & & & & \\
\mu_{n,0} & & & & &
\end{array}
$$

In practical applications, $n \leq 6$. In some cases, only the projection on the major principal axis is used ($M_{p,0}, 0 \leq p \leq n$). Other descriptors may adequately describe the shape from the silhouette moments of simple blob-like segments, being derived from the analysis of distributions, such as skewness $\left(\mu_{3,0}/\mu_{2,0}^{3/2}\right)$ or kurtosis $\left(\mu_{4,0}/\mu_{2,0}^2 - 3\right)$.

Alternative Moment Representation

An alternative silhouette representation is given by the rotational moments, which can be defined as:

$$F_{n,l} = \int_{-\pi}^{\pi} \int_{0}^{+\infty} r^n e^{jl\theta} f(r \cos\theta, r \sin\theta)\, dr d\theta \tag{3.18}$$

where $0 \leq l \leq n$ and $n - l$ is even. Note that obviously $r = \sqrt{x^2 + y^2}$ and $\theta = \text{arctg}(y/x)$. The rotational moments can be easily obtained from the conventional moments through a linear combination:

$$F_{n,l} = \sum_{j=0}^{n} a_j M_{n-j,j} \tag{3.19}$$

where $\{a_j\}$ are complex coefficients.

    Rotational moments are of interest as rotations are very easy to deal with, as well as reflections about an arbitrary axis. Being θ and φ the rotational angle and the angle of *the reflection line with reference to the y-axis, the normalizing equations are, respectively:*

$$F_{n,l}' = e^{il\theta} F_{n,l} \quad F_{n,l}'' = e^{-2il\varphi} F_{n,l}^* \tag{3.20}$$

where $F_{n,l}^*$ is the complex conjugate of $F_{n,l}''$. Unfortunately, translations are much more difficult with rotational moments than with conventional moments.

Other alternative moments representations are the orthogonal moments derived from conventional (Legendre) and rotational (Zernike) moments. Broadly speaking, the advantages of orthogonal moments consist of having a more adequate value range and precision, but a higher complexity of the computation required for translation, rotation, and scaling.

Gray-Level Moment

The moment approach is not only applicable to the silhouette, but also to gray-level images $g(x, y)$. In this case:

$$M_{p,q,r} = \iint_R x^p y^q g^r(x, y) \, dx \, dy \text{ for } p, q, r = 1, 2, \ldots \tag{3.21}$$

The gray-level distribution may contain useful information for segments classification. The moment sets resulting from the addition of a bias c ($g'(x,y) = g(x,y) + c$) to the gray level and with a factor d ($g'(x,y) = d\, g(x,y)$) are given, respectively, by:

$$M_{p,q,r}' = \sum_{j=0}^{r} \binom{r}{j} c^j M_{p,q,r-j} \tag{3.22}$$

$$M_{p,q,r}'' = d^r M_{p,q,r} \tag{3.23}$$

The standard gray-level moment set can be normalized with respect to luminance, by assuming c and d given, respectively, by:

$$c = -\frac{M_{001}}{M_{000}} \tag{3.24}$$

$$d = \sqrt{\frac{M_{002}}{M_{000}}} \tag{3.25}$$

The final SMS values (for the gray-level mean and variance) are then:

$$M_{001}' = 0, \quad M_{002}' = 1 \tag{3.26}$$

From what can be seen using SMS for gray-level silhouettes, the method can be easily extended to colored images, either considering each one of the RGB components or other possible representations.

The Linguistic/Syntactic Track

This method puts forward a structure-handling capability to compose details into a coherent, complete object. It is based on concepts derived from formal language theory [76].

Basic to the syntactic recognition approach is the decomposition of shapes into *subpatterns* or *primitives SP*. Each primitive is used as a possible symbol of a *grammar G*, the grammar featuring a set of syntax rules for the generation of sentences from the given set of symbols. The formal definition of a grammar *G* was already introduced in the section *Structural decision:*

$$G = (V_N, V_T, PR, S) \tag{3.27}$$

where V_N is a finite set of nonterminal symbols; V_T is a finite set of terminal symbols; *PR* is a finite set of production rules; and *S* is a starting symbol.

Given an incoming unknown target, a sentence representing the input shape, the recognition-based problem in this grammatical frame is that of deciding in which *language* (which grammar) among a limited set $\{G\}$ of *M* predefined grammars, each characterizing an expected pattern, the sentence holds.

In practice, for the classification in *M* classes, the problem then amounts to defining *M* languages (*M* grammars) such that:

- Any item in one of the classes be described by a sentence.
- The description satisfies the correspondent grammar, but not any other *M*-1 grammars.

In this case, the context can be defined as $Q \equiv (\{G\}, Os, \{PR\})$.

As an example of recognition-based retrieval, a case is presented by King-Sun Fu (1930–1985), one of the pioneers of this approach: the automation of the chromosome classification. Three context-free grammars were developed, each describing one class of chromosomes: metacentric (arms are roughly equal in length), submetacentric (length of arms is unequal), and acrocentric (the short arms are hard to observe). To this aim, $V_N = \{A-Z\}$; $V_T = \{a,b,c,d\}$, as shown in Figure 3.7; $S = AA$ (representing the contour symmetry); the three production rules *P* for each class are given in Figure 3.8.

In Figure 3.8, on the left the production rules corresponding to each chromosome type are listed, while an example of a chromosome belonging to each class is shown on the right.

Note that if a letter is repeated on both sides of a production rule, it implies a recursion. Following the chromosome contour clockwise, a circular string is obtained that fully describes the unknown chromosome. If the production rules *PR* are applied on the string until a complete coverage is obtained, the string is accepted by this grammar, and therefore the chromosome corresponds to this grammar class.

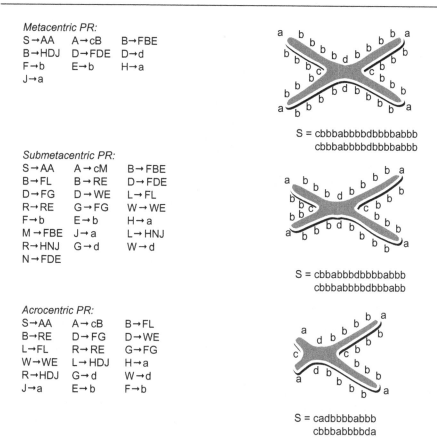

Metacentric PR:
S→AA   A→cB   B→FBE
B→HDJ   D→FDE   D→d
F→b   E→b   H→a
J→a

S = cbbbabbbbdbbbbabbb
    cbbbabbbbdbbbbabbb

Submetacentric PR:
S→AA   A→cM   B→FBE
B→FL   B→RE   D→FDE
D→FG   D→WE   L→FL
R→RE   G→FG   W→WE
F→b   E→b   H→a
M→FBE   J→a   L→HNJ
R→HNJ   G→d   W→d
N→FDE

S = cbbabbbdbbbbabbb
    cbbbabbbbdbbbabb

Acrocentric PR:
S→AA   A→cB   B→FL
B→RE   D→FG   D→WE
L→FL   R→RE   G→FG
W→WE   L→HDJ   H→a
R→HDJ   G→d   W→d
J→a   E→b   F→b

S = cadbbbbabbb
    cbbbabbbbda

Figure 3.7 Production rules for the three chromosome types: metacentric, submetacentric, and acrocentric.

Conversely, if the string is not fully covered, the chromosome does not belong to this class.

An alternative solution is given by exploiting an attributed grammar. An attributed grammar is a grammar where:

•   Each primitive or nonterminal symbol has a symbolic part and a value part that may have several attributes.
•   Each symbolic production rule has a corresponding set of attribute rules.

Adopting an attributed grammar, the number of production rules can be consistently reduced in spite of the management cost of the attributes [77]. As an example, considering the total curve length to be an attribute in the chromosome classification, the terminal symbols remain those of Figure 3.7, but b will be integrated with the length attribute; therefore, it will never be replicated locally. The sentences that describe the metacentric and submetacentric chromosomes will only differ on the attribute values.

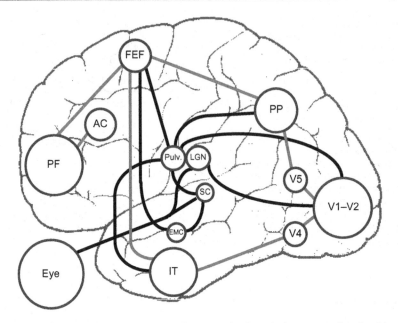

Figure 3.8 A simplified scheme of cortical areas and subcortical structures involved in human visual perception and attention; the localization is only indicative. The structures are AC—anterior cingulate area (in medial frontal cortex); EMC—eye motor control nuclei (in the pons); FEF—frontal eye field cortex; IT—inferotemporal cortex; LGN—lateral geniculate nucleus (in the thalamus); PF—prefrontal cortex; PP—posterior-parietal cortex; Pulv.—pulvinar nucleus (in the thalamus); V1—striate cortex; V2, V4, V5—extrastriate cortex; SC—superior colliculus (in the midbrain).

The Structural Track

When the structure of a pattern dominates the global shape, an alternative to grammatical techniques consists of accumulating partial information, elements of the structure. This operative fashion of the recognition follows a cumulative construction of this pattern. An additional benefit from such techniques is to be independent of the number-of-objects class. The Hough technique, already mentioned in the section *Cumulative matching* in Chapter 2, is particularly suited to recognize a pattern not *knowing the number of expected classes*, on the basis of local features independently extracted. The idea is that every observed detail supports the possible existence of a complex global pattern by contributing to measure a global compatibility from all detail peculiarities and locations. The richer the information supplied, the more precise the contribution to the pattern detection.

The Hough transform has been introduced in 1962 [78] for the detection of straight lines. Each contour point identified in an image can support the existence of the set of straight lines crossing its location. If a straight line is present in the image, and N of its points are detected, N sets of lines receive a contribution, but only the common single straight line receives N contributions. An edge detector may also provide the contour orientation; in this case, the possible detection is more effective with less spurious artifacts.

From the very first Hough transform version, many extensions were developed along the years. They range from more complex analytical curves (with a higher number of parameters (e.g., [79] for circles and [80] for parabolas)) up to the *generalized Hough transform* (GHT) [81], in which, under the assumption of rigid motion, any pattern can be represented and recognized.

The original approach of the GHT is based on these elements:

- An enriched edge detector (EED) to find contour pixels and some local properties as the gradient angle or local curvature (concavity and convexity).
- An array (in a parameter space) working as an accumulator of the contributions. Each element of the parameter space represents a possible instance of the searched object. In the GHT, each element corresponds to the parameters of the rigid motion that moves the reference point of the object on that location.
- A mapping rule that defines the contributions of the detected instance on the accumulator array. The simplest solution is to increment all the elements, corresponding to the pattern, compatible with the detected instance. A weighted contribution can be introduced on the basis of both the estimated precision (e.g., the further the location, the lower the contribution because of the edge detection orientation bias) and/or of the saliency of the detected instance.
- A discriminant criterion for the evaluation of the resulting final contribution in the parameter space DC. Knowing the expected maximum contribution, the common solution is by means of a threshold (local maxima over the threshold identify the presence of the pattern).

The GHT is applied when the pattern is not easily described by an analytical equation. In these cases, it is described through a reference table (RT) (see Figure 3.9). This table embodies the model set A of context Q, and defines the relative position and orientation (and eventually other peculiarities) of the border points with respect to a reference origin for the object. The RT is built offline, and contains as many border elements as necessary for the detection of that object in the context in which it must be found. Note that the maximum contribution achieved in

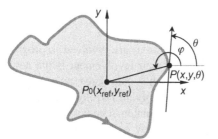

$$\rho = \sqrt{(x_{ref} - x)^2 + (y_{ref} - y)^2}$$

$$x_{ref} = x + \rho \cos(\varphi - \theta) \quad y_{ref} = y + \rho \sin(\varphi - \theta)$$

....	....	....	....
$P(x,y)$	ρ	$\varphi - \theta$	Other peculiarities
....	....	....	....

Reference table

Figure 3.9 GHT basics: a general object on the left, and RT and its content parameters on the right.

the parameter space is linearly dependent on the cardinality of RT (i.e., the *a priori* peculiarities of the border).

The parameter space in the GHT has the dimensionality given by the rigid motion parameters, which often in 2D correspond to the image space (just the translation parameters if scale variation is not applied and the object orientation is determined in a second phase).

In this case the context can be defined as $Q \equiv (RT, EED, DC)$.

The effectiveness of the GHT is well known, and several methods have been developed to reduce the computational burden, targeting realtime without compromising the quality of results. Among the different approaches developed, a dichotomy can be applied: the randomized ones (RHT) [82] and the deterministic ones. The former class includes Dynamic RHT (DRHT, [83]), Window RHT (WRHT, [83]), Connective RHT (CRHT, [83]), and so on; the latter ones, Fast HT (FHT, [84,85]), Adaptive HT (AHT, [86]), Hierarchical HT (HHT, [87]), Combinatorial HT (CHT, [88]), Curve Fitting HT (CFHT, [89]), and so on.

The Hough transform is widely used in motion detection and stereo reconstruction too, and further in the detection of any parameterized phenomenon. More generally, it supports a direct implementation of a decision mechanism based on the accumulation of evidence, from which comes its popularity.

Search-Based Retrieval

In this case, there is a general target that cannot be described with clearly defined images, icons, or parameters. A typical example is in surveillance systems against loitering: the goal is well defined (often in terms of avoiding dangerous situations), but what to look for can be expressed only in terms of special events, particular co-occurring relationships, and so on. Moreover, it may be, as in the quoted case of loitering, that there are other humans "playing the game" with the opposite goal. To solve these cases, the search is based on a bottom-up, data-driven, sophisticated strategy to extract useful, reliable, and timely information from highly dynamic environments.

The techniques chosen for these cases are high-level symbolic processing strategies, semantic networks, and simulated reasoning. This corresponds, in terms of the Q model, to the vanishing of A. The former contribution of A is now supported by O, and I is a predominant context actor.

Biological Context-Bound Interpretation

Considering the human brain, the prefrontal cortical areas are involved in programming high-order behavior. A basic requirement for their involvement is the degree of centralization needed for the current action: highly automated operations are executed without central control, whereas actions involving novelty need a central system that "modulates" the execution of predefined action schemes [90]. Novelty here refers to new actions, or actions executed in new environments, or actions effected with new perception schemes.

The frontal cortex is organized into a hierarchy of cortical areas in which premotor and motor areas are specialized in planning responses, whereas prefrontal areas are specialized as the working memory of sensory and temporal information [91]. Overall, the brain can be represented as an ascending hierarchy of sensory areas (responding to elementary features of the stimuli at the lowest level, and to symbolic and extra-personal spatial coordinate representations at the higher levels). A descending hierarchy of motor areas translates perception into action: the prefrontal cortex contains broad schemes of sequentially organized actions (e.g., syntactic and logical statements in spoken language); the premotor and motor cortices forecast more specific actions that are discrete in terms of somatotopy (e.g., morphemes and phonemes) and movements with their trajectories [92].

Some theories have been proposed for the prefrontal cortex. Norman and Shallice [93] postulated that at the highest level, action is represented by schemes such as scripts [94]. They are contextually activated in connection with environmental conditions. Temporally guided execution of subroutines implemented in specialized areas may also activate the scripts too (*A/O* in the *Q* model). A *supervisory attention system* (SAS) is needed to deal with intentions and decision making in new environmental conditions and to allow learning from errors. SAS operates by modulating the schemes quoted earlier (extended *I* in *Q*).

The *anterior attention system* (AAS) described in [95] is concerned with recruitment and control of the posterior areas of the brain that are responsible for sensory processing. These *executive functions* suggest that the executive AAS is informed of the processes taking place within the organization of specialized areas (phenomenologically this would correspond to *awareness*) and can achieve some control over the system.

The Automatic Behavior Analysis Track

The adaptation of a visual operator through machine learning techniques [96,97] allows developing image-understanding modules, assuming a training step. Nevertheless, it is beyond the current implementation level of systems in real conditions. Moreover, experience shows that a well-designed system taking advantage of expert knowledge of image understanding has a far better performance on focused applications than any solution based on machine learning.

The problem is that of controlling the global system configuration states rather than each single module. The latter problem stems directly from control theory and has been tackled by a large number of researchers.

In the following section, we describe the *context selection and commutation* approach [73], a strategy of global state control that switches from one configuration to another when the current configuration loses validity. The basic idea is that robustness can be increased by detecting a critical failure in one module and suspending its operation or by substituting it with an alternative solution until working conditions have been restored. To implement such a strategy, the system must be provided with a means of monitoring outer context and self-operation. This requires specialized algorithms named *daemons*, which pursue context analysis and trigger the switching process (Figure 3.10). Their role could be similar to that of the *executive functions* in the human AAS.

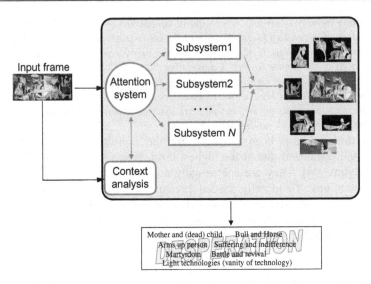

Figure 3.10 Control system strategy that switches the configuration, opportunistically optimizing the fitting of the system to a given context.

Applicative systems obey common-sense guidelines that can be implemented by the following sequence:

- Analysis of the application domain and normal operative versus critical situations.
- Selection of component modules and their organization into sets of subsystems.
- Definition of connections between contexts and their *a priori* transition probabilities.
- Design and selection of appropriate algorithms evaluating the state of the system and some world parameters that have an influence on system effectiveness (by analogy with thermodynamics and informatics; these processes are called daemons).

For the sake of clarity, the present behavior analysis track is illustrated by an example. It is focused on a restricted problem class concerning *context selection and commutation*; however, it should be clear that the methodology does not lose any generality.

Search-Based Retrieval: An Example

Consider a vision system for pedestrian detection and tracking on board a vehicle in an urban environment. Suppose that the application analysis has already identified both the normal and a few distinct critical contexts (still/low-/high-speed car, sudden break, bright/low lighting). In every context, some textured regions crossing the horizon are indicative of obstacles.

First Step

During the first step, it is important to collect knowledge from extensive training image sequences on *normal* and *critical* situations (e.g., lighting changes, shadows, and disturbing objects) in order to concentrate the optimization efforts on the class identification.

Normal operative conditions correspond to the "ideal" environmental state in which a system would work *most* of the time, but not at *all* times. Whenever the system does not operate properly, the explanation should be straightforward for a fair proportion of events, leaving room to system improvement: a situation is *critical* if it does not support system operation in the *reference configuration*, but allows system extension if a change in (A,O,I) is admitted.

Two tasks must be executed:

1. Identify a finite set of critical situations to which the system ought to adapt, that is, a set of contexts.
2. Supply for each situation, normal or critical, a description with working conditions (WC). Then, a context state q must be assigned to combinations of WCs; to express that the current context at time t is q_i, we write $Q(t) = q_i$, with $i = 1, \ldots, N$, being N the number of situations.

In essence, each given context q is a joint verification of a certain number of *working conditions,* and two contexts differ when their sets of verified *working conditions* are different.

At the end of the first step, the application domain has been decomposed into a set Q of contexts $q_i = (\{WC\}_i)$, with $i = 1, \ldots, N$ (see Table 3.1 for the pedestrian detection example).

Second Step

The second step consists in identifying the optimal triplet (A,O,I) for each situation. The result is a number of specialized *subsystems* focusing on some environmental or operative requirements. Each *subsystem* is optimized in harmony with the others in a spiral design progression.

In detail, for every q_i:

- The appropriate model set A_i that satisfies $\{WC\}_i$ must be specified.
- The appropriate operator set O_i, given the selected A_i and $\{WC\}_i$ must be identified.
- An appropriate decision policy I_i given A_i and O_i must be chosen.
- The structural architecture of the operator set O_i must be organized.

Table 3.1 A Possible Set of Five Contexts for the Pedestrian Detection Example

Context	Context Description
q_1	Still car, bright light
q_2	Still car, low light
q_3	Speed car below v^*
q_4	Speed car above v^*
q_5	Sudden break, vehicle perhaps out of control

Note that the normal operative conditions correspond to q_3. For the sake of clarity, the long list of $\{WC\}_i$ are not detailed; in particular, the set considers weather effects (e.g., rain, wind, lightning and sunset long shadows), features of the acquisition system (e.g., noise level, nonlinearities, and dissimilarities), temporally distributed features (e.g., background maintenance and optical flow), and so on.

At the end of this step, *contexts* have been defined in terms of all their basic components (see also Eqn. (2.2)): $q_i = (\{WC\}_i, \{d\}, P\{d\}, V\{d\}, \{o\}, I)_i$. In practice, an optimized *subsystem* s_i now corresponds to each context q_i. Each *subsystem* from set S is in a one-to-one correspondence to a *context* in Q. Tables 3.2–3.5 and Figure 3.11 exemplify the pedestrian detection problem.

Third Step

In the third step, transitions from one *subsystem* to another are tackled. Again, *a priori* transition probabilities can be estimated from large training sets of representative sequences.

Table 3.2 A Possible Group of *Model Set A*

Context	d	$P_d\ (\%)$	V_d
q_1	Color, silhouette, motion, texture	30	Linear
q_2	Color, silhouette, motion, texture	30	Linear
q_3	Silhouette, motion, texture	15	Linear
q_4	Silhouette, texture	15	–
q_5	Texture	40	–

If the car is moving at low speed and pedestrians are close, detectable cues are their characteristic motion and their vertical silhouettes. If the car is still at traffic lights, pedestrians are so close that the skin color of their faces is also detectable. Conversely, motion tracking becomes impossible at high speed. Finally, even silhouette detection is too difficult in the case of unreliable acquisition conditions, such as when the emergency break is used.

Table 3.3 Possible Choices in the Vision System for Pedestrian Detection, for the Operator Set O

Operator	Module Objective
o_1	Face detection through skin color
o_2	Shape detection by silhouette matching
o_3	Kalman tracking with a given evolution model
o_4	Attentive operator (textured regions)

Table 3.4 Contexts and Related Active Modules

Context	Context Description	Active Operators
q_1	Still car, bright light (skin color model 1)	$o_1(1), o_3, o_4$
q_2	Still car, dim light (skin color model 2)	$o_1(2), o_3, o_4$
q_3	Car speed below v^*	o_2, o_3, o_4
q_4	Car speed above v^*	o_2, o_4
q_5	Sudden break, vehicle perhaps out of control	o_4

Note that color segmentation o_1 is reliable only if the car is still and pedestrian faces are image regions greater than a minimal extension; o_1 also needs two color models, one for bright scenes and one for dark scenes; shape analysis o_2 is always very reliable, but with a limited frame rate; tracking o_3 is possible and reliable only up to a certain vehicle speed v^*; the attentive operator o_4 is the only really fast module that can deliver information with extremely short-time delay.

Table 3.5 A Likely Decision Table for the Example, Presenting the Operators o Related to Each Object Description d

Operator	d_1	d_2	d_3	d_4	d_5
o_1	1	1	2	2	3
o_2	0	1	0	1	0
o_3	1	2	2	3	1
o_4	1	4	4	3	2
o_5	0	2	2	1	0

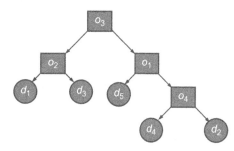

Figure 3.11 Decision tree derived from Table 3.5 on the basis of the questionnaires theory (example adapted from [6]).

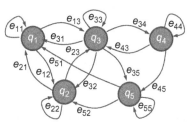

Figure 3.12 A directed graph of context transitions for an on-board vision-based pedestrian detector on a car. The transitions between q_1 and q_4, and the one from q_2 toward q_5 are not admissible.

To visualize the actual layout, an *oriented graph* is built. Generally speaking, an *oriented graph* is composed of a set of nodes $\{q\}$, representing in this case the contexts, and a set of oriented arcs $\{e\}$. Each arc stands for a relation and is represented by the couple of nodes it connects $e_{ij} = (q_i \cdot q_j)$, expressing that q_j can be reached directly with an *event* that corresponds to a particular *context change* ΔQ with respect to the current operative conditions. Obviously, the existence of e_{ij} does not necessarily imply the existence of e_{ji}. An arc e_{ii} indicates a self-connection of a node q_i with itself, corresponding to a stable context. Referring to the *pedestrian detection* problem, the admissible transitions between states are drawn in the graph of Figure 3.12.

In order to build the *transition matrix* E(3.28), it is necessary to quantitatively evaluate the *a priori event probability* for all the connections of the graph of Figure 3.12. Whenever two nodes are not directly connected, a zero probability is assigned to the transition. For other transitions $e_{ij} = (q_i \cdot q_j)$, probabilities $P(e_{ij})$ can be estimated by counting the frequency of *context changes* e_{ij} on training sequences that a human operator has marked with the appropriate *contexts*. The self-connection e_{ii} follows the same rule. Note the constraint for all $i: \sum_k P(e_{i,k}) = 1$. If no useful information is available, one can apply the *Laplace criterion* or *noninformative hypothesis* of Bayesian theory (all transitions exiting a *context* q_i are given the same probability). However, any abuse of this criterion is dangerous—for a discussion on this issue, see [98]. All *a priori* knowledge about transitions can be easily accommodated in a *transition matrix E*, such that $E_{ij} = P(e_{ij})$. Obviously, the sum of each row must give exactly 1.

In the case of the pedestrian detection, the transition matrix would be similar to what is shown in the sequel. The coefficients are just examples and have not been measured on real phenomena. Some of them depend on the car driver habits, training, or skills (e.g., transitions from and to limited car speed, q_3).

$$
E = \begin{matrix}
0.50 & 0.01 & 0.49 & 0.00 & 0.00 \\
0.01 & 0.50 & 0.49 & 0.00 & 0.00 \\
0.15 & 0.15 & 0.44 & 0.25 & 0.01 \\
0.00 & 0.00 & 0.50 & 0.49 & 0.01 \\
0.45 & 0.45 & 0.00 & 0.00 & 0.10
\end{matrix} \qquad (3.28)
$$

At the end of this third step, *contexts* are organized in an oriented graph in which arcs $(q_i \cdot q_j)$ represent *a priori* transition probabilities E_{ij} (i.e., the *transition matrix E*).

Fourth Step

The fourth and last step involves the identification of some *daemon algorithms* dedicated to the observation of features, from vision or other sensors, relating to the applicative context.

Now that the *a priori* information on commutations has been formalized, the system must be provided with means to observe the current frame and to deduce some features that determine which, among the possible transitions from the previous *context*, actually happened. For every *context* q_i, it is necessary to assign a group of *daemons* $\{\delta\}i$ able to measure the features specified by $\{WC\}i$. By measuring features related to *context*, daemon outputs finally provide a numerical meaning to *working assumptions*. In fact, each *context* is characterized by an expected set of daemon output values. Additionally, suitable *confidence measures* for *a posteriori* daemons and *similarity measures* for cross-validation daemons must be identified. Indeed, the evaluation by daemons can be completed after a given phase the system is in *a posteriori* or during it (e.g., in checking the consistency between several daemon results, *cross validation*) and needs, in turn, to be graded.

Once an estimate has been obtained for each context, a strategy can be devised to choose the current context at each step. Context change management, triggered by daemon detections, will be addressed, focusing on system control.

In the car application of the example, we need the three daemons described in Table 3.6. Daemon δ_1 is a vision-based daemon with a discrete output, measuring

Table 3.6 Example of the Expected Daemon Values for Each Context

Context	δ_1	δ_2	δ_3
q_1	90–255	0	0
q_2	0–145	0	0
q_3	Any	1	0
q_4	Any	2	0
q_5	Any	Any	1

the average intensity (gray level) in image pixels. Daemon δ_2 is a continuous ego-velocity sensor, whose output is digitized in three intervals by means of two thresholds. Daemon δ_3 is the binary on/off of the emergency break. Daemon δ_1 discriminates between q_1 and q_2. Daemon δ_2 distinguishes contexts related to car speed (q_1, q_2, q_3, q_4). Daemon δ_3 indicates that the emergency break is in use.

At the end of this step the system is fully represented by an oriented graph with N contexts described by triplets (Ai,Oi,Ii), some *WCs*, and a *transition matrix E*, together with N groups of *daemons* $\{\delta\}i$.

All these elements can be introduced into the framework of a hidden Markov model (HMM) for improving system adaptation. The aim of the HMM is the estimation of context state Q(t) by integrating daemon readings Φ(t) and the transition matrix E. HMMs support the integration of the whole information coming from the measurements of daemons and state transitions over time, to estimate the probability of each context q_i.

Contexts and New Technologies

Toward Multimedia: Image Retrieval via Context

Information channeling, as dealt with in multimedia (Chapter 4), will, from its very nature, extensively exploit contextual information, which mixes up several data types and appearances to the user's intent. In that matter, image retrieval, already outlined as the application where context is truly decisive, appears a key precursor worthy of further attention. It provides an actual link between image processing (Chapter 2) and context (Chapter 3) toward communication through images and other media (Chapter 4). In retrieving images and videos from databases and also from the Internet, the meanings for viewers must be considered in varied contexts. Obviously, the desired image depends on the level of analysis, that is, description, recognition, and interpretation [99]. The current section reconsiders techniques discussed in Chapter 2 within the specific frame of data retrieval, focusing on preferred ones in this application, those that are context oriented.

Image information retrieval was first textual [100] and then inefficient as it required a tedious and subjective indexing not easily automated. Current image retrieval involves structure, organization, and storage of numerical data in order to facilitate content analysis. Nevertheless, modern content-based image retrieval (CBIR) faces the problem of image semantics, and many systems mix text and image to get around the problem (*semantic gap*).

The system objective is to answer a user's query with pertaining images. Because accessing image documents is seldom straightforward (i.e., through a semantic description that is hard to define), most CBIR systems rely on the following actions:

- A low-level representation of the image content through color, texture, and shape.
- A comparison of the extracted such features.

According to Smeulders et al. [101], the basic functions of a CBIR system are as follows:

- *Representation and analysis*: This computation-demanding phase captures the image content to code it as a feature vector. Such a vector contains a summary in terms of regions or edges, attributed with colors or textures, and of spatial relationships between them. It provides an image signature and is mostly computed offline.
- *Indexing and feature storing*: This step requires a search strategy to be defined. Indexing has to be fast enough for real time and scalable as image databases vary in size.
- *User's query processing*: This is similar to the first step, but involves an image query. The user's query has to be expressed in a way compatible with the image database.
- *Similarity measure*: A distance is defined between the query image and the source images, in terms of features. Because image matching process may be complex, distances may actually require an adequate definition.
- *User interface*: This is the system showcase, displaying the results and dialog specific to the search (corresponding evaluation, parameter tuning, etc.). The interface should be integrated into the multimedia system and must be usable, accessible, and enjoyable (intuitive and comfortable).

The way a CBIR system will process a query depends on the information coding; queries can be designed in different ways, such as:

- *By example*: Images are ranked and presented according to their distance to the query image. No peculiar skills are required for using such systems.
- *By sketch*: This method uses explicit examples by means of drawings, synthesizing similar documents. Colors and textures as well as lighting properties may also be specified.
- *By feature*: Among all available features, users can choose some and provide their values (for instance, "Find all images with 50% blue, 25% gray, and 25% green" may be enough to retrieve images of a road in the countryside on a sunny day!).
- *By text and example*: The query image is integrated with a text that conveys additional information. Most systems limit the vocabulary to key words and adopt a simple grammar for interpretation. Images are gathered and indexed by groups. These groups of pertinence refer to a type or domain like "animals or vegetation," "urban or wild life," and so forth. Again, the text indexing gives room to subjectivity when context is not trivial.

Feature Extraction

This primary operation, according to Rui et al. [102], belongs to the classical-pattern recognition methods, including the segmentation phase (see Chapter 2).

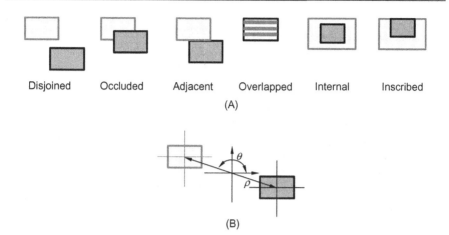

Disjoined   Occluded   Adjacent   Overlapped   Internal   Inscribed

(A)

(B)

Figure 3.13 Two examples of spatial relationships: (A) logical and topological relations; (B) distance and orientation relations.

Features can be low- or high-level ones; attributes such as color, texture, and elementary shape are the most common ones having a high discriminating power. Their effectiveness depends on the image nature and the application domain. Higher level features such as orientation, relative positions, global or local symmetries, and so on are used as refinement processes (Figure 3.13). A taxonomy of primitives has been suggested in [103]:

- *Physical features or primitives*: These are tangible variables that can be quantified. They usually stem from low-level processing: a region with a given color and shape is an example of such a primitive.
- *Logical features*: Higher level processing (e.g., context bound) provides such features. For instance, "sky" qualifying a region is a contextual feature to be interpreted in terms of its relative position in the image (upper part) and its color or transparency (e.g., blue, which is more questionable weather-wise!).

Low- and then high-level features extraction are now revisited in the frame of image retrieval.

The color feature: It is widely used for retrieval. Each color space has its specific discriminant properties. For instance, (H,S,V), explained in the section *Chromatic clues*, is the least correlated, which helps in separating between chromaticity and intensity, as the hue is invariant respective to lighting and shooting conditions. For retrieval, HSV is commonly considered the basis of perceptual spaces, allegedly close to human color sensing, at least after the Munsell's atlas (Albert H. Munsell, 1858−1918). Other spaces have been designed to be most uniform with regard to perception, such as CIE-(XYZ) or (LUV) [104].

Adams and Nickerson [105] originated a variant of XYZ called ANLAB-40 (A for Adams and N for Nickerson), Lab for short, where all three components are defined in proportion with the corresponding coordinate of the white. The transformation involves a discontinuous function: root cube for small values and then affine. In [106], a simplified version of the Karhunen–Loève transform (optimal for decorrelation) is proposed:

$$I_1 = \frac{R + G + B}{3}; \quad I_2 = \frac{R - B}{2}; \quad I_3 = \frac{2G - R - B}{4} \tag{3.29}$$

Note that for CBIR applications any color space is subsampled, most often to 6x6x6 bins.

After the choice of an adequate space, the histogram itself [107], or some variables computed from it, are used as a signature. Indeed, the first-order statistics is easy to compute and is scale and geometry invariant. Its main drawback is conversely to lose all information related to shape or topology (e.g., texture as a spatial color arrangement). Some systems aim at compensating for it, for example, [108], not being significantly more complex: [109,110] exploit moments of color, [111,112] use the so-called color constants, [113] elaborates a color signature, and [114] uses blob features arranged into a vector.

The texture feature: As already understood, this intuitive variable is easier to recognize by humans than to be formally defined. From a perceptive point of view, Tamura et al. [115] defines six attributes—coarseness, contrast, directionality, line-likeliness, regularity, and roughness—that can be in turn quantified, and their value embedded into a vector. Experimentally, derived measures appear to extract meaning efficiently compared to other low-level signal measurements. Beside these attributes, all usual image-processing techniques have been employed in CBIR: statistical, geometric, model-based, and spectral features.

- GLCM (gray level co-occurrence matrices) [116] are common in the field. Davis et al. [117,118] studied a generalized version based on structural prototypes as edge or line pieces.

  It was conjectured from the relation between GLCM and Gibbs fields [119,120] that a spectral histogram provides similar discriminative power as do Markov fields, but with less parameters to be computed. Al Janhobi [121] designed a process conjugating GLCM and the texture spectrum to be insensitive to light variations.

- In many image types, macro textures related to geometric properties of primitive patterns and to spatial constraints (placement rules) are more informant than pixel arrangements.

  The Voronoi's tessellation (Georgi F. Voronoi 1868–1908) is encountered in this matter. For instance, Zucker [122] considered a texture as a distorted version of an ideal tessellation coded by an isomorphic graph. The warping founds the compatibility measure between textures. Voorhees and Poggio [123] described the computation of the Laplacian of a Gaussian at different resolutions to extract small regions in which interrelations characterize the texture in an alleged anthropomorphic manner.

- Independently from CBIR applications, various processes for extracting primitives and embedding them in grammars are available.

- As defined in [124], synthesis-inspired techniques exploit a generative texture model of which the parameters provide discriminating features.

  Markov random fields (MRF) are popular here. They consider an image as a local realization of a random field, meaning that a pixel value depends solely on the intensity of neighbors and with given transition probabilities. Most often, they are considered Gaussian (GMRF) [125,126]. Krishnamachari and Chellapa [127] identified a GMRF at different resolutions, under the assumption that associated random variables are independent. A less greedy texture parameterization stems from the classical auto-regressive or simultaneous autoregressive model [128,129]. Comer and Delp [130] exploited an autoregressive Gaussian model at several resolutions, with correlation between adjacent layers, leading to a Gaussian Markov global representation. A different track is inspired from the Mandelbrot's fractal concept [131] of statistic surface generation. It was conjectured that most natural surfaces could be modeled as spatial isotropic fractals. Then, the fractal dimension captures some roughness of this surface and can serve as a feature [132–134].

• Conventional filtering can exhibit a repetition of motives as well.

Jernigan and D'Astous [135] tried the entropy of the normalized power spectrum for characterizing a textured region. Bovik et al. [136] defined channels depending on spatial frequencies and orientations to code images. Malik and Perona [137] designed banks of filters to exhibit frontiers between textured regions, while eliminating unlikely local responses, in a biologically plausible fashion. Most used filters in the field are Gabor's and wavelets [138–140]. Chen and Chen [141] adapted Gabor's filters to multiscaling. Smith and Chang [142] used the mean and variance of subbands of wavelets for features. Haley and Manjunath [143] mixed Gabor's filters with wavelets to provide rotation invariance. Thyagarajan et al. [144] mixed GLCM and wavelets to benefit from both statistics and frequency properties. Another technique manipulates spatial frequencies in the image domain—pixel or blob arrangements—at various scales: the authors in [145,146] indicated to scan the image according to recursively generated motifs that can be adapted, as they actually correspond to 4-adjacent pixel's permutations. The motif pattern (Z, N, α, γ, ⊃, Π) [147] is selected according to targeted properties such as maximal or minimal contrast along the scan, and then co-occurrences of motifs are used for textural index (Figure 3.14).

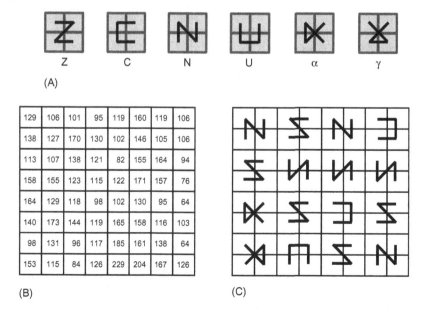

Figure 3.14 Texture representation by co-occurrence of motifs: (A) scan motifs to traverse a 2 × 2 grid; (C) motifs representing the 8 × 8 block (B).

Since the early research on texture sensing, and long before application to image retrieval, the different approaches have been compared and figures of merit were proposed [148−154]. Depending on the competing methods, the nature of test images— synthetic, natural, Brodatz, and so forth—and the classification used, the most efficient texture-finding technique varies. But experiments tend to prove that variants of GLCM or Gabor filters perform well in average. Smith and Burns [155] studied the accuracies of several texture-classification techniques and designed a free-access benchmark.

The shape feature: More than color or texture alone, in most situations, human beings would use a geometric and topologic description of a pattern, scene or context. Moreover, such a description is closer to a sketch, making it easier to build by a human−computer interfaces. Descriptions here are edge or region based, possibly attributed with color, texture, depth, or contour indexes. Geometric elements code a silhouette, generally associated to a measurement—length, curvature, continuity, and so forth—that contributes to the similarity analysis. Note that the concept of similarity [156] is weaker than that of distance and partly relies on coding and on a comparison tool (clustering, generalized distance (e.g., fuzzy or subjective [157])). A first constraint on object descriptions for CBIR is the invariance to geometric transforms such as translation, rotation, and scaling [158]. All previously detailed line codings are used, from the basic Freeman codes and skeletons to polar signatures [159,160]. Invariant moments show frequently for region-based descriptions [161−164].

Higher level descriptors: Several studies started more than a decade ago to enrich the machine image processing ability with a model of human perception to improve CBIR performance [165−168].

Relevance feedback methods are then used to bridge the semantic gap. Users are in the loop to retrieve images according to their preference [169−173]. Supervised learning techniques are thus spreading into CBIR systemmanagement under the form of neural nets, genetic algorithms, or more conventional clustering [165,174−176]. As a result, spatial relationship (Figure 3.15) between lower level features turns out to be a key descriptor, increasing the semantics of queries [177]. Chang et al. [178] described an image content thanks to chains of symbols called 2D strings: they result from a projection of "minimum bounding rectangles" of image objects on the axes, followed by coding their relative positions in using logical operators such as "before" (<), "confused with" (=), "intersecting" (:), and so on. Chang and Jungert [179] generalized the tool with more spatial operators and relations to specify inclusions or overlap, and so on. That allows a better description of confusing situations. The authors of [180] or [181] rather insisted on reducing the chain size by truncating rectangles or by marking the beginning and end of objects, respectively. Eventually, Gudivada [182] and El-Kwae and Kabuka [183] incorporate directions (angles) and topological relations (inclusions, intersections) for better rotational invariance. In all cases, the image resemblance is given by a graph-matching technique accounting for common objects, directional and topological similarity. Hafiane [184] designed a complete CBIR system exploiting Peano's motif co-occurrence matrices and Fuzzy C-means for texture segmentation, together with generalized $\theta−R$ strings in a multiresolution pyramid. Performances were compared with those of a group of nonexpert humans in a geographic satellite imagery application. It was found that errors are comparable in nature and proportion. The system variant exploiting relational strings for texture supports comparison between several techniques within the now classical TREC EVAL frame [185].

An example of image description for retrieval is analyzed in Chapter 4, *Multimedia exploitation—Pictorial indexing*.

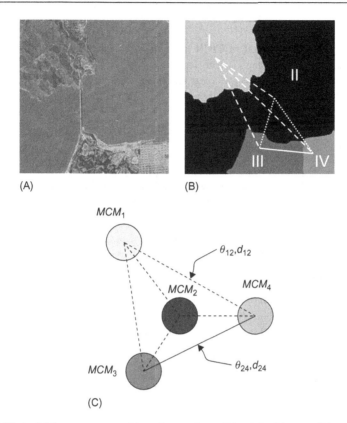

Figure 3.15 Aerial image segmented into four regions: (A) original image; (B) results of texture segmentation; (C) ARG: nodes represent regions, and edges carry relations.

Similarity Measures and Matching

Similarity between images can be measured by comparing them inside the feature space. This measure is often a distance with low computational complexity, because CBIR is likely to be computed in real time. Images are considered similar if this distance is small enough. However, other parameters are influential in the choice of a distance or of a more sophisticated decision process, such as the feature space or the base sizes. A naïve search computes the distances between the query and all images in the base, before sorting them. The resulting complexity is in $O(N)$, that is, proportional to the base size. Content indexing techniques allow to lower this complexity. Whether it is a straight distance computation, or it exploits some prior clustering, the similarity obeys the following properties:

- *Perceptive*: a small measure points out similar images.
- *Effective*: the computation is easy and the answer is quick.
- *Scalable*: the waiting time does not depend on the base size.
- *Robust*: the measure does not depend on unwanted conditions (e.g., image acquisition).

Distances Encountered in CBIR

Classical distances exploited in CBIR are listed from the simplest analytic ones to the information-related ones. In the formula q and i stand for the query and the searched image, respectively; n is their size, and l, the number of gray levels.

Among distances of the Hilbert' or Minkowski's family, parameterized by p,

$$d_p(q, i) = \left(\sum_{j=1}^{n} |q(j) - i(j)|^p \right)^{\frac{1}{p}} \qquad (3.30)$$

weighted forms D of the quadratic distance are tried to stress image parts a priori, if they are locally more similar.

$$D_A(q, i) = \sqrt{(q - i)^t A(q - i)} \qquad (3.31)$$

where A is the similarity matrix.

For instance, $d_{i,j} = 1 - (d_{i,j}/\max d_{i,j})$ has been proposed for the elements of A, with $d_{i,j}$ a distance between pixels i and j of images q and i, respectively, from representative samples in the application field. Such a distance is allegedly close to human color perception and suitable for CBIR according to Flickner et al. and Carson et al. [111,186]. A peculiar case is the Mahalanobis distance, where A is a covariance to account for the correlation between the distribution of classes.

A somewhat simpler way to introduce image distributions is through their histograms again. Swain and Ballard [187] designed one of the first such distances in CBIR, evaluating the histogram intersection $d_{h\cap}$:

$$d_{h\cap}(q, i) = \frac{\sum_{j=1}^{l} \min(h_q(j), h_i(j))}{n} \qquad (3.32)$$

where h_x is the histogram of x.

Note that this might not be a distance, as the symmetry criterion may not be met. Smith [188] used a symmetric version.

Among distances bound to a process, operation-cost based distances are known to be peculiarly efficient, such as the Levenstein's distance associated to dynamic programming. Another such distance frequently used in CBIR is the Earth mover distance (EMD) that is bound to linear optimization. The idea is to minimize the cost of transforming a distribution into another, under constraints on the class shift [189]

$$EMD(q, i) = \frac{\sum_{j,k} g_{jk} d_{jk}}{\sum_{j,k} g_{jk}} \qquad (3.33)$$

where d_{jk} is the dissimilarity between $h_q(j)$ and $h_i(k)$, g_{jk} the flow between them.

The cost $\Sigma g_{jk}d_{jk}$ is minimized under the following constraints:

$$g_{jk} \geq 0; \sum_j g_{jk} \leq h_i(k); \sum_k g_{jk} \leq h_q(j); \sum_{j,k} g_{jk} = \min(h_i(k), h_q(j)) \qquad (3.34)$$

Eventually, classical stochastic distances can be helpful as well:

- The Kulback–Leiber divergence *DKL* expresses the relative entropy between two distributions:

$$DKL(q, i) = \sum_j h_q(j) \log \frac{h_q(j)}{h_i(j)} \qquad (3.35)$$

with its symmetric and more stable form, the Jeffrey's divergence DJ:

$$DJ(q,i) = \sum_j h_q(j) \log \frac{h_q(j)}{\widehat{h}(j)} + h_i(j) \log \frac{h_i(j)}{\widehat{h}(j)} \Big/ \widehat{h}(j) = \frac{h_i(j) + h_q(j)}{2} \qquad (3.36)$$

The Battacharia's distance deals with Gaussian approximations:

- On the cumulated distributions *C*, one can compute the Kolmogorov–Smirnov *DKS* or Cramer–Von Mises *DCvM* distance:

$$DKS(q,i) = \max_j (C_q(j) - C_i(j)) \text{ and } DCvM(q,i) = \sum_j (C_q(j) - C_i(j))^2 \qquad (3.37)$$

CBIR-Oriented Matching Techniques

Measuring the similarity of images often requires us to pair entities extracted from them: regions, lines related with objects (contour or skeleton), or vectors of attributes of images subparts (regions or blocks). An image is then a graph embedding the entities (e.g., regions) as its vertices with weighted edges (e.g., inter-distances and relative angles). The matching concerns bipartite graphs. Two types of pairing are envisioned:

- One query's element to one target element, the 1:1 assignment problem.
- Several query's elements with many target elements, the *N:N* assignment problem.

On top of already introduced matching algorithms such as the *stable marriage* paradigm—especially fitted to bipartite graph matching—we list here two more methods common in CBIR.

- *Hungarian algorithm*: It was first designed by Kuhn [190]. Let $G(X, Y, X \times Y)$ be a weighted graph. The weights $w(x_i, y_j)$ are arranged in the distance matrix *D*. Assuming that

$|X| < |Y|$, every node x_i in X shall be associated a node y_j of Y such that the total distance D_H be minimized.

$$D_H = \sum_{i=1}^{|X|} w(x_i, y_j) \tag{3.38}$$

The method works in five steps:

1. *Line reduction*: Subtract its minimum to every line.
2. *Column reduction*: Subtract its minimum to every column.
3. *Minimal coverage*: Find the minimum number of lines and columns to cover all zeros.
4. Until the minimal coverage is equal to the dimension of the reduced matrix:
   find the uncovered minimal cell;
   subtract it from all uncovered cells;
   add it to cells at the intersection of covering lines and columns.
5. 0 valued cells mark the optimal assignment.

This algorithm accepts adding constants to lines or columns without affecting the optimum.

- *Attributed graph matching*: Although it is not a specific algorithm, the extension of bipartite graph-matching techniques to edge-attributed graphs has been peculiarly worked on. In general, as weights represent more than a mere distance between entities, the stress is put on, first, the way to cumulate edge attributes along pairing attempts; and second, how to incorporate the result to the distance between query and target elements. Examples can be found in [191−194]. A special mention is due to Li et al. [195], where Li constructs a significance matrix (s_{ij}) of the individual similarity between q_i and tj, out of significance credits (the intrinsic importance of p_i and p_i' of an entity in its image Q or T; for example, a foreground subject is likely more decisive for pairing than the background). The problem of defining a distance between region sets is then converted into defining the significance matrix. This is implemented through the following constraints and computations:
  - Checking constraint $\sum_j s_{i,j} = p_i$
  - Pairing process $p - \min(p, p') \rightarrow p$
  - Evaluating the significance credits of regions by assigning as much significance as possible to the region link with minimum distance. The overall distance is then:

$$D_{IRM}(q_i, t_j) = \sum_{i,j} s_{ij} d(q_i, t_j) \tag{3.39}$$

where d is the basic distance.

Human−Computer Interaction

The CBIR logically requires a user's intervention. It depends on the type of search (nature of data, purpose, constraints on precision or exhaustiveness, etc.), on the tools and functions made available, on the programming environment. CBIR usually addresses more the description and search algorithms than interaction and environment design. But today's users demand a variety of actions, a multiplicity of choices, and some comfort or realism comparable to those of games, for instance. The main issue of interaction in CBIR is the selection of the query space, represented in [101] as a 4-tuple (I, F, S, Z):

- Selecting I as the query space.
- Defining the set of features F and associated processing.
- Defining the similarity and associated processes S.
- Featuring the elements of the semantics (set of object tags and features Z) through a high-level language.

F is actually the entity most subject to human choices, also because it conditions S. This subject will be fully addressed in Chapter 4, in the *Human–Computer Interaction* section. Two state-of-the-art examples of practical query retrieval from a given image are shown in Figures 3.16 and 3.17.

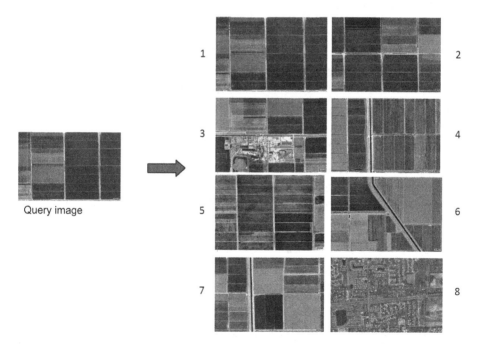

Figure 3.16 An example of query by single region. The ranking corresponds to searching the global texture of the query image. To evidence the relative semantic level reached, when the query image is the third one (second left) the ranking becomes 1, 5, 2, NR, 4, NR, NR, 8. NR means that retrieved images did not come out in the first selection.

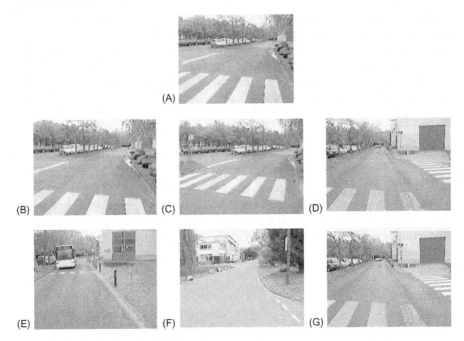

Figure 3.17 Road scene retrieval in a system memory organized by situations (e.g. *turn and cross-way*). (A) query image; (B) through (G) the best retrieved similar situations, in order, from a query by single region.

Cooperative Data Analysis

Among the new technologies, one emerging issue is distributed sensor networks and cooperative data analysis. Wireless technology has made it possible to connect smart, small, and inexpensive sensors with the ability to talk, listen, and interact with the data. Combining these achievements with new software and algorithms that exploit the proximity of devices to drastically improve the accuracy of detection and tracking, wireless sensor networks (WSN) having up to 10,000 nodes (smart elementary sensors) per entire network, with 99.9% end-to-end reliability, have been conceived. These new network techniques are suitable for highly dynamic environments that allow information processing to extract useful, reliable, and timely information from the deployed sensor network [196,197]. For the most forward-looking observer, future scenarios with *ubiquitous sensing* or *sentient objects* or even *sentient world*, or of an *Internet of things*, are definitely attractive challenges.

Even if the scalability of a local approach must be taken into account, the naïve strategy of collecting all data in a central computing node, with a high computational power, may turn out to be often not convenient. In many cases, the raw data are not needed, and the demand is limited to estimating a small number of parameters: in these cases, a better approach is having each node contributing to calculus and processing. The typical sensor local processing allows us to [198]:

- transmit only if the event is happening (event-of-interest detection);
- transmit only a limited spatial region (region-of-interest identification);
- transmit only a feature vector, edge maps, and so on (feature or metadata extraction);
- send only the differences in time or among sensors (data compression);
- send only compact high-level models (model building, e.g., in camera networks from 2D views).

In this connection, *decentralized* and *distributed* algorithms are two common solutions, but in decentralized algorithms, scaling is difficult. Note that the total number of links is $O(n^2)$, where n is the number of sensors. Distributed algorithms based on networks, the number of links is $O(n)$ or at most $O(n \log(n))$ can be allowed in terms of communication costs.

The strategy of data management strongly depends on the metaphor used to understand a sensor network. Up to this point, the proposed paradigms are as follows:

- *Distributed database*: This strategy is definitely the most popular [199−202]. Data gathering is formulated as a database retrieval problem. Sensors are seen as distributed storage points, which can be addressed on user demand.
- *Agent system*: Sensors are agents interacting according to social paradigms. Macroprogramming is based on modifying global parameters of social behaviors [203].

The database view of sensor networks has so far attracted more attention.

The problems depicted highlight the need to adopt new software paradigms for distributed computation and data fusion [204]. The peculiar approaches so far proposed are distributed hypothesis and decision formation [205], collaborative signal and information processing, and consensus filtering [206] (a consensus filter consists of the fusion of a set of sensor measurements). In particular, Duarte et al. [205] propose a distance-based fusion algorithm applied to moving vehicles: sensors far from the target have a significantly lower chance to produce a reliable value. Willet et al. [212] proposed two stages: coarse to fine network analysis.

Interesting studies regarding the management of these rich networks are related to the role of groups: among autonomous elements, group creation becomes the problem of providing all the information required for individuals to decide whether they can usefully contribute to the group. The group protocol includes the group creation announcement information on the task to be performed and a set of task-specific joining requirements like creating a group and advertising its membership criteria; joining or leaving a group; reevaluating whether to remain in the group (whenever another enters or leaves, or the criteria are modified, the group members are notified of the change and may need to reevaluate their own membership); modifying the membership criteria; terminating a group; sending and receiving messages within a group [207].

Wireless connection facilitates implementation and makes the data remotely accessible by creating a network layer between the sensors. These networks can support various *self*-* properties; for example, they can be adapted to a variety of functions: *self*-configuration (the WSN determines the arrangement of its constituent parts); *self*-localization (randomly distributed nodes determine a global coherent positioning); *self*-optimization (the WSN monitors and controls resources to ensure optimal functioning); *self*-awareness (the WSN has a sense of its own behavior, a knowledge of its components, its current status, and its goal); *self*-healing (it can repair itself or at least take actions so that faults that appear in the WSN do not hinder its performance); *self*-tuning; *self*-maintenance; *self*-(re-)production; *self*-regulation; *self*-steering; *self*-reference; *self*-empowerment; *self*-protection; and so on [208].

An advanced research example of an intelligent network is the *Eye Society* project (http://web.media.mit.edu/ ~ warlock/eye_society.html). The "society" consists of small, cheap, autonomous wireless mobile cameras, each controlled by an embedded processor. Each camera can independently pan and tilt and move along an overhead lighting track, and is in constant communication with its fellow cameras; and each is independently capable of analyzing its own data and sharing information on what it sees with its fellow robots.

The fundamental principles behind the Eye Society project are as follows [198]:

- It is possible to put sufficient processing into an information capture device such that a central processing server is not needed for many sophisticated tasks.
- A user or programmer does not need to think in terms of an identifiable individual device but of the overall system.

There are various application scenarios, ranging from the obvious military applications, such as distributed battlefield sensing or frontier control, to peaceful and civilian uses like multimedia distribution, daily weather reports, and health applications. Among these lasts, examples are habitat monitoring (birds [209], whales [210]), home intelligence (e.g., local climate control and smart appliances), biomedical [211], patient tracking, disaster relief, surveillance, fire control, agricultural, and industrial control.

Distributed sensor networks are indeed an attractive technology, even if runtime execution cannot be achieved for complex pattern recognition problems because of the technological limits of the sensor program/stack memory and the battery life. The future scenarios of a "sentient world" or of an "Internet of things" are both future and realistic scenarios standing good chances to be implemented within 10 years from now. All authors also pointed to the difficulties and the technological challenges posed by the increasing, and necessary, sensor miniaturization. Besides the hardware-related challenges, all sensor data will have to be stored, compressed, and analyzed. Sensor networks may provide, in the future, very heterogeneous information and multimedia data: 3D image, sound, distance, acceleration—perhaps even smell or others.

References

[1] F. Melgani, S.B. Serpico, A statistical approach to the fusion of spectral and spatio-temporal contextual information for the classification of remote-sensing images, Pattern Recognit. Lett. 23 (2002) 1053–1061.

[2] X. Merlo, Techniques probabilistes d'intégration et de contrôle de la perception en vue de son exploitation par le système de décision d'un robot, PhD Thesis, Université de Paris Sud (Paris XI), Paris, France, 1988.

[3] P. Tissainayagam, D. Suter, Contour tracking with automatic motion model switching, Int. J. Pattern Recognit. 36 (2003) 2411–2427.

[4] H. Kruppa, M. Spengler, B. Schiele, Context-driven model switching for visual tracking, in: Proc. Ninth Int. Symp. Intell. Robotics Sys., Toulouse, France, 2001.

[5] C. Coutelle, Conception d'un système à base d'opérateurs de vision rapides, PhD Thesis, Université de Paris Sud (Paris XI), Paris, France, 1995.

[6] A. Lanusse, Contribution à l'étude de processus décisionnels en robotique, PhD Thesis, Université de Paris Sud (Paris XI), Paris, France, 1989.

[7] R.D. Rimey, Control of selective perception using Bayes nets and decision theory, available at http://citeseer.nj.nec.com/rimey93control.html, 1993.

[8] K. Toyama, E. Horvitz, Bayesian modality fusion: probabilistic integration of multiple vision algorithms for head tracking, in: Proc. ACCV'00, fourth Asian Conf. Comp. Vision, Tapei, Taiwan, 2000.

[9] T.M. Strat, Employing contextual information in computer vision, in: Proc. DARPA93, 1993, pp. 217–229.

[10] T.M. Strat, M.A. Fischler, Context-based vision: recognizing objects using information from both 2D and 3D imagery, IEEE Trans. Pattern Anal. Mach. Intell. 13 (10) (1991) 1050–1065.

[11] I. Horswill, Analysis of adaptation and environment, Artif. Intell. 73 (1–2) (1995) 1–30.

[12] B.A. Draper, J. Bins, K. Baek, ADORE: Adaptive Object Recognition, in: Proc. ICVS99, 1999, pp. 522–537.

[13] C. Shekhar, S. Kuttikkad, R. Chellappa, Knowledge based integration of IU algorithms, in: Proc. Image Understanding Workshop, ARPA, v. 2, 1996, pp. 1525–1532.

[14] J. Kittler, J. Matas, M. Bober, L. Nguyen, Image interpretation: exploiting multiple cues, in: Proc. Int. Conf. Image Processing and Applications, Edinburgh, UK, 1995, pp. 1–5.

[15] C.O. Jaynes, Seeing is believing: computer vision and artificial intelligence, available at http://www.acm.org/crossroads/xrds3-1/vision.html, 2007.

[16] V.M. Bove Jr., J. Mallett, Collaborative knowledge building by smart sensors, Biotechnol. J. 22 (4) (2004) 45–51.

[17] M. Savini, Active vision, in: V. Cantoni (Ed.), Human and Machine Vision: Analogies and Divergencies, Plenum Press, New York, 1994, pp. 159–170.

[18] V. Cantoni, V. Di Gesù, A. Setti, D. Tegolo, Human and Machine Perception (3): Thinking Deciding and Acting, Kluwer Academic/Plenum Publishers, New York, 2001.

[19] J.K. Tsotsos, There Is No One Way to Look at Vision, CVGIM: Image Understanding 60 (1994) 95–97.

[20] L. Yarbus, Eye Movements and Vision, Plenum Press, New York, 1967.

[21] C.H. Anderson, D.C. Van Essen, B.A. Olshausen, Directed visual attention and the dynamic control of information flow, in: L. Itti, G. Rees, J. Tsotsos (Eds.), Neurobiology of Attention, Elsevier, San Diego, CA, 2005, pp. 11–17.

[22] J.M. Findlay, Global processing for saccadic eye movements, Vis. Res. 22 (1982) 1033–1045.

[23] J. Burt, C.H. Anderson, J.O. Sinniger, G. van der Wal, A pipeline pyramid machine, in: V. Cantoni, S. Levialdi (Eds.), Pyramidal Systems for Computer Vision, Springer-Verlag, Berlin, Federal Republic of Germany, 1986, pp. 133–152.

[24] V. Cantoni, G. Caputo, L. Lombardi, Attentional engagement in vision systems, in: V. Cantoni, S. Levialdi, V. Roberto (Eds.), Artificial Vision, Academic Press, London, UK, 1996, pp. 3–42.

[25] S. Levialdi, From natural to artificial picture processing, in: Proc. EUROCON, A 3–4, Lausanne, 1971, pp. 1–2.

[26] C. von der Malsburg, W. Schneider, A neural cocktail-party processor, Biol. Cybern. 54 (1986) 29–40.

[27] A. Treisman, G. Gelade, A feature-integration theory of attention, Cogn. Psychol. 12 (1980) 97–136.

[28] S.J. Luck, S.A. Hillyard, Spatial filtering during visual search: evidence from human neurophysiology, J. Exp. Psychol. Hum. Percept. Perform. 20 (1994) 1000–1014.

[29] S.J. Luck, S.A. Hillyard, The role of attention in feature detection and conjunction discrimination: an electrophysiological analysis, Int. J. Neurosci. 80 (1995) 281–297.

[30] E.L. Schwartz, Computational anatomy and functional architecture of striate cortex: a spatial mapping approach to perceptual coding, Vis. Res. 20 (1980) 645–669.

[31] Y. Yeshurum, E.L. Schwartz, Shape description with a space variant sensor: algorithms for scan-path, fusion, and convergence over multiple scans, IEEE Trans. Pattern Anal. Mach. Intell. 11 (1989) 1217–1222.

[32] S.L. Tanimoto, A. Klinger (Eds.), Structured Computer Vision: Machine Perception Through Hierarchical Computation Structures, Academic Press, New York, 1980.

[33] A. Rosenfeld (Ed.), Multiresolution Image Processing, Springer-Verlag, Berlin, Federal Republic of Germany, 1984.

[34] R. Dyer, Multiscale image understanding, in: L. Uhr (Ed.), Parallel Computer Vision, Academic Press, Orlando, FL, 1987, pp. 171–213.

[35] V. Cantoni, M. Ferretti, Pyramidal Architectures for Computer Vision, Plenum Press, New York, 1994.

[36] P. Burt, Attention mechanisms for vision in a dynamic world, in: Proc. Eleventh Int. Conf. on Pattern Recognition, Rome, Italy, 1988, pp. 977–987.

[37] V. Cantoni, L. Cinque, C. Guerra, S. Levialdi, L. Lombardi, Describing objects by a multi-resolution syntactic approach, in: A. Nakamura, M. Nivat, A. Saudi, P.S.P. Wang, K. Inoue (Eds.), Parallel Image Analysis, Springer-Verlag, Heidelberg, Federal Republic of Germany, 1993, pp. 54–68.

[38] K. Nakayama, The iconic bottleneck and the tenuous link between early visual processing and perception, in: C. Blakemore (Ed.), Vision: Coding and Efficiency, Cambridge University Press, Cambridge, MA, 1990, pp. 411–422.

[39] V. Concepcion, H. Wechsler, Detection and localization of objects in time-varying imagery using attention, representation and memory pyramids, Pattern Recognit. 29 (9) (1996) 1543–1557.

[40] M.J. Bravo, K. Nakayama, The role of attention in different visual-search tasks, Percept. Psychophys. 51 (1992) 465–472.

[41] B.B. Bendenson, R.S. Wallace, E.L. Schwartz, A miniaturized active vision system, in: Proc. Eleventh Int. Conf. on Pattern Recognition, The Hague, The Netherlands, 1992, pp. 58–61.

[42] T. Baron, M.D. Levine, Y. Yeshurum, Exploring with a foveated robot eye system, in: Proc. of Twelfth Int. Conf. on Pattern Recognition, vol. D, 1994, pp. 377–380.

[43] V. Cantoni, M. Mosconi, Approaches for Allocation of Attention in Computer Vision Systems, WOPPLOT, Springer-Verlag, Heidelberg, 1995.

[44] B.A. Draper, A. Hanson, E. Riseman, Knowledge-directed vision: control, learning and integration, Proc. IEEE 84 (11) (1996) 1625–1681.

[45] D. Marr, Vision: A Computational Investigation into the Human Representation and Processing of Visual Information, W.H. Freeman, New York, 1982.

[46] D.H. Hubel, T.N. Wiesel, Receptive fields, binocular interaction and functional architecture in the cat's visual cortex, J. Physiol. 160 (1962) 106–154.

[47] A. Treisman, S. Gormican, Feature analysis in early vision: evidence from search asymmetries, Psychol. Rev. 95 (1988) 15–48.

[48] A. Treisman, Search, similarity, and integration of features between and within dimensions, J. Exp. Psychol. Hum. Percept. Perform. 17 (1991) 652–676.

[49] A. Treisman, N. Schmidt, Illusory conjunctions in the perception of objects, Cogn. Psychol. 14 (1982) 107–141.

[50] A. Cohen, R. Ivry, Illusory conjunctions inside and outside the focus of attention, J. Exp. Psychol. Hum. Percept. Perform. 15 (1989) 650–663.

[51] M. Green, Visual search, visual streams, and visual architectures, Percept. Psychophys. 50 (1991) 388–403.

[52] J. Duncan, G.W. Humpheys, Visual search and stimulus similarity, Psychol. Rev. 96 (1989) 433–458.

[53] K.R. Cave, J.M. Wolfe, Modeling the role of parallel processing in visual search, Cogn. Psychol. 22 (1990) 225–271.

[54] A. Treisman, S. Sato, Conjunction search revisited, J. Exp. Psychol. Hum. Percept. Perform. 16 (1990) 459–478.

[55] K.S. Haird, K. Steiglitz, A linear programming approach to noisy template matching, in: Proc. IEEE Computer Society Conf. on Pattern Recognition and Image Processing, Las Vegas, NV, 1982, pp. 50–57.

[56] Z. Pylyshyn, The role of location indexes in spatial perception: a sketch of the FINST spatial-index model, Cognition 32 (1989) 65–97.

[57] B. Julesz, Texton gradients: the texton theory revisited, Biol. Cybern. 54 (1986) 245–251.

[58] S. Yantis, J. Jonides, Abrupt visual onsets and selective attention: evidence from visual search, J. Exp. Psychol. Hum. Percept. Perform. 10 (1984) 601–621.

[59] S. Yantis, J. Jonides, Abrupt visual onsets and selective attention: voluntary versus automatic allocation, J. Exp. Psychol. Hum. Percept. Perform. 16 (1980) 121–134.

[60] M.I. Posner, S.J. Boies, Components of attention, Psychol. Rev. 78 (1971) 391–408.

[61] M.I. Posner, Orienting of attention, Q. J. Exp. Psychol. 32 (1980) 3–25.

[62] C.W. Eriksen, J.D. St. James, Visual attention within and around the field of focal attention: a zoom lens model, Percept. Psychophys. 40 (1986) 225–240.

[63] D. La Berge, V. Brown, Theory of attentional operations in shape identification, Psychol. Rev. 96 (1989) 101–124.

[64] H.B. Barlow, Single units and sensation: a neuron doctrine for perceptual psychology, Perception 1 (1972) 371–394.

[65] L. Uhr, Highly parallel, hierarchical, recognition cone perceptual structures, in: L. Uhr (Ed.), Parallel Computer Vision, Academic Press, London, UK, 1987, pp. 249–287.

[66] D.C. Van Essen, C.H. Anderson, D.J. Felleman, Information processing in the primate visual system: an integrated systems perspective, Science 255 (1992) 419–423.

[67] W.H. Merigan, J.H.R. Maunsell, How parallel are the primate visual pathways? Annu. Rev. Neurosci. 16 (1993) 369–402.

[68] M.S. Livingstone, D.H. Hubel, Psychophysical evidence for separate channels for the perception of form, color, movement and depth, J. Neurosci. 7 (1987) 3416–3468.

[69] V.P. Ferrera, T.A. Nealey, J.H.R. Maunsell, Mixed parvocellular and magnocellular geniculate signals in visual area V4, Nature 358 (1992) 756–758.

[70] E.K. Miller, L. Li, R. Desimone, A neural mechanism for working and recognition memory in inferior temporal cortex, Science 254 (1991) 1377−1379.

[71] L.G. Ungerleider, M. Mishkin, Two cortical visual systems, in: D.J. Ingle, M.A. Goodale, R.J.W. Mansfield (Eds.), Analysis of Visual Behavior, MIT Press, Cambridge, MA, 1982, pp. 549−585.

[72] A.D. Milner, M.A. Goodale, Visual pathways to perception and action, in: The Visually Responsive Neuron: From Basic Neurophysiology to Behavior, T.P. Hicks, S. Molotchnikoff, T. Ono (Eds.), Prog. Brain Res, 95, Elsevier, Amsterdam, The Netherlands, 1993, pp. 317−338.

[73] P. Lombardi, 2004, A model of adaptive vision system: Application to pedestrian detection by an autonomous vehicle, PhD Thesis (cotutelle), Universities Paris XI, France and Pavia, Italy.

[74] A.P. Reeves, A. Rostampour, Shape analysis of segmented objects using moments, in: Proc. Pattern Recognition Image Processing Conf., Dallas, TX, 1981, pp. 171−174.

[75] R.J. Prokop, A.P. Reeves, A survey of moment-based techniques for unoccluded object representation and recognition, CVGIP: Models and Image Processing 54 (5) (1992) 438−460.

[76] K.S. Fu, Recent developments in pattern recognition, IEEE Trans. Comput. 29 (10) (1980) 845−854.

[77] W.H. Tsai, K.S. Fu, Attributed grammar—a tool for combining syntactic and statistical approaches to pattern recognition, IEEE Trans. Syst. Man Cybern. SMC-10 (12) (1980) 873−885.

[78] P. Hough, 1962, Methods and means for recognizing patterns. US Patent, 3,069,654.

[79] R.O. Duda, P.E. Hart, Use of the Hough transformation to detect lines and curves in pictures, Commun. ACM 15 (1972) 11−15.

[80] H. Wechsler, J. Sklansky, Finding the rib cage in chest radiographs, Pattern Recognit. 9 (1977) 21−30.

[81] D. Ballard, Generalizing the Hough transform to detect arbitrary shapes, Pattern Recognit. 13 (1981) 111−122.

[82] L. Xu, E. Oja, P. Kultanen, A new curve detection method: randomized Hough transform (RHT), Pattern Recognit. Lett. 11 (5) (1990) 331−338.

[83] H. Kalviainen, P. Hirvonen, L. Xu, E. Oja, Probabilistic and nonprobabilistic Hough transforms: overview and comparisons, IVC 13 (4) (1995) 239−252.

[84] H. Li, M.A. Lavin, R.J. Le Master, Fast Hough transform: a hierarchical approach, Comput. Vis. Graph. Image Process. 36 (1986) 139−161.

[85] H. Li, M.A. Lavin, R.J. Le Master, Fast Hough transform, IEEE Trans. Pattern Anal. Mach. Intell. 9 (5) (1987) 690−698.

[86] J. Illingworth, J. Kittler, The adaptive Hough transform, Image Vis. Comput. 13 (4) (1995) 239−252.

[87] J. Princen, J. Illingworth, J. Kittler, A hierarchical approach to line extraction based on the Hough transform, Comput. Vis. Graph. Image Process. 52 (1) (1990) 57−77.

[88] D. Ben-Tzevi, M.B. Sandler, A combinatorial Hough transform, Pattern Recogn. Lett. 11 (3) (1990) 167−174.

[89] P. Liang, A new transform for curve detection, in: Proc. Third Int. Conf. Comput. Vision, Osaka, Japan, 1990, pp. 748−751.

[90] W. Schneider, M. Pimm-Smith, M. Worden, Neurobiology of attention and automaticity, Curr. Opin. Neurobiol. 4 (1994) 177−182.

[91] J. Quintana, J. Fuster, Mnemonic and predictive functions of cortical neurons in a memory task, NeuroReport 3 (1992) 721−724.

[92] J. Fuster, The Prefrontal Cortex: Anatomy, Physiology, and Neuropsychology of the Frontal Lobe, Raven, New York, 1989.

[93] D.A. Norman, T. Shallice, 1980, Attention to action: willed and automatic control of behavior, Center for Human Information Processing, Technical Report no. 99.

[94] R.C. Schank, R. Abelson, Scripts, Plans, Goals and Understanding, Lawrence Erlbaum Associates, Hillsdale, NJ, 1977.

[95] M.I. Posner, S.E. Petersen, The attention system of the human brain, Annu. Rev. Neurosci. 11 (1990) 25−42.

[96] M. Ebner, A. Zell, Evolving a task specific image operator, in: Proc. First European Workshops on Evolutionary Image Analysis, Signal Processing and Telecommunications, Springer-Verlag, Göteborg, Sweden, 1999, pp. 74−89.

[97] A. Guarda, C. Le Gal, A. Lux, Evolving visual features and detectors, in: Proc. Int. Symp. Comp. Graphics, Image Processing, and Vision, Rio de Janeiro, Brazil, 1998, pp. 246−253.

[98] B.Y. Zavidovique, First steps of robotic perception: the turning point of the 1990s, Proc. IEEE 90 (7) (2002) 1094−1112.

[99] S. Shatford, Analyzing the subject of a picture: a theoretical approach, Catalog. Classif. Q. 6 (3) (1986) 39−62.

[100] K.S. Jones, P. Willett, Readings in Information Retrieval, Morgan Kaufmann Publishers, San Fransisco, CA, 1977.

[101] A.W.M. Smeulders, M. Worring, S. Santini, A. Gupta, R. Jain, Content base image retrieval at the end of the early years, IEEE Trans. Pattern Anal. Mach. Intell. 22 (12) (2000) 1349−1380.

[102] Y. Rui, T.S. Huang, S.F. Chang, Image retrieval: current techniques, promising directions and open issues, J. Vis. Commun. Image R. 10 (1999) 39−62.

[103] V.N. Gudivada, V.V. Raghavan, Design and evaluation of algorithms for image retrieval by spatial similarity, ACM Trans. Inform. Syst. 13 (2) (1995) 115−144.

[104] Colorimetry, second ed., CIE publication 15.2. Vienna Bureau Central CIE, 1986.

[105] E.Q. Adams, X−Z planes in the 1931 ICI system of colorimetry, J. Opt. Soc. Am. 32 (1942) 168−173.

[106] Y. Ohta, T. Kanade, T. Sakai, Color information for region segmentation, Comput. Graph. Image Process. 13 (1980) 222−241.

[107] M. Swain, D. Ballard, Color indexing, Int. J. Comput. Vis. 7 (1) (1991) 11−32.

[108] L. Cinque, S. Levialdi, A. Olsen, A. Pellicano, Color based image retrieval using spatial-chromatic histograms, Image Vis. Comput. 19 (13) (2001) 979−986.

[109] M.A. Stricker, M.J. Swain, The capacity of color histogram indexing, IEEE, Conference on Computer Vision and Pattern Recognition, 1994, pp. 704−708.

[110] K. Ravishankar, B. Prasad, S. Gupta, K. Biswas, Dominant color region based indexing for CBIR, in: Proc. Int. Conf. on Image Analysis and Processing, Venice, Italy, 1999, pp. 887−892.

[111] M. Flickner, H. Sawhney, W. Niblack, J. Ashley, Q. Huang, B. Dom, M. Gorkani, J. Hafner, D. Lee, D. Petkovic, D. Steele, P. Yanker, Query by image and video content: the QBIC system, IEEE Comput. 28 (9) (1995) 23−32.

[112] M. Worring, T. Gevers, Interactive retrieval of color images, Int. J. Image Graph. 1 (3) (2001) 387−414.

[113] J. Kender, B. Yeo, Video scene segmentation via continuous video coherence, IEEE CVPR, Santa Barbara, CA, 1998, pp. 367−373.

[114] S.F. Chang, W. Chen, H.J. Meng, H. Sundaram, D. Zhong, VIDEOQ: an automated content based video search system using visual cues, in: Fifth ACM International Multimedia Conference, Seattle, WA, 1997, pp. 313−324.

[115] H. Tamura, S. Mori, T. Yamawaki, Textural features corresponding to visual perception, IEEE Trans. Syst. Man Cybern. 8 (6) (1978) 460–473.

[116] R.M. Haralick, K. Shanmugam, I. Dinstein, Textural features for image classification, IEEE Trans. Syst. Man Cybern. 3 (6) (1973) 610–621.

[117] L.S. Davis, M. Clearman, J.K. Aggarwal, Computer description of textured surfaces, IEEE Trans. Pattern Anal. Mach. Intell. 1 (3) (1979) 251–259.

[118] L.S. Davis, S.A. Johns, J.K. Aggarwal, Texture analysis using generalized cooccurrence matrices, IEEE Trans. Pattern Anal. Mach. Intell. 3 (2) (1981) 214–221.

[119] I.M. Elfadel, R.W. Picard, Gibbs random fields, co-occurrences and texture modeling, IEEE Trans. Pattern Anal. Mach. Intell. 16 (1) (1994) 24–37.

[120] S.C. Zhu, X.W. Liu, Y.N. Wu, Exploring texture ensembles by efficient Markov chain Monte-Carlo: toward a "trichromacy" theory of texture, IEEE Trans. Pattern Anal. Mach. Intell. 22 (6) (2000) 554–569.

[121] A. Al Janhobi, Performance evaluation of cross-diagonal texture matrix method of texture analysis, Pattern Recognit. 34 (1) (2001) 171–180.

[122] S.W. Zucker, Toward a model of texture, Comput. Graph. Image Process. 5 (1976) 190–202.

[123] H. Voorhees, T. Poggio, Detecting textons and texture boundaries in natural images, in: Proc. First Int. Conf. on Computer Vision, Gran Canaria, Spain, 1987, pp. 250–258.

[124] G.C. Cross, A.K. Jain, Markov random field texture models, IEEE Trans. Pattern Anal. Mach. Intell. 5 (1) (1983) 25–39.

[125] R. Chellappa, S. Chatterjee, Classification of textures using Gaussian Markov random fields, IEEE Trans. Acoust. Speech Signal Process. 33 (1985) 959–963.

[126] R. Chellappa, A.K. Jain, Markov Random Fields: Theory and Applications, Academic Press, New York, 1993.

[127] S. Krishnamachari, R. Chellapa, Multiresolution Gauss–Markov random field models for texture segmentation, IEEE Trans. Image Process. 6 (2) (1997) 251–267.

[128] R. Chellappa, R.L. Kashyap, Texture synthesis using 2D non causal autoregressive models, IEEE Trans. Acoust. Speech Signal Process. 33 (1985) 194–203.

[129] J. Mao, A.K. Jain, Texture classification and segmentation using multiresolution simultaneous autoregressive models, Pattern Rcognit. 25 (2) (1992) 173–188.

[130] M. Comer, E. Delp, Segmentation of textured images using a multiresolution Gaussian autoregressive model, IEEE Trans. Image Process. 8 (3) (1999) 408–420.

[131] B. Mandelbrot, Fractal Geometry of Nature, Freeman, San Francisco, CA, 1982.

[132] S. Peleg, J. Naor, R. Hartley, D. Avnir, Multiple resolution texture analysis and classification, IEEE Trans. Pattern Anal. Mach. Intell. 6 (1984) 518–523.

[133] A. Pentland, Fractal-based description of natural scenes, IEEE Trans. Pattern Anal. Mach. Intell. 6 (1984) 661–675.

[134] L. Kam, J. Blanc-Talon, Multifractal Multipermuted Multinomial Measures for Texture Characterization and Segmentation, Nova Science Publishers, Commack, NY, 2001.

[135] M.E. Jernigan, F. D'Astous, Entropy based texture analysis in the frequency domain, IEEE Trans. Pattern Anal. Mach. Intell. 6 (2) (1984) 237–243.

[136] A.C. Bovik, M. Clark, W.S. Gessler, Multichannel texture analysis using localized spatial filters, IEEE Trans. Pattern Anal. Mach. Intell. 12 (1) (1990) 55–73.

[137] J. Malik, P. Perona, Preattentive texture discrimination with early vision mechanisms, J. Opt. Soc. Am. 7 (1990) 923–932.

[138] D. Dunn, W. Higgins, J. Weakley, Texture segmentation using 2-D Gabor elementary functions, IEEE Trans. Pattern Anal. Mach. Intell. 16 (2) (1994) 140–149.

[139] D. Dunn, W. Higgins, Optimal Gabor filters for texture segmentation, IEEE Trans. Image Process. 4 (7) (1995) 947–964.

[140] M. Unser, Texture classification and segmentation using wavelet frames, IEEE Trans. Image Process. 4 (11) (1995) 1549–1560.

[141] C.C. Chen, D.C. Chen, Multi-resolutional Gabor filter in texture analysis, Pattern Recognit. Lett. 17 (10) (1996) 1069–1076.

[142] J.R. Smith, S.F. Chang, Transform features for texture classification and discrimination in large image bases, in: Proc. IEEE ICIP, 1994, pp. 407–411.

[143] G.M. Haley, B.S. Manjunath, Rotation invariant texture classification using a complete space frequency model, IEEE Trans. Image Process. 8 (2) (1999) 255–269.

[144] K.S. Thyagarajan, T. Nguyen, C. Persons, A maximum likelihood approach to texture classification using wavelet transform, in: Proc. IEEE ICIP, 1994, pp. 640–644.

[145] N. Jhanwar, S. Chaudhuri, G. Seetharaman, B. Zavidovique, Content based image retrieval using motif co-occurrence matrix, Image Vis. Comput. 22 (14) (2004) 1211–1220.

[146] A. Hafiane, S. Chaudhuri, G. Seetharaman, B. Zavidovique, Region based CBIR in GIS with local space filling curves to spatial representation, Pattern Recognit. Lett. 27 (4) (2005) 259–267.

[147] B. Zavidovique, G. Seetharaman, Z-trees and Peano rasters for scan adaptive image processing, Int. J. Pure Appl. Math. 38 (1) (2007) 123–151.

[148] J. Weszka, C.R. Dyer, A. Rosenfeld, A comparative study of texture measures for terrain classification, IEEE Trans. Syst. Man Cybern. 6 (4) (1976) 269–285.

[149] O.D. Faugeras, W.K. Pratt, Decorrelation methods of texture feature extraction, IEEE Trans. Pattern Anal. Mach. Intell 2 (4) (1980) 323–332.

[150] R. Conners, C. Harlow, A theoretical comparison of texture algorithms, IEEE Trans. Pattern Anal. Mach. Intell. 2 (1980) 204–222.

[151] J. Du Buf, M. Kardan, M. Spann, Texture feature performance for image segmentation, Pattern Recognit. 23 (1990) 291–309.

[152] P. Ohanian, R. Dubes, Performance evaluation for four classes of textural features, Pattern Recognit. 25 (8) (1992) 819–833.

[153] T. Ojala, M. Pietikainen, D. Harwood, A comparative study of texture measures with classification based on feature distributions, Pattern Recognit. 29 (1) (1996) 51–59.

[154] C.C. Chen, D.C. Chen, Filtering methods for texture discrimination, Pattern Recognit. Lett. 20 (8) (1999) 783–790.

[155] G. Smith, I. Burns, Measuring texture classification algorithms, Pattern Recognit. Lett. 18 (14) (1997) 1495–1501.

[156] A. Tsversky, Features of similarity, Psychol. Rev. 84 (1977) 327–352.

[157] D. Oliva, I. Samengo, S. Leutgeb, S.A. Mizumori, Subjective distance between stimuli: quantifying the metric structure of representations, Neural Comput. 17 (2005) 969–990.

[158] B.M. Mehtre, M.S. Kankanhalli, W.F. Lee, Shape measures for content based image retrieval: a comparison, Inform. Process. Manag. 33 (3) (1997) 319–337.

[159] P.J. Van Otterloo, A Contour-Oriented Approach to Shape Analysis, Prentice Hall International, London, UK, 1991.

[160] E.R. Davies, Machine Vision: Theory, Algorithms and Practicalities, Morgan Kaufmann Publishers, San Francisco, CA, 2004.

[161] M.K. Hu, Visual pattern recognition by moment invariants, IEEE Trans. Inf. Theory 8 (2) (1962) 179–187.

[162] C.H. Teh, R.T. Chin, On image analysis by the methods of moments, IEEE Trans. Pattern Anal. Mach. Intell. 10 (4) (1988) 496–513.

[163] X.Y. Jiang, H. Bunke, Simple and fast computation of moments, Pattern Recognit. 24 (1991) 801–806.

[164] G. Taubin, D.B. Cooper, Object recognition based on moment (or Algebraic) invariants, in: J. Mundy, A. Zisserman (Eds.), Geometric Invariance in Computer Vision, MIT Press, Cambridge, MA, 1992.

[165] T. Minka, R. Picard, Interactive learning using a "Society of Models," Pattern Recognit. 30 (4) (1997) 565–581.

[166] I.J. Cox, M.L. Miller, T.P. Minka, P.N. Yianilos, An optimized interaction strategy for Bayesian relevance feedback, IEEE Conf. Comput. Vis. Pattern Recogn. Trier, D, (1998) 553–558.

[167] T.V. Papathomasa, T.E. Conway, I.J. Cox, J. Ghosn, M.L. Miller, T.P. Minka, et al., Psychophysical studies of the performance of an image database retrieval system SPIE'98 (Human Vision and Electronic Imaging), 1998, pp. 591–602.

[168] Y. Rui, T.S. Huang, M. Ortega, S. Mehrotra, Relevance feedback: a power tool for interactive content-based image retrieval, IEEE Trans. Circuit Syst. Video Technol. 8 (1998) 644–655.

[169] G. Ciocca, R. Schettini, Content-based similarity retrieval of trademarks using relevance feedback, Pattern Recognit. 34 (8) (2001) 1639–1655.

[170] S.D. MacArthur, C.E. Brodley, A.C. Kak, L.S. Broderick, Interactive content-based image retrieval using relevance feedback, Comput. Vis. Image Understand. 88 (2) (2002) 55–75.

[171] I. King, J. Zhong, Integrated probability function and its application to content-based image retrieval by relevance feedback, Pattern Recognit. 36 (9) (2003) 2177–2186.

[172] Y.H. Kwak, J.S. Cho, Relevance feedback in content-based image retrieval system by selective region growing in the feature space, Signal Process. Image Commun. 18 (9) (2003) 787–799.

[173] G. Giacinto, F. Roli, Bayesian relevance feedback for content-based image retrieval, Pattern Recognit. 37 (7) (2004) 1499–1508.

[174] W.Y. Ma, B.S. Manjunath, Texture features and learning similarity, in: Proc. CVPR'96, 1996, pp. 425–450.

[175] W.Y. Ma, B.S. Manjunath, Edge flow: a framework of boundary detection and image segmentation, in: Proc CVPR'97, 1997, pp. 744–749.

[176] R.W. Picard, T.P. Minka, Vision texture for annotation, Multimedia Systems: Special Issue on Content-based Retrieval 3 (3) (1995) 3–14.

[177] D. Hernández, E. Clemetini, P. Di Felice, Qualitative distances, in: A. Frank, W. Kuhn (Eds.), Spatial Information Theory: Theoretical Basis GIS, Springer-Verlag, Heidelberg, Germany, 1995, pp. 45–57.

[178] S.K. Chang, Q.Y. Shi, C.W. Yan, Iconic indexing by 2D strings Source, IEEE Trans. Pattern Anal. Mach. Intell. 9 (3) (1987) 413–428.

[179] S.K. Chang, E. Jungert, Y. Li, Representations and retrieval of symbolic pictures using generalized 2D-strings, in: Proc. SPIE on Visual Communications and Image Processing, 1989, pp. 1360–1372.

[180] S.Y. Lee, F.J. Hsu, 2D C-String: a new spatial knowledge representation for image database systems, Pattern Recognit. 23 (10) (1990) 1077–1087.

[181] S.Y. Lee, M.C. Yang, J.W. Chen, 2D B-string: a spatial knowledge representation for image database systems, in: Proc. ICSC'92 Second International Computer Science Conference, 1992, pp. 609–615.

[182] V.N. Gudivada, Theta R string: a geometry based representation for efficient and effective retrieval by spatial similarity, IEEE Trans. Knowl. Data Eng. 10 (3) (1998) 504–512.

[183] E.A. El-Kwae, M. Kabuka, A robust framework for content-based retrieval by spatial similarity in image databases, ACM Trans. Inform. Syst. 17 (2) (1999) 174–198.

[184] A. Hafiane, Caractérisation de textures et segmentation pour la recherche d'images par le contenu. PhD Thesis, Université de Paris Sud (Paris XI), Paris, France, 2005.

[185] A. Hafiane, B. Zavidovique, Local relational string and mutual matching for image retrieval, Inform. Process. Manag. 44 (3) (2008) 1201–1214.

[186] C. Carson, M. Thomas, S. Belongie, J.M. Hellerstein, J. Malik, Blobworld: A system for region-based image indexing and retrieval, in: VISUAL '99: Proc. Third Int. Conf. on Visual Information and Information Systems, London, UK, 1999, pp. 509–516.

[187] M. Swain, D. Ballard, Color indexing, Int. J. Comput. Vis. 7 (1) (1991) 11–32.

[188] J.R. Smith, Integrated spatial and feature image systems: retrieval, analysis and compression, PhD Thesis, Columbia University, New York, 1997.

[189] Y. Rubner, J. Puzicha, C. Tomasi, J. Buhmann, Empirical evaluation of dissimilarity measures for color and texture, Comput. Vis. Image Understand. 84 (1) (2001) 25–43.

[190] H.W. Kuhn, The Hungarian method for the assignment problem, Nav. Res. Logist. Q. 2 (1955) 83–97.

[191] B. Bhanu, O. Faugeras, Shape matching of two-dimensional objects, IEEE Trans. Pattern Anal. Mach. Intell. 6 (2) (1984) 137–156.

[192] H.A. Almohamad, S.O. Duffuaa, A linear programming approach for the weighted graph matching problem, IEEE Trans. Pattern Anal. Mach. Intell. 15 (5) (1993) 522–525.

[193] B.T. Messmer, H. Bunke, A new algorithm for error-tolerant subgraph isomorphism detection, IEEE Trans. Pattern Anal. Mach. Intell. 20 (5) (1998) 493–504.

[194] E.G.M. Petrakis, C. Faloutsos, Similarity searching in medical image databases, IEEE Trans. Knowl. Data Eng. 9 (3) (1997) 435–447.

[195] J. Li, J.Z. Wang, G. Wiederhold, IRM: integrated region matching for image retrieval, ACM Multimedia (2000) 147–156.

[196] V. Cantoni, L. Lombardi, P. Lombardi, Challenges for data mining in distributed sensor networks, in: Proc. ICPR2006, vol. 4, Hong Kong, China, 2006, pp. 378–385.

[197] V. Cantoni, L. Lombardi, P. Lombardi, Future scenarios of parallel computing: distributed sensor networks, J. Vis. Lang. Comput. 18 (2007) 484–491.

[198] J. Mallet, V. M. Bove, Eye Society, International Conference on Multimedia and Expo (ICME 2003).

[199] S. Madden, M. Franklin, J. Hellerstein, W. Hong, TinyDB: an acquisitional query processing system for sensor networks, ACM Trans. Database Syst. 30 (1) (2005) 122–173.

[200] S. Nath, Y. Ke, P.B. Gibbons, B. Karp, S. Seshan, IrisNet: an architecture for enabling sensor-enriched Internet service, Technical Report IRP-TR-03-04, Intel Research Pittsburgh, PA, 2003.

[201] Y. Yao, J.E. Gehrke, The Cougar approach to in-network query processing in sensor networks, ACM Sigmod Record 31 (3) (2002) 9–18.

[202] R. Newton, M. Welsh, Region streams: functional macroprogramming for sensor networks, in: Proc. First Int. Workshop on Data Management for Sensor Networks (DMSN), Toronto, Canada, 2004.

[203] G. Mainland, D.C. Parkes, M. Welsh, 2005, Decentralized, adaptive resource allocation for sensor networks, in: Proc. Second USENIX/ACM Symposium on Networked Systems Design and Implementation (NSDI 2005).

[204] M.G. Rabbat, R.D. Nowak, Quantized incremental algorithms for distributed optimization, IEEE J. Sel. Areas Commun. 23 (4) (2005) 798–808.

[205] M. Duarte, Y.H. Hu, Distance based decision fusion in a distributed wireless sensor network, Telecommun. Syst. 26 (2–5) (2004) 339–350.

[206] R. Olfati-Saber, R.M. Murray, Consensus problems in networks of agents with switching topology and time-delays, IEEE Trans. Autom. Control 49 (9) (2004) 1520–1533.

[207] J. Mallet, The role of group in smart camera network, PhD Thesis, MIT Press, Cambridge, MA, 2006.

[208] A. Pilpré, Self-* Properties of multi sensing entities in smart environments, PhD Thesis, MIT Press, Cambridge, MA.

[209] A. Mainwaring, D. Culler, J. Polastre, R. Szewczyk, J. Anderson, Wireless sensor networks for habitat monitoring, in: Proc. First ACM Int. Workshop on Wireless Sensor Networks and Applications, 2002, pp. 88–97.

[210] T. Small, Z.J. Haas, The shared wireless Infostation model: a new ad hoc networking paradigm (or where there is a whale there is a way), in: Proc. Fourth ACM Int. Symp. Mobile Ad Hoc Networking Computing, 2003, pp. 233–244.

[211] L. Schwiebert, S. Gupta, J. Weinmann, Research challenges in wireless networks of biomedical sensors, in: Proc. Int. Conf. Mobile Computing and Networking MOBICOM2001, Rome, Italy, 2001, pp. 151–165.

[212] R. Willett, A. Martin, R. Nowak, Backcasting: Adaptive Sampling for Sensor Networks, in: Proc. International. Symposium on Information Processing in Sensor Networks (IPSN 2004), pp. 124–133.

4 Channeling the Information

Filling the Channels

In time, artists discovered cues that helped them to compile their work so as to favor the user interpretation, solving the "inverse problem" of image analysis. A few centuries later, aiming to enhance image understanding, artists fully exploited the contextual knowledge, even if physics laws of the visual representation were often violated. Capitalizing on cues and contexts, artists have developed tools and techniques for image processing and computer vision. In the present chapter, dealing with the vision—perception—action path, more recent approaches by other artists are introduced.

Here, in the active side of communication, multiple channels and media are considered, where:

- Images are not the only information carriers.
- Texts, sounds, and other communication means must be integrated to improve knowledge transfer.

Because technology is continuously generating new tools and facilities to improve broadcasting information, new strategies for achieving optimal delivery are coming to the forefront. In order for the artist to effectively transmit his or her concepts, he or she will select the proper channels to actively and effectively put out the intended information (the direct problem). The first problem is to choose the number and types of channels to be used. The aim is to design a coarse-to-fine process that, starting at a high symbolic level, will lead to the detailed definition of all the necessary actions to convey the intended meaning.

An emblematic case will be considered, as done previously, where "seduction" is the action to be represented. This notion is primarily personified by the character of Don Juan. Note that Don Juan is already an abstraction of a real human as, for instance, Giacomo Casanova, and has inspired many art pieces ranging from paintings (Auguste Leroux) and books (Lydia Flem), to movies (Federico Fellini, Joseph Losey, Carlos Saura, etc.), and even music (Richard Strauss), theater plays (Molière), and operas (Wolfang Amadeus Mozart).

The Don Juan character was conceived by Tirso de Molina in 1630, in *El burlador de Sevilla y convidado de piedra* (on the basis of a Sevillian folk tale), who placed his protagonist in Spain of the fourteenth century. Molière was inspired by this character and wrote a preliminary version *Dom Juan ou les Festin de Pierre* in

3C Vision. DOI: 10.1016/B978-0-12-385220-5.00004-8

1665. In this play, Don Juan, differently from Molina's character, is an atheist who does not repent his libertine behavior. At that time, the play was considered objectionable by the Roman Catholic Church and therefore censored. The original uncensored version of the play was performed for the first time only in 1884.

Note that this same character had multiple versions, ranging from a totally seducing personality (*Don Juan De Marco*, 1995, film with Johnny Depp) to a man totally seduced by women (Lord Byron's poem 1819–1824). There is even a humorous version of this character in the film *Don Juan*, 1955, with the French comedian Fernandel.

Other character facets have been considered from the moralist, the romantic (a lover), the libertine, or the adventurous knight (*Don Juan*, 1948, film with Errol Flynn) to the negative masculine figure such as the swindler (*Casanova*, 1976, film by Federico Fellini). One trait considered has been guiltiness, whereby the character can be seen as a victim of women, society, or destiny (*Don Juan Tenorio*, 1844, by José Zorrilla). Along this line, he has even been portrayed as a hangman who enjoys subduing his female partners and ignoring their sufferings (*Don Giovanni*, 1979, by Joseph Losey, reproducing Mozart's opera of 1787). A recent film by Carlos Saura, *Io, Don Giovanni* (2009), is centered on the scriptwriter of the Mozart opera, Lorenzo da Ponte, who had a very multisided personality. He was a converted Jew who adopted the name of his baptizer, later becoming a priest. Nevertheless, he had a mistress and children, causing his forced exile from Venice. In Vienna, he met Mozart and Casanova, the latter inspiring him to write the opera script. As the title of the film suggests, da Ponte identified himself with Don Juan and, like him, understood that lecherous behavior must be banned.

Only films and theatrical and opera productions have been quoted so far, but Don Juan's legend has been a source of inspiration for many other intellectuals such as Ernst Hoffmann, Alexander Pushkin, Søren Kierkegaard, George Bernard Shaw, and Albert Camus, to name a few.

With reference to the communication problem, the idea here is that some concepts such as amorality, seduction, and redemption require more than a single context to be fully conveyed. At this point, the context is driven by (common) culture. The question becomes how to trigger such understanding, employing advanced communication technology, when the common cultural reference (history, memory, education, etc.) does not preexist. And what degree of efficacy can be achieved?

Pablo Picasso (painting) or Fritz Lang (mute film) relied on context to suggest or transmit a feeling of horror. For instance, one could imagine that their artistic creation would only be a part of today's possible realizations through multimedia. Another way to understand the relevance of the advent and spread of multimedia systems is to wonder how more ordinary creators, not such as the quoted genius, or not only the artistically motivated—for example, those with economic or political intentions—would transmit such a complex feeling. In that sense, computer-aided interaction at the basis of information multichanneling may appear a kind of prosthesis, facilitating and enhancing human communication.

Here we analyze five different aspects of multimedia information content to be transmitted and received along different channels such as audio, video. Next, features optimizing the conveyance of meaning through a multimedia environment will be considered.

Multimedia Exploitation

In the last two centuries, the Don Juan character has been portrayed in books, scripts, drawings, musical compositions, and posters; later, in photography and films, enriching the information carried by media. Moreover, many films are subtitled for audiences that do not understand the original film language, a trivial combination of text and image (Figure 4.1).

The **imdb** portal (www.imdb.com) advertising the film *Don Juan De Marco* by Jeremy Leven is a plentiful example of a multimedia information channel embodying Don Juan's character, corresponding to the homepage that will be now analyzed; it can be seen in Figure 4.2.

Once the browser is queried by the film title, **imdb** is the most detailed informative page. On the far left, a vertical column sponsored by Amazon advertises the DVD of the film with an undersized cover from the film posters. Underneath the "buy" button, the links to learn more about the film, and other links for the trailers and videos and memorable quotes, can be found. Moreover, links providing detailed information on the cast, crew, and credits are also included.

All these textual links put together different pieces of information, which can be classified through a taxonomy of information types [1] (Figure 4.3). Three axes, corresponding to media type, context, and media expression, are displayed with a set of different attributes. The Y-axis represents, with increasing complexity, the single media. The X-axis is related to representation levels, from a concrete (raw) data (low level) up to a higher level of abstraction. In fact, raw data require a stronger effort from the observer, who must "elaborate" such information stemming from the data. Finally, the Z-axis, labeled context, includes different aspects that describe the circumstances and factors generating communication. This taxonomy can be used as a preliminary guideline to sketch out the main features of multimedia content, whereas a deeper analysis would require a higher dimensionality to cover all the different aspects in a homogeneous and congruent manner. For instance, the multimedia content should be described either from the content producer side or from the viewer side, without mixing them, as done on the X- and Z-axes. For example, on the X-axis, elaboration is assumed as a viewer's activity, whereas abstraction is performed by the content producer. The audience on the

Z-axis is directly connected to the viewer, whereas discipline relates to the considered topic; furthermore, quality is a communication attribute.

Coming back to the analysis of the **imdb** portal and using one of the taxonomies reported in [1], the provided information pieces on the Don Juan portal correspond to semantic relationships because menus and links, text, and images integrate the multimedia information about Don Juan; on the right side, a publicity space presents commercial advertisements.

The first row of the central frame of the homepage gives a set of images that can be seen in sequence both statically or sequentially on three distinct subject

Figure 4.1 Different pictorial representations of the Don Juan character along the years.
(A) Don Juan Tenorio from José Zorrilla's script; (B) Don Juan statue in Sevilla;
(C) Molière's Don Juan; (D) *The Finding of Don Juan by Haidee* (1878) by Ford Madox
Brown, from Lord Byron's poem; (E) Poster advertising the film *Don Juan* (1926), starring
John Barrymore and Mary Astor; (F), (G), and (H) two posters and the cover of the soundtrack
recording of the film *Adventures of Don Juan* (1948), starring Errol Flynn and Viveca Lindfors;
(I) Poster of the film *Don Juan* (1956), starring Fernandel and Carmen Sevilla; (J) Poster of the
film *Don Juan De Marco* (1994), starring Johnny Depp, Faye Dunaway, and Marlon Brando;
(K) Poster of the play *Don Juan in Chicago* (2003) written by David Ives.

(F)   (G)

(H)   (I)

(J)   (K)

Figure 4.1 (Continued).

Figure 4.2 Homepage of the **imdb** portal for Don Juan De Marco on June 24, 2009.

matters: the actors party, the film shots, and the film posters and a CD cover. The second row displays, by means of yellow stars, the users' rating of the film, including a link to the statistics of votes. In the following, both credits and a plot description are presented, with links allowing access to more extended information. Next, a three-column presentation is included, with pictures, the actor's name, and corresponding character; most of these labels are links. Recalling the previous taxonomy, the combination of the actor's photo and his name corresponds to the graphics/concrete intersection. Moreover, a number of technical details (such as film runtime and language) are given, corresponding to the intersection of text and a few context attributes of the Z-axis. Finally, there are links to funny stuff (like goofs and quotes), and also to a CD containing the film soundtrack. A last interesting media channel is provided with both frequently asked questions and user comments, giving the audience feedback on the film appreciation.

The richness of this site also stems from its commercial aim, that is, encouraging us to see the film and buy the DVD or the CD, and convincing the site user to enjoy the performance of the high-quality acting.

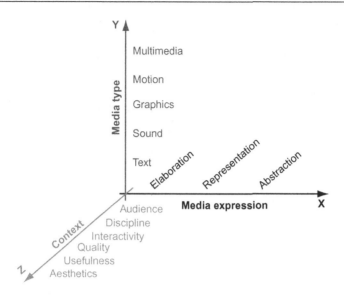

Figure 4.3 The taxonomy of information types according to Heller et al. [1].

Icons and Metaphors

There are many ways to express and represent meanings, for instance, by means of icons, provided they are easily and uniquely interpreted. An analysis of the poster of Fernandel's Don Juan shows a sword spearing three hearts to express the seductive power of Don Juan, because hearts are the classical icon for love. Furthermore, in Errol Flynn's Don Juan, the fire flames as icons represent human passion. In the poster of Moliere's play, Don Juan has his right hand resting on his heart, therefore conveying a romantic feeling.

Content Structure

Lord Byron portrays in his poem a man seduced by women, giving another interpretation of Don Juan. A shipwrecked man lying on a rock can be seen in

Figure 4.2 (a fragment of *The Finding of Don Juan by Haidee*, 1878, by Ford Madox Brown). This reclining languid figure, saved by a woman trying to resurrect him by putting her left hand on his chest while the right one is waving in front of him. The following components (patterns) can be distinguished: the rocky coastline in the background; the kneeling lady next to the naked horizontal body; and curiously, the man's leg across the wooden oar in an unnatural position. The pattern arrangement indicates a man in a helpless state, half asleep, aided by a willing woman in the bottom left part of the painting. This picture can be described using another multimedia taxonomy based on content structuring patterns such as the intersection of graphics/spatial or geographical coordinates.

Social Interaction

In past centuries, user feedback was hard to obtain, in fact readers, observers, and spectators could only write letters to authors: these can be called offline interactions. Later on, with more advanced communication technologies like the telephone, and particularly with Internet, nowadays everybody is connected to everybody else. By means of social platforms (like Facebook, Linkedin, and Twitter) authors may find online readers' and spectators' opinions of their works. Note that in the **imdb** page for *Don Juan De Marco* the audience appreciation and comments are still offline, even though they are easily accessible. Today's authors can still continue their own version of a story or work collaboratively with readers (coauthoring). The message can be exchanges, also using different media and references, between spectators, audiences, plot creators, movie directors, and so on.

Role Rendering

As can be seen in [1] on another taxonomy of the media role, the partition of media can be considered as well as their combined usage—text, sound, graphics, and motion are the basic ingredients of the *Y*-axis. Reflecting on Don Juan as exemplified by Errol Flynn's poster in Figure 4.1G, in the integration of text with graphics, words are written in different fonts and sizes to attract a candidate viewer to see the film. For instance, in the bottom right part of the poster, a (red) silhouette of

Don Juan in the air between the title words of the film exhibits the adventurous nature of the character. The fast development of today's technology allows the combination of different media in such a way to optimize both representation and expression, to efficiently and economically communicate an enriched role portrayal. Sound and image integration also underlines specific role features, as found, for example, in Mozart's opera, but also on the soundtracks of all films.

Multimedia Exploitation

When describing the content within a multimedia environment, the impressive potential of the online direct manipulation (as it is called by Shneiderman [2]), such as an interaction paradigm, should be taken into account. Interaction may be defined as a mutual or reciprocal action, or influence, between two human subjects and machines, or even a combination of the two. An interesting kind of interaction is the social one, where the degree of sociality determines the behavior, for example, in human−computer network via Facebook, Linkedin, and others. "Human−computer interaction (HCI) is a discipline concerned with the design, evaluation, and implementation of interactive computing systems for human use and with the study of major phenomena surrounding them" (working definition of ACM SIGCHI curricula for HCI, 1997). The main scope of HCI today is to make information searching from the web as fluent and natural as possible through software engines. Typically, the interactive use plays an important role in discussion groups, lists of FAQs, chats, videoconferences, blogs, VoIP, and so on. As new applications gain interactivity, this applied research area expands in importance and dimensions.

In Figure 4.4, a modified version of the diagram in [62], containing a global view of multimedia HCI, is illustrated. Four interrelated aspects are pointed out: the working context features, the human characteristics, the computer system and the interface architecture traits, and the software development cycle.

The top part of Figure 4.4 represents the working context features, which include social, organizational, and working environments; as for the application areas, they include navigation database access, web navigation and exploration, social networking, and such; the adaptation of both hardware and software to human needs; and usability and accessibility.

The middle part of the figure points on the left to the essential human features of mental data processing, language expression, and interaction capabilities with devices. On the right, the computer world is represented, including electronic input−output devices that may enhance interaction, like the mouse, joystick, keyboard, monitor, head-mounted display for virtual reality, and haptic interfaces. Furthermore, dialog techniques, graphical representations, and icons aim to facilitate interaction, possibly exploiting special-purpose computer architectures.

The lower part of the figure represents the well-known software production cycle, comprising specification, implementation, validation, and evaluation, supported by their corresponding tools.

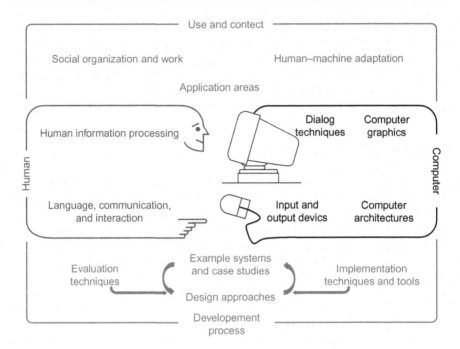

Figure 4.4 HCI components within a multimedia environment.

Seeing Through the Web

In 2006, Tim Berners-Lee [3] theorized the transition from computer science to web science, which can be intended to "understand what the Web is, engineer its future, and ensure its social benefit." For this reason, a new initiative was born and later became the Web Science Trust. The main differences in content between classical computer science (CS) and the new web science (WS) are the following:

- The principal subject matter deals with computer networks in CS, and social networks in WS.
- CS relates to packet-switching networks, whereas voice/video over IP relates to WS.
- Information is the essential brick of CS, but relationships are the main ingredient of WS.
- Programming languages are the basic tools of CS; the wikis, blogs, and tags are their dual in WS.
- Databases with operating systems are the typical applications of CS, e−*, where the * designates governance, business, games, learning, and so on, in WS.
- Compilers are basic tools in CS, corresponding to domain knowledge translation (from medical, financial, geographical, etc., domains) in WS.
- 3D computer graphics and rendering are supported in CS, and facilities for the creation and sharing of the generated multimedia objects, in WS.
- Computational geometry and maps are handled in CS; animation, music, photos, and video-clips, in WS.

Three typical parameters to evaluate the computing performance on a quantitative way for CS systems are Moore's Law, the algorithm complexity, and the information quantity involved. Conversely, for WS systems the number of visited web pages, quantity of visitors per month on a site, and the number of downloaded songs, videos, and so on, are the basic features.

The web allows multimedia information to be downloaded by the user (such as films, video) exploiting the human senses. Among such senses, vision is the most important because it occupies the largest cortical area of the brain; next, the ear is the second best. A great step toward the use of multimedia objects on the web was achieved through the availability of image-generating programs and audio/video recording. The richness of means and contents allows fast and cheap communication between very large communities of users. Moreover, the possibility of using different interaction paradigms supports and enhances a wide number of activities like: e-learning, teleworking, health monitoring, multiplayer gaming, and so on. Advanced HCI requires the integration of social, cognitive, and perceptive knowledge.

Starting in the 1970s, the choice of the desktop metaphor has become widespread; the icons of the desktop, in the *direct manipulation* metaphor [2], are considered real objects that can be displaced on the screen, superimposed, or thrown in the garbage can (*drag and drop*). The advantage of such a paradigm is an increase of working speed and a memory aid to remember the performed actions by seeing the obtained results immediately. Furthermore, a visual control of the computer state can be seen in the so-called *WYSIWYG* method (*What you see is what you get*, coined by Flip Wilson in the late 1960s) meaning that a printout exactly corresponds to the screen dump: nothing less and nothing more. Finally, by using *WYSIWYG* both navigation and browsing can be easily performed on e-newspapers and e-games.

Images on the web are designed to achieve many purposes: commercial, educational, conversational—even emotional. A standard way to transmit an emotional state, even by e-mail, is by employing emoticons, as shown in Figure 4.5. Each emoticon represents with only a few pixels a self-description of an elementary coded feeling.

Figure 4.6 shows another example to communicate the perception of a polluted environment, including all the relative possible consequences. The message sent by this image is that by breathing the air in this industrial neighborhood, a person's lungs may be severely damaged.

In order to speak the language of the general public, the visual rhetoric uses metaphors and descriptors providing affective images and targeting the audience emotion. Affective imagery impacts on large communities, enabling them to share crucial opinions and general-purpose ideas [4].

Looking with the Web

A few years ago, image management was restricted to the main computer-based application, that is, databases; image querying and retrieval were the only two

Figure 4.5 A set of standard emoticons.

Figure 4.6 An image of a highly polluted neighborhood in an industrial town.

possible tasks. Nowadays, thanks to the Internet, a nearly infinite distributed source of images and videos is available, casted into real-time applications of many kinds, directly from the PC or from a smart phone, iPad, or other device.

By means of Internet connectivity, geographical location finders provide photographic views, satellite pictures, and road maps and navigation facilities, even congruently in orientation and position, and possibly superimposed. Moreover, turning to image databases, there are many novel techniques for image retrieval, exploiting color, texture, shape, and movement, even from biometric features for human recognition in video surveillance.

Digital and web cameras provide image and videos from everywhere at all times, so that a large quantity of images and videos must be processed, organized, and stored to allow easy retrieval and sharing from anywhere. Presently, the request increases for video surveillance and identity verification, for industrial inspection and traffic control; these applications have enormously augmented the information traffic and, consequently, the bandwidth demand.

When considering software displaying geo-maps that can be used for business and tourism, competitive programs can be found, all having nearly the same features, for example, Google Maps™, MapQuest™, Multimap™. Generally maps are free, fast, and easy to use, and some are integrated with content from other sources like GPS data, meteoforecasting, and points of service.

As an example, Google Maps visualizes a searched world place, providing street maps (showing photos, videos, Wikipedia data, and webcam videos in the area), satellite images with or without labels, and terrain images. This program also provides directions from one point of the map to another desired one, by car, public transport, or walking. Another feature allows seeing the location through Street View, by shifting a "tag man" on the desired street; once there, it is possible to pan and zoom, navigating in the neighborhood. This visualization scheme corresponds to augmented reality (see later on), which provides extra information on the site and its local neighborhood. Moreover, Google offers another interesting site visualization program called Google Earth, which allows us to fly to anyplace in the world. Whereas Street View (Figure 4.7A) presents the road environment at a human viewing angle, Google Earth provides a landscape's top view (Figure 4.7B). Recently a new Google program, Google Sky, has been integrated into Google Earth, allowing us to see, at any time instance, planets, constellations, nebulae, and so on, and to travel in space from an earth location toward any wanted place, with the possibility of recording such a trip. Any given star in space is documented through links to corresponding information. A similar, more recent, program by Microsoft is called WorldWide Telescope [5]. In addition, there is also the possibility to navigate underwater through Google Ocean, also integrated into Google Earth.

Another interesting application (3D Warehouse™) permits us to create 3D models by the user, or even select one (from a database), matching a building to be integrated into Google Earth, to be displayed in 3D. An example may be seen in Figure 4.7C, which was created after positioning ourselves, through Google Earth, on Saint Peter's Church in Rome (Vatican State). After selecting the corresponding model (among more than 1000 church models available), it was dragged on the displayed church. The program automatically integrated and reconstructed the church inside the model. Next, the date and time of rendering were selected (November 30 at 7:40 A.M.), and the program provided the corresponding lighting conditions.

In a completely different application, that is, visualizing multiple statistical data, Trendalyzer™ (bought by Google in 2007) can be used for displaying, through the years, the evolution of data (yearly since 1800) related to economics, demography,

Figure 4.7 Examples of Google Maps integrated facilities. Saint Peter square in Rome seen through: (A) Street View, (B) through Google Earth, and (C) 3D Warehouse.

education, and so forth, for a high number of countries. Looking at Figure 4.8, two charts can be seen showing the evolution of born children per woman since 1800 for China (red), Egypt (green), India (blue), Italy (orange), and the USA (yellow), against the income per person in US dollars, until the year 2008 (Figure 4.8A). Moreover, the circle sizes are proportional to the number of women in the chosen population for each country; note that the X-axis is on a logarithmic scale. In Figure 4.8B, the life expectancy at birth per year is shown within the same framework and representation modalities.

One of the most brilliant success stories in video sharing is YouTube™, originated in 2005 (bought by Google in 2006), where a very large community on the web is able to upload (if registered) and download (unregistered) videos of almost any format, including user-generated videos, movie clips, TV clips, and music videos, as well as amateur content such as video blogs and short original videos. Videos may be retrieved by key words or from geographical maps and viewed with standard video players. Presently (2011), there are nearly 1 billion videos available on YouTube. As an example, by connecting to YouTube and requesting videos on Don Giovanni, 60,200 of them will be retrieved, and by choosing the trailer of the film by Joseph Losey (1979), it can be discovered that this trailer has been visited

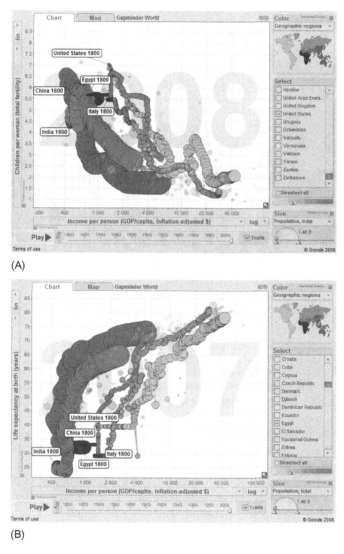

(A)

(B)

Figure 4.8 Trendalyzer: a statistical data visualizer. Income per person in the *x*-axis related to (A) number of children per woman and (B) life expectancy at birth on the *y*-axis.

33,660 times. A beautiful image from this trailer, a Venetian gondola, can be seen in Figure 4.9.

Because the initial programs were only for image retrieval on a PC, we have come a long way, and now vast possibilities can be found for downloading, retrieving, editing, and sharing images and videos generated by any user with his or her own webcam and an Internet connection, to be viewed by anyone, anywhere, at any time.

Figure 4.9 An image from Losey's *Don Giovanni* film trailer as downloaded from YouTube.

Ambient Intelligence

Ambient intelligence, or AmI, was first developed in the 1990s. The term refers to "electronic environments that are sensitive and responsive to the presence of people" (Wikipedia) and stands for a futuristic technological scenario based on consumer electronics, telecommunications, and computing. In this framework, devices support people in carrying out their everyday life activities, tasks, and rituals in an easy, natural way, using information and intelligence hidden in the network connecting these devices. As devices become smaller and smaller, they can be more interconnected and integrated into our environment; the technology becomes transparent and therefore easily perceived by the user.

The ambient intelligence paradigm builds upon ubiquitous computing, profiling practices, and human-centric–computer interaction, and is essentially guided by Internet marketing. The main features of ambient intelligence are the following:

- *Embedded*: Many networked devices are integrated into the environment.
- *Context aware*: These devices can recognize you and your situational context.
- *Personalized*: They can be tailored to your needs.
- *Adaptive*: They can change in response to you.
- *Anticipatory*: They can anticipate your desires without conscious mediation.

In AmI, there are no borderlines between the physical and virtual worlds where connections may be controlled, varying in time and with context: the ambient becomes the interface. Human–ambient interaction takes place through sight, hearing, touch, taste, smell, temperature, kinesthetic sense, pain, balance, and acceleration.

Figure 4.10 Intelligent shop window related to an experience economy.

The Internet may be considered extended to active everyday objects, sometimes called the *Internet of things* [6].

Two basic research guidelines can be envisioned: first, integrating the rich content of the digital networked world into our everyday substantial life, and second, augmenting the digital world with information coming from different new technological gadgets.

In the first case, a project within the area of "experience economy" is illustrated; in particular, a project on "ambient narratives for smart retail environments" is considered in the PhD thesis by Mark van Doorn [7]. The intelligent shop window prototype, with authoring environment, was built and evaluated in ShopLab at the High Tech Campus in Eindhoven (Figure 4.10).

Generally, the shop itself is seen as the stage, and the increasingly interactive, dynamic lighting, audio, and video, with special effects, enhances the shopping experience for customers. In this experience economy, following a multisensorial trend, a co-creation environment has been designed. In this context, the consumer becomes an active producer in the construction of the experience that is offered to him. From a literary and semiotic perspective, such a co-creation environment can be considered as an interactive narrative experience, consisting of interrelated social scripts, associated to device actions. By interacting with this dynamically changing narrative ambient (performing social scripts), players or viewers construct their own story or ambient intelligence experience.

Figure 4.11 The hanging device, a gestural command, and a keyboard projection of a
virtual phone.

In the second case, a good example is the Sixth Sense project at MIT within the
Fluid Interfaces group lead by Pattie Maes and built by Pranav Mistry [8]. To
achieve this extra sense, a new exciting device has been developed as a wearable
gestural interface that augments the physical world around us with digital information and lets us use natural hand gestures to interact with that information.

The human sensing capabilities include a 1D input—output (audio), and a 2D
single input (sight); the new gadget empowers human sensoriality by providing
multi-inputs (webcam, mobile) and a variety of outputs through a mini-projector.
This device can be controlled by gestures, recognized by the webcam via pattern
recognition, so that useful data can be obtained. Such data augment information on
physical objects (books, newspapers) or generate virtual objects (mobile keyboard),
for instance on the hand (Figure 4.11), allowing us to interact with them.

These two projects represent the topmost technological achievements, yet people
should be able to manage their lives in the future to allow for security, privacy, and
creativity.

It is worthwhile to remember the statement by Weiser [9], who said: "The most
profound technologies are those that disappear. They weave themselves into the
fabric of everyday life until they are indistinguishable from it."

Augmented Reality

This term was coined around the 1990s and refers to the addition of computer-
generated imagery to real-world environments on a digital viewing system like, for
instance, a virtual set. An extended definition from Wikipedia is *"[A]ugmented reality
is a term for a live direct or indirect view of a physical real-world environment whose
elements are *merged* with (or augmented by) virtual computer-generated imagery—
creating a mixed reality (MR). The augmentation is conventionally in real time and in
semantic context with environmental elements."*

In many instances, it may be useful to combine real objects of a TV study with
virtual images taken at another place and even at another time. It is also possible to
implement, starting from existing blueprints, whole virtual buildings integrated
with existing physical structures, as can be seen in Figure 4.11, where the Sixth

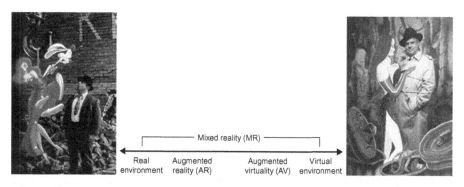

Figure 4.12 Virtuality continuum following Milgram and Kishino. Two images from the film *Who Framed Roger Rabbit* (1988) directed by Robert Zemeckis.

Sense Project allows the superimposition of a physical hand on an active phone keyboard.

Integration can be performed in two ways: either by starting from the real environment and superposing a virtual object (augmented reality) or by superimposing a real object on a virtual environment (augmented virtuality). Figure 4.7C illustrates the integration in a real scenario (the Vatican State) of a virtual model (St. Peter's church). This MR can be defined, following Wikipedia, as a system "encompassing both augmented reality and augmented virtuality." New environments and visualizations may be produced where physical and digital objects coexist and interact in real time. Moreover, Paul Milgram and Fumio Kishino, in 1994, defined an MR as [10] "anywhere between the extrema of the virtuality continuum," where the virtuality continuum extends from the completely real to the completely virtual environment, with augmented reality and augmented virtuality ranging between. In Figure 4.12, this continuum is linearly represented by a segment highlighting two case extremes in which animation is combined with live action: on the left, a real physical scenario includes two cartoon characters, whereas on the right, a totally virtual scene includes an actor.

Pictorial Indexing

As seen earlier, images may be described in many ways: by a pictorial copy, color, text, structural components, spatial organization, contents, and so on. A cluster, or a single one of these features, may characterize an individual image within a collection, as may be seen in Chapter 3, *Toward multimedia: image retrieval via context*. Looking at Figure 4.13, the reproduction of a film poster of the latest Saura's film, *Io, Don Giovanni* can be seen, and considered as an image to be technically described. Such descriptions are generally used for retrieval purposes from an image database. The first works on this subject were performed at MIT during the 1980s, and a recent review of all the different approaches to image captioning, indexing, and content-based retrieving (CBIR) can be found in [11]. Recently,

(A)   (B)

Figure 4.13 A film poster of *Io, Don Giovanni* (2009), illustrating chromatic components.

because the number of digital images has grown exponentially (due to digital cameras, webcams, iPhone, etc.) new programs available on the web can be used to recover specific wanted images.

A successful example of a web-based social image repository, which can be queried by anyone, is flickr (www.flickr.com). Images can be found through appropriate *tags* that describe the image contents as labeled by the creator of such an image.

Other ways than CBIR, in which an image can be described, to be later identified and retrieved, will be now shortly revisited through Figure 4.13. Sometimes, in order to reduce the computational burden, special pictorial features can be chosen, such as object contours, chromatic components, morphological parameters.

Turning now to our chosen image (Figure 4.13), we see that it has a dark background and two main characters, strongly lit, with white text at the bottom. In Figure 4.13A, the color components (RGB) of its top part are evaluated and displayed on top of Figure 4.13B, whereas the bottom of Figure 4.13A, containing written text, is on the bottom of Figure 4.13B. The first color histogram basically reports that color hues concentrate along the grey axis (R = G = B), with a secondary pink component reflecting the light color of the skin. The second color histogram has a large dark digital blob, centered on the origin, because of the black rectangle that is the text background. A small white sphere on the vertex, opposite to the origin of the 3D histogram space, corresponds to the white written letters. The color histogram may have specific features (like the color hues distributed along one axis and the two blobs), which can be used when performing image retrieval.

A textual description can be given both as a set of key words (Don Giovanni, Carlos Saura, actors' names, etc.) or as metadata (2009 film, Mozart's opera, etc.). The image structure corresponds to a couple of characters looking at each other, hand-in-hand and face-to-face. The three red circles enclose the above-mentioned structural components, which can be searched and recognized both as single elements or, with a stronger selective power, with their relative locations in the image describing the spatial organization.

Low-level features have been considered so far. Now, high-level ones will be used to facilitate the formulation of the image query by users, at a higher level of abstraction, closer to natural language. This method corresponds to a semantic retrieval and may be exemplified as "a couple of lovers of the seventeenth century." The main problem is to reformulate the query with a new set of peculiarities translated into the corresponding low-level features.

Two basic parameters are used to evaluate the image retrieval efficiency: the result's *accuracy* (how many of the images found were correct) and the *coverage* (how many of the correct images were found). In order to achieve best results, it may be convenient to combine the different descriptors listed earlier into one single query by means of the set theory operators (see Chapter 3, the *CBIR* section).

Annotation

The image interpretation requires meta-information (typically context, author, and motivation) to be fully envisaged and profited. In fact, perusing an illustrated book it is common practice to annotate both text and images for a later use. Such annotations are strictly personal, modify the printed pages, and can only be changed by physical erasure. Conversely, digital annotation can be shared (or remain private), does not modify the original version, and may be easily modified or updated: this is the goal of a number of projects, starting from the first version of Annotea [12] and continuing with a variety of approaches recently based on the Web 2.0 paradigm.[1] A couple of systems representing leading projects in this area will be mentioned. The first one is Webnotes [13], which also allows annotating Adobe files and Diigo [14], that includes a variety of available functions, typically belonging to a social content site, like knowledge sharing, collaborative research, and a number of retrieving capabilities.

---

[1] "The term 'Web 2.0' is commonly associated with web applications that facilitate interactive information sharing, interoperability, user-centered design, and collaboration on the World Wide Web" (Wikipedia), as, for example, Facebook, Linkedin, Youtube.

More specifically, the possibility of annotating text, images, and videos, with writing, drawing, or voice recording greatly enriches the metadata associated with the original object. Last, because annotations can be stored in a database on a server, it is possible to query it from any computer in the world, for example, by date, author, or even by content, regardless of their physical dimensions. As an example, the photography of a statue (Figure 4.14) is annotated with its basic facts in "Étienne Marcel riding a horse."

Annotation is crucial in many cases because metadata provide the necessary information for image interpretation such as in biomedical images. Figure 4.15 shows a chest frontal view X-ray, taken on a male patient (RadiologyInfo, Radiological Society of North America).

As can be seen from the picture, informative values of the X-ray are completely given by the metadata on the right side; without them the picture would lose its significant value.

A few years ago, a university project for multimedia annotation of web pages was started under the name of MADCOW (Multimedia Annotation of Digital COntents on the Web) [15]. Further improvements were continuously made, as described in [16]. This approach followed the definition of the Rhetorical Structure Theory [17], in which annotations on natural language text (the nucleus) may be considered as satellites. In fact, a corresponding taxonomy was defined as described with the following functions:

- *Explanation*—clarifies some documents' concepts on sentences, images, or videos.
- *Comment*—provides the same personal opinions related to the document content.
- *Question*—presents a doubt about a given document, paragraph, or section.
- *Integration*—presents information completing the document content.

Annotated metadata

Étienne Marcel on horse back

Hotel de Ville,Paris

Author : Jean-Antoine-Marie (Antonin) Idrac (1849 - 1884)

Statue finished on 1872

Foto author: John Williams, Date: May 19, 2009

Figure 4.14 Annotated picture enriched by the corresponding metadata.

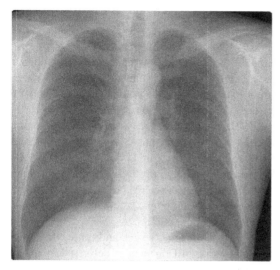

Patient:	John Williams
Frontal view	
Date:	May 15, 2009
Radiologist:	Michael Schmith
Diagnostic:	Negative
Oncologist:	Burt Wisdom
Diagnostic:	

Figure 4.15 Annotated chest X-ray.

- *Example*—contains some specific instances explaining some document concepts.
- *Summary*—provides an abstract of the document content.
- *Solution*—describes a possible answer to a problem found in the document.
- *Announcement*—contains information related either to events or significant facts for users.
- *Memorandum*—includes information about something to be remembered.

Each function is represented by means of a specific icon, thereby facilitating the user choice of the function to be performed by the annotation. Every annotation starts with a selection of the multimedia component (text, image, or video); the user next chooses the annotation function and fills in a floating screen box with his or her annotation. The system automatically provides the date, and the annotation may be posted on the web to a server. This annotation is marked on the web page and can be easily retrieved only by the user (if private) or by everyone else (if shared) [18].

Multimedia Communication

Because the number, type, and size of messages to be sent increases by the day, one single channel is not sufficient: multiple channels of communication are required in order for the transmission to be effective. Among the channels that can be considered today are letters and text messages, press releases, newsletters, brochures, books and reports, photos and slide shows, TV and radio programs, sms's and e-mails, blogs, corporate websites, interest groups, videos, social-networking sites, podcasts, e-books, and so on.

Note that "multichannel" has many different, but related, meanings. A first definition corresponds to the case in which "there are two or more communication channels over the same path, such as a communication cable, or a radio transmitter, which can broadcast on two different frequencies, either individually or simultaneously" (Answers.com).

Within the commercial environment, the definition of multimedia communication for improving sales, as given by Talvi™ (Helsinki, Finland), is the following: "a term for actions that combines multiple digital channels, utilizes unique benefits of Internet and Web 2.0, and uses digital content creation to provide value to the audience in the marketing or corporate communications ... when trying to promote a new product release, they could send out an e-mail message or TV-commercial campaign individually. This, if properly executed, could yield positive results. However, this same campaign could be exponentially improved if multiple message types and interactive communities are implemented—a TV commercial, a cinema commercial, a radio commercial, mobile, microsite, blogs, web communities, viral, banners, e-mail campaign, search engine campaign, etc."

Historically, encompassing a wider context of time, space, and sense, the multimedia communication process is like the notion of Don Juan as delivered by means of theater, novel, film, music, opera, and so on.

Remediation

The title name describes a process by which new media technologies improve upon, or remedy prior technologies, as for example, in the case of using the Internet for telephone calls (or voice over Internet protocol (VoIP)), which remedies the standard telephone channels [19]. Another definition considers remediation to mean the formal logic by which new media refashions prior media forms. Along with immediacy and hypermediacy, remediation is one of the three traits of our genealogy of new media. Remediation can also be seen as "an agent of the teleological evolution as we invent media that improve on the limits of prior media." This definition [20] may be further specified by the process during which "media develop 'anthropotropically' that is, to resemble the human."

An impressive example of remediation is online newspapers, which provide news and a number of extra services, as with Times Reader 2.0 of *The New York Times*, to be found on (http://www.nytimes.com/pages/todayspaper/index.html). The provided "digitally remastered" editions include 7 days of the paper (to read previously published missed news); news can also be browsed by headlines, sections, and even pictures; the digital version is updated hourly. Moreover, even leisure aspects are covered innovatively, for example, the crossword puzzle can be written/erased without pencil through mouse and keyboard.

Repurposing

This term is often used in the entertainment industry to describe the practice of adapting a "brand" to a number of different media venues, for example, a Disney's creation, a Broadway musical, a Saturday morning cartoon, and a complete line of

Figure 4.16 The Hello Kitty icon and some derived franchises (from mobiles to beers).

Figure 4.17 The Simpsons and some derived franchises (from human and dog cloths to bed covers).

children's products. A typical example of repurposing is Hello Kitty (Yuko Shimizu, 1974, Japan), reproduced in a large variety of objects, drawings, furniture, mobiles, and so on (Figure 4.16). Another example (Figure 4.17) having an incredible success and a worldwide audience is the Simpsons (Matt Groening, 1989, USA), fictional characters launched by TV.

Icons and Metaphors

The etymology of the word icon is *eikon*, a Greek word that stood for an image carrying some meaning, as in typical portraits of sacred persons within the Orthodox Church, Figure 4.18.

This icon illustrates the concept of unity representing the Holy Trinity, as well as the fact that the characters are neither men nor women having conventional poses. Literal or figurative meaning is usually associated to religious, cultural, political, or economic standing. More broadly, "the term is used in a wide number of contexts for an image, picture, or representation; it is a sign or likeness that stands for an object by signifying or representing it either concretely or by analogy, as in semiotics" (Wikipedia).

Figure 4.18 The icon of the Holy Trinity painted in the fifteenth century by Andrei Rublev.

Following Umberto Eco [21]:

Semiotics is concerned with everything that can be taken as a sign. A sign is every-thing that can be taken as significantly substituting something else. This something else does not necessarily have to exist or to actually be somewhere at the moment in which a sign stands in for it. Thus semiotics is, in principle, the discipline study-ing everything that can be used in order to lie. If something cannot be used to tell a lie, conversely it cannot be used to tell the truth; it cannot in fact be used "to tell" at all. I think that the definition of a "theory of the lie" should be taken as a pretty comprehensive program for a general semiotics.

Long ago, during the 1930s, an operational definition of icon was given by Charles Peirce [22] as "anything that stands for something else, to somebody, in some respect or capacity." Being so general, it covers most traditional practices, typically linking linguistic, pictorial (or even auditory) expressions to a *meaning* that needs to be *interpreted* by a human. See Figure 4.19 for a couple of examples of icons representing different religions and peace.

Hymns and flags are used as icons for countries, and peculiar songs like "Roses of Alabama," for the South in the USA during the secession time. The Gregorian style or Bach's oratorios are the archetype of Christian prayers; similarly, "A Love Dream" by Franz Liszt and some particular poems by Alphonse de Lamartine or Lord Byron are all icons representing Romanticism.

More generally, an icon may imply an idol (as a pop star) or a symbol (the Rotary wheel worn on coat lapels) that represents a group of persons, or even a

Figure 4.19 Religious icons (A) and peace icons (B).

Figure 4.20 A computer icon bar.

lifestyle (the Nike symbol for sports). Eventually icons appear as the ultimate condensed form of a previously mentioned culture, with related drawbacks like their uniqueness, because other alternative icons could also be equally representative (e.g., Hector Berlioz could challenge Franz Liszt to better represent romanticism, and Ugo Foscolo and Wolfgang Goethe could challenge Alphonse de Lamartine and Lord Byron).

Current Icons

Within HCI, the common understanding of an icon is to consider it as a visual metaphor representing a file, a directory, a window, a mode, or a program. Whenever a number of icons are presented together, this group is referred to as an icon bar, generally at the top or bottom of the page in most web browsers; see Figure 4.20 with the basic icon bar of Mac OS X Software.

Note that the interpretation of an icon meaning is subjective and dynamic; there is no unique meaning corresponding to a class of signs. Peirce's sign taxonomy considers, first, the icon (where a mental process is required to understand it); then, the index (having a causal relationship to its signified, like smoke for fire); and finally, the symbol (having a totally arbitrary relationship, like a red cross for the corresponding international medical organization).

The icon is wrongly considered to be similar to what it signifies; typically, by looking at the icon one should derive information about its significance, yet this is rarely the case, because different meanings may be attributed to an icon depending on context, time, and observer. This fact provides a possible approach to ambiguity management in human–computer interfaces by restricting the user model to a given class of users. The design of effective icons should be performed after an accurate study of the cultural background, age, and motivation of the potential users.

The Blending Approach

A rather recent concept, which establishes a theoretical foundation for both HCI and software engineering, is the *blend*. In short, the blend is an operation [23] "that is applied to two input spaces, which results in a new, blended space." Blending can also be seen as a conceptual integration having the following properties: composition, integration, and elaboration. The first one describes the consequences of the projections toward the blended space, generating new relations; the second one, by using cognitive and cultural models, produces a composite structure on the blended space; and finally, the third one processes the newly formed patterns, bringing into being new views and abstractions.

A concrete example of blending from two input domains is described here: the early electronic mail and the ordinary mail domain. These two initial spaces blend into a virtual system generating new functions, as can be seen in Table 4.1. This table is analogous, but not equal, to the one in chapter 8 from [23]. Five columns are represented, namely, the first one showing the initial icon as found on the screen; and the second final icon column, displaying the transformed icon after the evoked execution. The third column describes the corresponding user activity, while the fourth reports the obtained results. Finally, the fifth column explains the allowed user function.

It is easy to see that new one-shot functions (absent in the two original domains) appear in the new blended space (like forwarding a message, or replying to all the involved people, or triggering a chat when a message is received by an online user) only implemented today in some systems.

Table 4.1 Blending Post Office Functions with Internet Facilities for Generating Electronic Mail

Initial Icon	Final Icon	Action	Effect	Operation
		Two mouse clicks	Documents now can be read	Reading the message contents
		One mouse click	Document is deleted	Undesired mail user cancelled

(Continued)

Table 4.1 (Continued)

Initial Icon	Final Icon	Action	Effect	Operation
		One mouse click	Answering is set up	A reply message can be written
		One mouse click	Answers to all	A reply to all can be performed
		One mouse click	Allows to forward a message	Sending the forwarded message
		One mouse click	Connects an attachment	Sending the attachment
		One mouse click	Choosing a priority level	Fast sending of messages
		No operation	Outward message	Partially sent message
		No operation	Sent message signal	Message has been sent
		No operation	Delivered message signal	Message has been delivered
		No operation	Colored icon	The message has been read
		One mouse click	Deleted message	Not available message

Structuring the Content

Using multiple media, with different modalities for communicating, is a very natural process, as, for instance, in a TV program, where images, sound, and text are usually fully integrated and broadcasted. Communication may involve all our senses, not only the classical five (sight, touch, hearing, taste, and smell), and should also include the feelings of balance, acceleration, temperature, and pain as well as the kinesthetic sensation. These last ones are nowadays used in entertainment (e.g., IMAX in *Harry Potter* and *The Transformers*). Sometimes the same medium (which differs from the others in lexicon, syntax, and pragmatics) may be perceived by more than one sense (e.g., sounds having low frequencies are perceived also through the belly).

Adding a New Channel

When a new channel is opened, this may be done for three different purposes [24]: to capture the attention (*attentive function*), support information understanding (*explicative function*), and improve information retention (*mnemonic function*).

The addition of a channel for the text and figures case can be seen in this chapter by paying a quick visit to ancient books and treaties like the *Trattato della Pittura*. This book was written by one of the disciples of Leonardo da Vinci (probably Francesco Melzi), around 1550, directly from Leonardo's notes and drawings. The examples that follow are taken from specific chapters.

Whenever a new channel is introduced, as shown in Figure 4.21, the presentation plays an active role in helping to drive the user's attention to the currently relevant information. When something changes on the computer screen, the attention is immediately focused on the changing "loci" [25]. According to the spotlight metaphor, the areas around the "loci" are directly looked over; meanwhile, the area surrounding the focus of attention can capture the user's interest by means of an "interrupt" technique (e.g., a discontinuity in time such as an abrupt onset and offset, like blinking publicity banners). To obtain a good result, the user should only see variations on the new relevant information he or she requires; this design constraint follows the principle of least astonishment. Such principle states that the result of performing any operation (e.g., a query) should be obvious, consistent, and predictable [26,27].

From: **"Dell' uomo che porta un peso sopra le spalle"**

On the man who is carrying a weight on his shoulders
The man's shoulder carrying the weight is always taller than the other shoulder; and this is shown in the figure on the left side ...

Figure 4.21 Drawings taken from chapter XX of the *Treaty*, displaying the three basic functions of communication to integrate text with images.

Adding Pictures

Pictures are common in everyday life, such as in publicity (branding), on the computer desktop, and even on common products. In [28,29], the different roles that a picture can take are described; an illustration through examples can be found in "Degli Alberi e delle Verdure," "On Trees and Vegetation," chapter VI of the *Trattato:*

• *Representation*—inserts redundancy in the transmitted information, recalling the same ideas in a different form. Figure 4.22A provides, at a glance, the relationship between the viewing angle, the perception of the black portion of spheres, and consequently, the obscurity change due to the shadow occurring when representing trees at a distance.
• *Organization*—underlines the figure structure to highlight the internal relationship in order to elicit a wanted meaning. The level curves in Figure 4.22B draw attention to the branching texture, pointing out the main structure and the genesis of the "living" object.
• *Interpretation*—supplies analogies and sketches to facilitate concept comprehension. The clue for understanding the formation of a concavity in the junction of three branches is the main purpose, illustrated in Figure 4.22C. The hole generated by the three circles, on the triangle gravity center, clarifies the creation of a concavity; the drawing on the right justifies the shape of the tree growth.

(A)

Degli alberi posti sotto l'occhio.

On the trees placed below the eye.
The trees placed below the eye, having the same height, color and branch development, will become darker with distance...

(B)

Della ramificazione delle piante.

On tree's branching
The trees' ages, ... , may be captured through their main branching; as abcdef circles, for every new main branching...

(C)

All'albero giovane non crepa la scorza.

Young tree has no bark cracks
Since the main bough will be subdivided in many branches at the same height, then the junction borders will be raised, meanwhile deep concavities will remain in the center ...

(D)

Quali termini dimostrino le piante remote dell'aria che si fa lor campo.

Which aspects show distant trees due to the air in between.
Trees with branches in sunny air: the more distant they are the more spherical they become ...

(E)

Figure 4.22 Different roles played by inserting a picture, from *On Trees and Vegetation* by Leonardo.

- *Transformation*—facilitates human information storage by inducing mnemonic transformations, for example, losing details and modifying shapes by turning them into geometrical primitives as the viewer's distance increases. As shown in Figure 4.22D, the sequence of trees appears to be at an increasing distance by reducing their size, losing the foliage details, and smoothing them toward a circular shape.
- *Decoration*—adds aesthetic elements to increase the user's pleasure. The spiral with leaves in Figure 4.22E frequently decorates the titles in a given edition of the *Trattato*'s chapters, and in other old books the first letter of a chapter is typically illuminated.

Notice that this classification is not based on image features, such as the degree of realism or their metric properties, but it is rather built on the evoked response to the images in terms of active mental processes.

It is worth mentioning that memory retention can be increased whenever images are carefully designed, because their exploration will provide image chunks in short-time memory, merging and storing them in long-term memory. According to the principle of "expectation violation," an effective technique is to set up an image that is readily identifiable and that creates visual expectations in the viewer. If such expectations are violated, the user's attention is attracted, because they seem wrong or unusual. Regular images, when scanned, are difficult to remember; for this reason, whenever differences between presented and expected images appear, such images will be easily stored by the viewer. In conclusion, abnormality turns out to be more effective than normality for memory retention.

Representation Grammars

To efficiently transmit a specific content, the organization of single and multiple media must be carefully designed. An audience can easily see this fact in verbal communication and music, because the structure of such representations may totally alter their understanding. A single pictorial media organization will be now considered: the set of rules and techniques to be used to properly design a presentation can be called a "representation grammar." The grammar used to describe a knowledge transfer through graphic elements is given in [29], where some basic primitive actions are defined. Their parallel counterparts can be found in the *Trattato* (in chapter 3, entitled "De' vari accidenti e movimenti dell'uomo e proporzione di membra" ("On the various human accidents and movements and limbs proportions")), as shown in Figure 4.23:

- *Grouping*: By arranging symbols in clusters, they are perceived as belonging to the same conceptual category. Figure 4.23A shows the cluster of the "convex noses" category, showing an instance for each possible class.
- *Detailing*: By changing the degree of detail, the attention of the "user/observer" can be driven toward the single elements (highly detailed) or to the whole structure (at a lower detail). It is well known that when a single symbol is used for all possible electronic circuit components, this will facilitate the understanding of its topology, whereas when each component is specified, the global topology will often be hidden. Figure 4.23B is a paragraph illustrating the strength of men, by two men wrestling, and a detail on the muscles around the elbow.

(A)

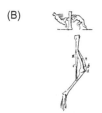

Del fare un'effigie umana in profilo dopo averlo guardato una sola volta.

How to draw a face profile after just one look.
Convex noses vary in three modalities: some of them bent above, others in the middle, and others below...

(B)

Della forza composta dall'uomo, e prima si dirà delle braccia.

On man composite strength, firstly speaking about the arms.
Muscles extending and retracting the arm, start in the middle of the bone called abductor, ...

(C)

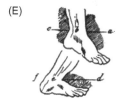

Delle misure del corpo umano e piegamenti di membra.

On human body measurements and bending limbs.
The lengthening and shortening of the arm comes from the bone protruding the arm juncture...

(D)

Del fare un'effigie umana in profilo dopo averlo guardato una sola volta.

How to draw a face profile after just one look.
First lets speak about nose, that are of three types: straight, concave, and convex. The straight one has four cases: long, short, high with a tip, and low. Concave noses are of three types: the ones that have the concavity in the higher part, the ones that have it in the middle, and others in the lower part...

(E)

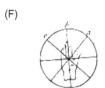

Delle giunture de' piedi, e loro ingrossamenti e diminuzioni.

On feet's junctions, their swelling and reduction.
... whenever the junction angle turns out to be more acute the d-e-f section increases and vice versa as shown with dimension a-b-c.

(F)

Che e' impossibile che una memoria riserbi tutti gli aspetti e le mutazioni delle membra.

How is it impossible that memory stores all features and limbs transformations
... the eye movement, going from a to b, looking at the hand shifts around an ab space that is a continuum, ... , and in circling around it hovers the hand...

Figure 4.23 Representation of grammar primitives. Examples of the organization of different graphic elements integrated with a text (alongside). Most English captions of the examples are free translations from the fifteenth century Italian.

- *Sequencing*: By ordering the various graphic elements from left to right or from top to bottom, information is transmitted in temporal sequences (each event happens *after* another one) or in causal relationships (each event happens *because* of another one). Three-arm positions (unfolded, folded, and straight), explaining the distance variations between elbow and shoulder, are given in Figure 4.23C. Note that, besides representing the three bones, the five horizontal lines produce a *pop-out* phenomena of the different distances.
- *Hierarchizing*: By organizing different elements within a hierarchy, their inheritance becomes explicit and consequently their affiliation as well (if they occupy the same level). Broadly speaking, hierarchical taxonomies are very effective for describing the inheritance of properties and subset components. Figure 4.23D illustrates a two-level hierarchical classification of noses, with suitable features for immediate recognition purposes. The first level has straight, concave, and convex noses, whereas the second level has two classes with three cases corresponding to the concave and convex noses (each with the curvature appearing at the top, in the middle, or at the bottom) and another class, difficult to be seen on the figure (straight noses), with four cases.
- *Comparing*: By placing together two, or more, related pictures the "user/observer" is induced to compare them so as to investigate similarities and differences. This is the case shown in Figure 4.23E, in which the cross section of the feet junctions changes in size, according to the leg–foot angle.
- *Directing*: By properly using directional graphic elements (e.g., arrows), driving human spatial exploration (or navigation paths). The hand anisotropy is easily discovered on the basis of the eight compass lines crossing the hand representation, as shown in Figure 4.23F; in fact, these lines capture the eye's attention and guide the perception process.

Media Organization

To improve human understanding and learning as outlined earlier, there must be a synergy between text, pictures, and sound (and combinations of other media) by a true integration. The designer therefore has to enable the observer to access all the available sources.

For example, a possible technique consists in leaving some gaps in the written communication to be filled in by pictorial information (colored images or even animated ones) and, vice versa, by labeling images with tags.

Implicit and explicit media integration should be distinguished: in the first case, the designer exploits the different media to favor the understanding of a whole concept (like a painting style of an historical period concerning a picture of the same period). In the second case, the designer provides links to information chunks to different media; the observer will be aware of the single media contribution and solicits the integration (e.g., links to seminars or references to books on the main subject of the painting period).

Nevertheless, the integration is not only a matter of contents, as has been already said, but also the presentation mode plays an important role because the same contents may be understood differently when transmitted through different media (see McLuhan "The medium is the message" [30]).

An interesting media taxonomy, suggested in [31], helps designers better understand the impact and added value by each individual medium to a multimedia presentation. This taxonomy (which appears in a 2D space) presents three expression categories for each media type (text, graphics, sound, motion), ranging from a fully described *elaboration* category, through a *representational* one, to a metaphorical *abstraction* category.

If the designer of a multimedia presentation selects two or more media using the same expression category, the probability that what is said in the different media represents mere duplicates of each other greatly increases. In many software packages, the print icon and the word "print" are of the same expression category, even if with different media; hence, the information is not increased. On the contrary, by using a different expression category for each media, the impact of the presentation will be strengthened (turning to our printer example, by adding "hp color Laser Jet 2550 PS" to the icon, the information is certainly enriched).

The way in which different media may be combined together may provide specific information [32]. This is well known by graphic designers, who can benefit from a rich literature on composing text with graphics [33]. Nevertheless, this literature lacks a minimal guidance to avoid improper coordination of media, such as a text presentation on one topic with images on another topic, simultaneously [32]. Moreover, another significant design issue concerns the order in which different media are presented.

The order in which media are presented strongly influences the perceived meaning of the presentation, as already observed above in regard to visual and textual information. An image before a difficult text generally facilitates understanding by providing a useful *platform* for the interpretation of that text, where most of the ambiguities are removed.

Another important role of a figure before a text is that of providing an *analysis criterion*. In other words, a figure can drive the strategy for the analysis of text, suggesting which hierarchy to be followed for a fast and exhausting appreciation.

Finally, the observer's aptitudes must be taken into account because they certainly influence his or her investigation approach. For instance, if the observer has already built his *mental image*, a new input figure could be perceived as an unwanted, annoying interference. Moreover, some people tend to approach problems first using visuals, whereas others prefer to *read the instructions* in order to anticipate meaning.

Sometimes, instead, it is quite important to conclude a presentation by a picture summarizing the concepts previously introduced; this is also helpful in human memory storage and retrieval.

Social Interaction

Although the previously described interactions were intended between an author and his audience through the Internet, the interaction between the system designer

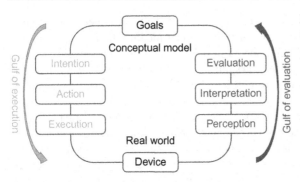

Figure 4.24 The HCI model
according to Lieberman [33].

and the user of such system, as taking place in HCI, is discussed here. Broadly speaking, interaction may be defined as a mutual or reciprocal action or influence, where the agents may be humans or humans with computers. A number of authors have suggested different models to describe the interaction process; among them, one of the first to be published was [34]; see Figure 4.24.

The overall conceptual map of HCI is made of two separate, symmetric parts called execution and evaluation gulfs. Each gulf is subdivided in a sequence of three sequential steps, from top to base and vice versa. Traversing from the top (the desired goal) toward the bottom (the device) the intention to act must be formulated. The necessary sequence of actions and, finally, the execution of such actions covers the execution gulf. Conversely, on the right part of the figure, the gulf of evaluation is composed of a sequence of three steps, namely perceiving the state of the world, interpreting such a perception, and evaluating it.

Another model [35] simplifies the interaction cycle, eliciting the computing system describing the input−output execution phases. Nevertheless, this model is flexible and adaptable to the user system, accepting the choice of different strategies to achieve the goal.

Because the interaction process may be seen as a sequence of situations (equivalent to computational states), according to Tondl [36] the interpretation of meaning is strongly linked to the corresponding situation type (i.e., the initial state of affairs, solution methods, effective means, and available resources).

Finally, a model stemming from the visual language literature [37] explicitly considers the sequence of image transformations, $i(t_1)$, $i(t_2)$, ..., $i(t_n)$ flowing from the human (H) toward the computer (C) and backward at each interaction stage. The image *materializes* the meaning intended by the sender (human vs. computer), which must be *interpreted* by the receiver (computer vs. human) (Figure 4.25).

Usability

Around the 1970s, "a property reflecting the ease of use of an information system" was introduced by Miller [38] and called "usability," soon becoming a very important feature of any computer-based system. Demonstrating the devastating effects of unusability, during the same years Jacques Carelman published a book [39] containing a

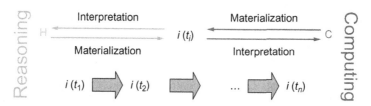

Figure 4.25 The human−computer visual model describing two basic functions: interpretation and materialization.

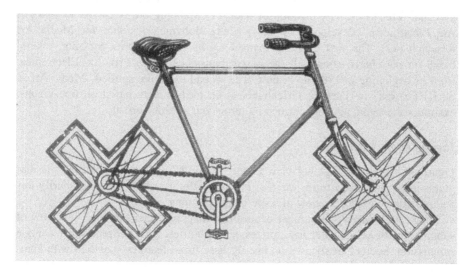

Figure 4.26 Bicycle to climb stairs by J. Carelman.

large set of impossible objects, similar to a sales-product catalog, where most objects would be considered unusable, impossible, irrational, or simply peculiar. As an example, Figure 4.26 shows a stairs-riding bicycle taken from his book.

A broader view of usability is "the effectiveness, efficiency, and satisfaction with which specified users can achieve specified goals in a particular environment" [40]. This definition was further enriched by Bevan and Holdaway [41] to include "the level of efficacy, efficiency, and satisfaction reached by a product which is employed by a class of users in order to reach given goals in specific environments."

The main attributes of such definitions are *effectiveness* for the precise accomplishment of the wanted goal; *efficiency*, the ratio between the required human resources (memory load) and the task complexity; and *efficacy*, the computational demands needed to reach the goal.

For instance, with reference to icon usability, and particularly to the interpretation of ambiguity, consider the iPhone icons (Figure 4.27). It can be noted that the

Figure 4.27 Usable and nonusable icons.

left one clearly represents a standard calendar, whereas the right one, being a flower, may signify a flower dealer, a holiday resort, the countryside, or some such—but certainly not the picture-displaying function.

The visualization of information must satisfy the usability requirements as described earlier. A recent development of such activity, under the name of Information Aesthetics (started a few years ago), can be illustrated with two examples that refer to the visualization of data for "Mapping the Archive: 30 years of Ars Electronica," developed by the Ludwig Boltzman Institute for Media Art Research [42]. The first example, named "X by Y" by Moritz Stefaner, mainly based on pie charts, shows all the past submissions of the Prix Ars Electronica, from its beginning in 1987 up to now. The second example, entitled "Media Art as Social Process" by Dietmar Offenhuber et al. [43], mainly based on tree graphs, examines the social network formed by jurors and awarded artists.

The Pie Chart Approach

Figure 4.28 presents a global view of the "X by Y" approach exploiting pie diagrams in a compressed form, whereas Figures 4.29 through 4.33 further clarify this and provide an exploded view of some image portions.

Figure 4.28 displays a number of different diagrams representing a full view of submissions by years, categories, prizes, and countries; each dot represents a single submission. Each chart focuses on one of these listed features specified with numbers, colors, prize names, and country names. The top left chart includes all submissions, while the top right one indicates, on an abstract world map, the submissions by country. The size of each circle corresponds to the number of submissions by country, and the slice color represents the category. The image portion corresponding to the European submissions is expanded in Figure 4.29 to show the contributions of each country.

In Figure 4.30, the first six pies belong to the years 1987−1992, whereas the last six pies belong to the years 2004−2009. The colors, as before, represent categories, and the central number corresponds to the total number of submissions. Figure 4.31 provides information on the type, number, and category to which prizes were assigned; in fact, the large pie represents the no-award submissions.

A matrix version having the time line on the x-axis provides the different submission categories on the Y-axis (Figure 4.32), whereas a quantitative analysis of submissions by category is shown in Figure 4.33.

The Tree-Graph Approach

An interesting method for visualizing large data quantities employing graph-based engines is SemaSpace [44], which semantically explores structured data and

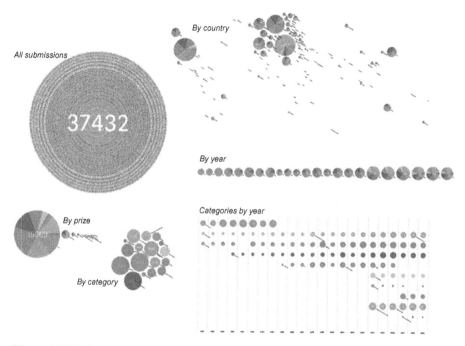

Figure 4.28 Full view of "*X* by *Y*" representations: along a clockwise order from the top left: all submissions, by country spatially corresponding to the geographical distribution, by year with sizes proportional to number of submissions, categories by year, category, and prize.

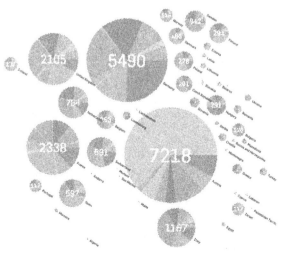

Figure 4.29 Exploded view: pie charts representing submissions by each European country.

Figure 4.30 Exploded view: pie charts representing submissions by year.

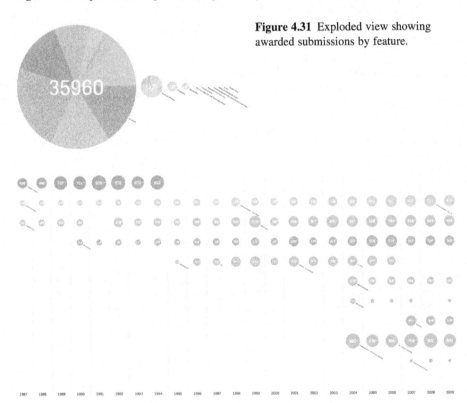

Figure 4.31 Exploded view showing awarded submissions by feature.

Figure 4.32 Exploded view: time line of submissions by category.

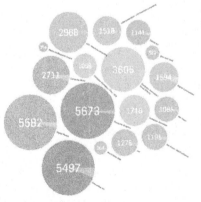

Figure 4.33 Exploded view: pies showing submissions by category.

memory spaces solving the problem of handling large amounts of nodes, up to several thousands—even if the nodes are represented by images. The authors of SemaSpace describe their project as follows: "SemaSpace is a fast and easy-to-use graph editor for large knowledge networks, specially designed for the application in nontechnical sciences and the arts. It creates interactive graph layouts in 2D and 3D by means of a flexible algorithm. The system is powerful enough for the calculation of complex networks and can incorporate additional data such as images, sounds, and full texts."

On the Media Art as Social Process website [45], it is possible to find not only the tool but also an interesting application to the 30 years of Ars Electronica [46]. The complete relationship set, between candidate jurors and jury committees along the years (Figure 4.34) for each Prix category, is shown. In Figure 4.35 another graph, displaying the complete relationship set between the awarded artists

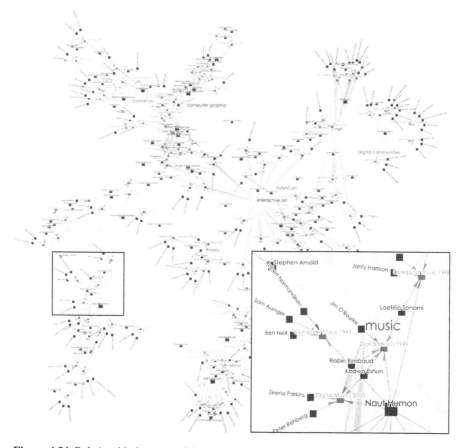

Figure 4.34 Relationship between all jurors and the juries they have participated in; the smaller subgraph on the bottom right displays a portion of the same relationships concerning the music category.

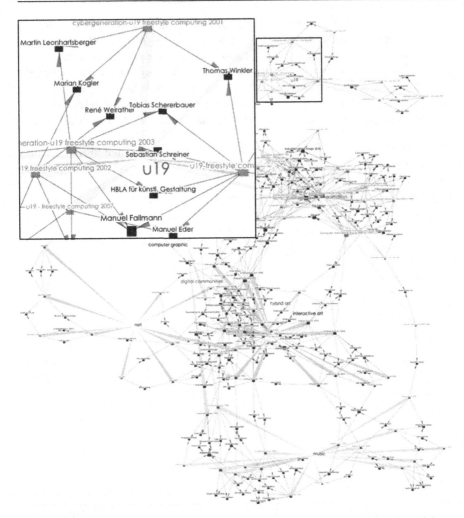

Figure 4.35 Network graph displaying the awarded artists and the jury sessions in which they received the award: on the top left a subgraph, showing a portion of the U19 category, is presented.

and the jury committees, is illustrated. Note that, in both cases, all the editions along the years and every Prix category are represented; from these graphs it appears that awarded artists become very often jury members.

By merging all the information displayed above, it is possible to see in Figure 4.36 a bipartite graph network, referring only to the Ars Electronica categories. The hinge of the graph is a juror, Golan Levin, who served throughout the history of the competition and, as an artist, received awards. Arrows exiting from the person node indicate he has served as a juror; arrows entering the node imply he has received an award. In practice, Levin has received five awards and has

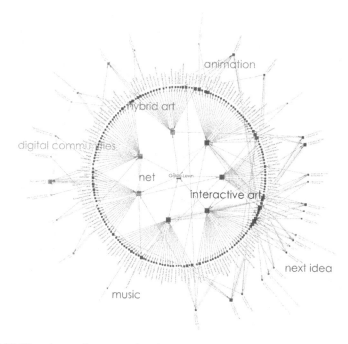

Figure 4.36 Bipartite graph representing the juror role and received awards for a given artist.

participated in two juries. As before, colors refer to categories where the influence of such a juror is globally seen.

As exposed in the Ars Electronica Festival, many submissions aim not only to communicate effectively through pictorial elements, but also to produce pleasant artistic results for the observer along the years. In the last edition, moving from a common database of submissions, awards, juries, and categories, the aim was to visually represent not only all the data, but specifically and interactively all the relationships. The result can be termed *usable* and produces effective, efficient, and pleasant representations providing the information in an aesthetic, captivating, and even emotional mode.

Accessibility

According to Wikipedia, accessibility is a general term used to describe the degree to which a product (e.g., device, service, and environment) is accessible by as many people as possible. It can be viewed as the "ability to access" or the functionality, and possible benefit, of some system or entity. It is often used to focus on people with disabilities and their right of access to entities, often through the deployment of an assistive technology.

According to Microsoft, accessibility makes the computer easier to see, hear, and use. Bill Gates' position is: "Our vision is to create innovative technology that is accessible to everyone and that adapts to each person's needs. Accessible technology eliminates barriers for people with disabilities and it enables individuals to take full advantage of their capabilities."

Worldwide, 57% (74.2 million) of computer users are likely, or very likely, to benefit from the use of accessible technology because they have mild or severe difficulties/impairments. As an example, for users having gestural problems, virtual keyboards (Figure 4.37) may be employed visually. The user must fixate a single key on the screen for a short period, called dwell time, until the next letter is fixated. Two main drawbacks are present: first, because a correct letter selection is needed, the virtual keys must have a rather large size, and second, because the virtual keyboard is on the screen, it will occlude any other present information.

Another system for issuing commands is Eye-S [47], which allows a general input to be provided to the computer also through a gaze-based approach. Thanks to the adopted *eye graffiti* communication style (Figure 4.38), this technique can be used both for writing and for generating other kinds of computer commands. In Eye-S, letters and other computer commands are created through sequences of fixations on nine screen areas, called *hotspots*. Because the sensitive regions are

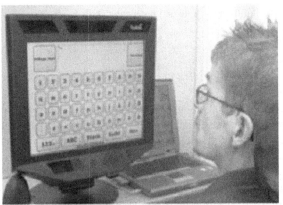

Figure 4.37 Visual writing by a gaze finder, through a virtual keyboard displayed on the monitor.

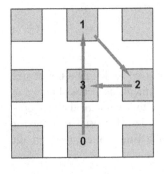 

Figure 4.38 Sequence of visual hotspots on the screen (left) and the corresponding P letter (right).

usually not visible, they do not interfere with other applications, and therefore all the available screen area can be exploited.

When the user looks at a hotspot for more than a defined threshold time (e.g., 400 ms), a *sequence character/command recognition process* starts. After the first hotspot has been watched for a predefined *dwell time* next, other hotspots are looked at, within predefined time intervals. The sequence of watched hotspots must belong to the set of predefined sequences (stored in a database).

Another project designed to help people with amyotrophic lateral sclerosis (ALS, or Lou Gehrig's disease) is the EyeWriter [48]. This system is a low-cost, eye-tracking apparatus and custom software that allows graffiti writers and artists to draw only using their eyes. The long-term goal is to create a professional/social network of software developers, hardware hackers, urban projection artists, and ALS patients. Such members around the world who use local materials and open-source programs may generate both distributed creativity and produce eye art (Figure 4.39).

Because web pages are the most popular reference source of information, their accessibility is essential for an easy and fast knowledge recovery. There are over 200 tools for testing accessibility of web pages, both commercial and free for use. Nevertheless, not all problems may be revealed automatically, and human intervention is required. In some cases, a tool bar is integrated to the web browser to facilitate the task. An interesting example is the WAVE tool developed by the University of Utah and the Center for Persons with Disabilities [49].

The performance of automatic accessibility testing by the WAVE tool, on the homepage of the *New York Times (NYT)* on the web, is shown in Figure 4.40. In Figure 4.41, the result of applying the WAVE tool to a small part of the *NYT* homepage (i.e., Figure 4.40) is displayed. Figure 4.42 explains the meaning of the accessibility flaw icons.

Note that the selected *NYT* area includes different objects like images, text, lists, hyperlinks, and search boxes. The title page of Figure 4.41 indicates 32 accessibility errors considered on the *NYT* full page, all of red color. Indeed, a severity index from high (red icons) to low (light blue icons), with a variety of cases, is also

Figure 4.39 A patient with ALS (left) creating graffiti and the resulting artifact on the screen (right).

Figure 4.40 Top left part of the *NYT* home page.

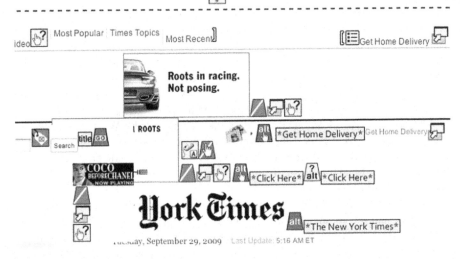

Figure 4.41 Results of WAVE accessibility analysis of the top part of the *NYT* home web page.

provided. With reference to the picture having an advertisement with a partial car, the system produced three flaw icons. The first is the red icon with a white diagonal line indicating, "Alternative text is not present for an image," which means that because the picture contains text, the required explanatory words are absent. Moreover, the included words are vague and do not convey an obvious meaning. Furthermore, it should be remarked that no automatic tool may infer such meaning.

The next yellow icon, with a white arrow toward another window, is less risky and is signaled as "A link is set to open in a new window." In fact the link is hidden, and more information is given by the next yellow icon, having a question mark, which means "Link text does not make sense out of context, contains

WAVE 4.0 Icons, Titles, and Descriptions

- All RED icons indicate accessibility ERRORS. Their presence will almost certainly cause accessibility issues.
- All YELLOW icons indicate ALERTS. They may or may not be accessibility issues, but typically indicate an area where accessibility is often an issue or where it may be made better. They should each be checked for possible issues.
- All GREEN icons indicate ACCESSIBILITY FEATURES that the author should check for accuracy.
- All LIGHT BLUE icons indicate STRUCTURAL, SEMANTIC, or NAVIGATIONAL ELEMENTS that may aid accessibility. They should checked for proper use.
- All trapezoid shaped icons (alt, for example) relate to images.

Figure 4.42 Five classes of flaw icons, according to WAVE, in order of critical damage.

extraneous text (such as "Click here"), or is the same as another link on the page, but links to a different location." In practice, once the link is discovered, there is no idea where it will drive and what will be found.

The next red icon, containing a label, refers to the search box on the left of the page. This icon conveys the following meaning: "A form < input >, < select >, or < textarea > does not have a corresponding label." In practice, there is no guide to what a user may search for. The next light blue icon, referring to the link button, indicates "A title attribute is present," which indicates only that an event can be triggered, but being in light blue indicates a navigational tool that should be checked for proper use.

Finally, the next icon is green, containing the label GO, which explains that "Alternative text is present in an image input element," but requires us to check whether such text is fitting and encourages the designer to verify the text.

From the earlier examples, it can be seen that the tool summarizes the types of problems encountered as well as the positive aspects that should be continued or expanded on the site. It also recommends follow-up steps, including full conformance evaluation, which takes into account the validation of markup and other tests, and ways to address any identified problems. In conclusion, note that accessibility software tools are efficient in terms of time and simplicity to identify problems, but the indications provided by the tool must be interpreted and, if necessary, fixed by the web-page designer.

Cognitive Networks

In Wikipedia, a Cognitive Network (CN) includes "a cognitive process that can perceive current network conditions and plan, decide, act on those conditions, learn from the consequences of its actions, all while following end-to-end goals." Following the pioneers [50], the cognition loop senses the environment; plans actions according to sensor input and the network policy, deciding which scenario best fits its end-to-end purpose, using a reasoning engine; and finally acts on the chosen scenario.

These networks use machine learning techniques to improve their performance, learning from the past, combining communication with computation to achieve flexibility, and tuning to user needs (based on location, time, goal, and profile).

Role Definition for Virtual Realism

New technologies allow users to virtually enter a specified scenario, where they can play different roles: trainee, practitioner, troubleshooter, and so forth. In fact, new tools (e.g., head-mounted display, special glasses, and cave set-up) may generate real-looking environments that, provided the user suspends his belief, become totally credible.

Reality and Illusion

Before providing reality definitions, it is worth mentioning that, for different persons and even for a single one, the interpretation of reality may change due to the psychological, emotional, physical, or other personal states of mind. This fact has been widely shown in literature, for instance by Luigi Pirandello (Nobel prize, 1934) who has portrayed, in many of his theatrical works, different reality perception of his characters, often driving them to a dramatic outcome.

On the other hand, whenever the subject's immersion in reality is a total one, he or she feels inside it; nevertheless, the concept of presence is a complex one, requiring specific definitions according to both physical and technological circumstances.

When tracking the concept of presence for different realities, it can be noted that in order to be somewhere else, a variety of both old and new media must be exploited. This may be performed through novels, films, TV sequels, and video games, all of which may turn out to be useful not only for leisure but also for therapeutic aims. Differently from the possibilities for interaction offered by the media, by means of the creation of a virtual environment, novel realities (i.e., virtual realities) can be obtained. This can be achieved by analyzing the human ways for perceiving reality, requiring the introduction of a convincing scenario. In fact, reality is not directly derived by perceptual and memory storage, but by a continuous mental judgment process [51].

Some definitions of presence will be provided according to different sources, starting from the Webster^{TM} dictionary: "being at a specified or understood place"; "the person's perception of being at a specified or understood place" [52,53]; "a mediated experience allowing the perception of a different physical/virtual place" [54]; a "subjective sensation of being present in a remote or artificial environment but not in the surrounding, physical environment" [55].

Note that the perceived scenario plays a fundamental role in the perception of presence so that each context will determine a moment-to-moment different reality [52]. The basic state of consciousness is given, in a physical context (i.e., being there), even spatially apart, yet in a time-immediate mode. The presence in a virtual context is mediated by special-purpose technology and within an imaginary environment, having reduced distal stimuli without being influenced directly by the media; such presence is achieved by internally generated mental images. Whenever representations that look, sound, and feel real, a "real" presence is obtained.

For instance, social realism reflects events that are true to life, as in the film *The Truman Show* (1998, directed by Peter Weir), where the main character believes that he is living in a real scenario, but in fact, it is only a virtual set (Figure 4.43).

On the other hand, perceptual realism depicts objects and people to look "sound" (even if their behavior is unrealistic), as in the film *Crouching Tiger, Hidden Dragon* (2000, directed by Ang Lee), where the characters are real but, during fencing scenes, violate the law of gravity (Figure 4.44A and B).

Finally, in behavioral realism, credible agents that are not perceptually real, yet behave in a human-like way, as in the film *Ice Age: Dawn of the Dinosaurs* (also known as *Ice Age 3*, 2009, a 3D computer-animated film directed by Carlos Saldanha), where the squirrel behaves emotionally as a human (Figure 4.45).

If different approaches are considered, the user lives such experiences in the third person because he or she observes and controls all actions (as in video games) externally. On the other hand, another presence style is to live it in first person by using some or all of the human senses.

The feeling of full immersion can be obtained if convincing evidence is provided to a subject on "being there" [56]; as mentioned earlier, it can be achieved through technological means like head-mounted displays using a 3D representation of a surrounding environment, and so on. In this *real* experience, participants externalize the received precepts, attributing them to distal sources. Using Thuresson's

Figure 4.43 An image from *The Truman Show* film, where an impossible shadow on the sky reveals a false reality.

(A)   (B)

Figure 4.44 Two images from the *Crouching Tiger, Hidden Dragon* film, where the basic laws of physics are violated.

Figure 4.45 An image from the film *Ice Age 3* showing the squirrel's human-like emotions.

definition [57], "Immersion is an objective description of the system and presence a subjective phenomenon in the user's experience." IMAX™ is an example of a full-immersion technology that delivers a 3D movie experience, enabling viewers to experience objects seemingly leaping off the screen ("into the laps of the audience"), further enhancing the feeling of being inside the movie (Figure 4.46). Nevertheless, even using the latest immersion technology with highly sophisticated solutions, physical presence always provides richer and stronger sensations.

A final, very important virtual presence, from the economical point of view, is provided by web user visibility. Billions of people daily want to find products and services on the web, aiming to optimize their choice. The search engine marketing (known as SEM) model of presence is widely studied in order to gain commercial priority and selling power for a given product, in such a way offering "the sense of being there" [58]. Another example calling for presence is that of an investor who

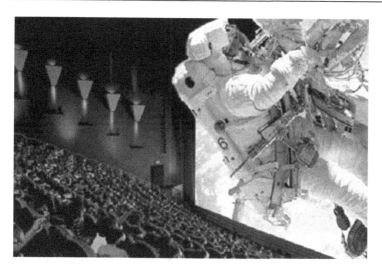

Figure 4.46 An image showing a moon-landing operation in the IMAX theater.

Figure 4.47 Stock exchange values on the iPhone by Bloomberg™.

would like to be inside the stock market exchange room but must accept reading the stock and share values through TV or newspapers on the Internet and multimedia facilities—even on a mobile phone (Figure 4.47), which shows stock exchange values for the iPhone.

Games

The role of images in all games is instrumental. Without them, a game would lose all its appeal. The first games played with a computer were called PC games and used the computer monitor to visualize, with elementary graphics, the scenarios in which the player would be challenged, either increasing scores or winning simple competitions. The computer was used for generating images and processing the players' actions, whereas today, with the advent of special-purpose consoles and graphic processors (GPU), the games became highly sophisticated and can be considered the most advanced computer graphic applications; some include sound (SoundBlaster^{TM}) and 3D, enhancing the player's experience.

As games develop, players may be always more involved in the game until becoming fully immersed in it. A good example of a full immersion environment is the flight simulator used for pilot training, which has now proliferated into a wide set of sport-based video games, as, for example, for skiing or car racing.

The player can either see him- or herself in the game scenario (third-person player) or, by means of a real full immersion, the player is integrated into the environment where the game is being played (first-person player).

An interesting possibility is the one of creating virtual personal characters when playing in the third person, called *avatars*. This name comes from the Sanskrit language and means *incarnation*. There are many programs for generating avatars, picking up features of the person to be represented like skin color, hair fashion, and so on, or even caricatures of their faces. In this way, there is a stronger involvement of the player because the avatar impersonates the player and can be considered an *identicon*.

A kind of game known as a role-playing game involves a given set of characters performing tasks related to the basic goals: finding strategies, exploiting discoveries, and using a local area network (LAN) or even the Internet to enable multiplayer participation. Some players like to change some parts of the game without a necessary agreement with the software house, thereby slightly modifying the game; these personal options are called *mods*. Because playing is becoming always more complex and hard, particularly for experienced players, there is a tendency to cheat in many different ways like lowering the entry levels for ascending categories or even transforming the "soldier−player" into an immune character or a superhero.

Most video games are shooting games, a gender known as *militainment*, like *America's Army*; see Figure 4.48, showing the official game homepage.

There are also other games having educational purposes, like the *Civilization* series or others explicitly declared as nonviolent, like *A Force More Powerful*. This game is the sequel of a documentary on a number of dictators around the world whom the player should defeat. In this game, real characters and country landscapes are intermingled with virtual players, implementing a mixed, or alternate, reality (Figure 4.49).

Some authors support the idea that games can be helpful for education purposes by engaging attention, providing immediate feedback, and following the personal learning rhythm. Conversely, other authors believe that games cannot really substitute the social interactions available in a classroom, the personal contact with an instructor, and the possibility of formulating questions: this subject is known as the *game controversy*. Moreover, it has been demonstrated that, most times, computer games can become addictive, and players have a strong resistance to interrupt their game; in such situations, their mental health can be damaged.

Figure 4.48 *America's Army*: official homepage of the computer game.

Animation

For many years, creative artists have designed animated cartoons for film screening. Nevertheless, only recently, by using computer programs, new techniques have been developed to increase realism and involvement. Even when animal characters are represented, having a different appearance from real-living ones and with behavior closely similar to the human one, they are extremely credible.

Two main streams of animation have been followed: computer assisted and computer animated [59]. In the first case, animation is at first performed by hand, initially producing *key-frames*. These are then joining them by *tweening*; that is, *in-between frames* are generated by interpolation. Another possibility refers to clay or pongo models, which are photographed in slightly different positions, creating the illusion of movement (see an example in Figure 4.50): this technique is called *stop motion*. An improvement of this method, enhancing the effect of movement, is *go motion*, in which the capture of sequential scenes is obtained by slight movements of the model, producing a *blurring effect*.

Turning now to computer-generated animation, the process starts by building an articulated *wireframe* model of the character (see Figure 2.8 and the corresponding Digital Marlene video clip: http://www.danielrobichaud.com/marl_mov.htm), which, by programming, is animated with movements simulating the physical laws of

Figure 4.49 A set of images from *A Force More Powerful* game.

Figure 4.50 An image from the film *A Grand Day Out*, by Nick Park, Wallace and Gromit, BBC, 1993.

dynamics. It is also possible to create a virtual environment where gravity, force, mass, and so on, can be properly simulated.

Real-life scenarios (houses, roads, gardens, etc.) can be generated in detail to create near photographic quality (Figure 4.51). To further increase realism,

Figure 4.51 A computer-generated outdoor scene by Industrial Light and Magic (from the Getty Images collection).

particularly whenever crowds, herds, or flocks are present, special probabilistic algorithms are applied, thereby avoiding having to program every single detail. One special technique has been developed at Vanderbilt University (Center for Constructive Approximation) for *particle systems*, to recreate smoke, fire, or water. Some fixed parameters like amplitude and darkness of *waves* can be programmed to generate the dynamics and multiplicity of clouds, flames, and billows.

One of the most successful digital animation studios (founded in 1986) is Pixar. A screen shot of a recent movie entitled *Up* is shown in Figure 4.52. Pixar developed a digital tool called RenderMan^{TM}, which was designed to achieve high-performance programs, for example, high-speed and low computer memory. Note that, a 90-min film at 24 frames/s requires the generation of 130,000 frames. Other RenderMan^{TM} traits are the creation of blur and a variable depth of field, the generation of realistic fur and hair, and the full control of displacement needed for a realistic (nonregular) presentation.

To make a full-feature animated film, a high number of graphic artists, musicians, and technicians are required. Furthermore, even if computer technology and human skill highly contribute to animation quality, the story told nevertheless still remains the most important issue for audience entertainment.

Cyberspace

This term was introduced by William Gibson [60] in his science fiction novel *Burning Chrome*, 1982, where the action takes place in a fictitious world.

In the *cyberspace* world, space is not physically occupied but lies in the surfer's conceptual frame, and navigation may take place by exploring links, eventually going toward unknown or unexpected sites. Images on the screen represent an

PIXAR ANIMATION STUDIOS

UP | Publicity Image | Pixar Creative Services
generated from element: final_comp
u315b_1cpubAComp.pub8.119.tif · 2008:11:25 18:16:56 · (4096 x 3188

Figure 4.52 A scene from the film *Up*, the latest digital animation created by Pixar (2009).

empty space in which a number of virtual objects and characters live, work, and play, allowing the surfer to interact with them. At the same time, the surfer may modify the cyberspace and establish relationships with *cyberborgs*. Within this abstract world, virtual communities can be launched, which are born and die following the surfer's commands.

A good example of a cyberspace implementation is *Second Life* [61] developed at Linden Laboratories Inc. in 2003. There are many activities that can be performed in this imaginary world, such as doing business, playing with friends, going shopping, organizing parties. See Figure 4.53, depicting a living room in Second Life. According to different sources, the number of Second Life users ranges from 4 to 7 million, with a downturning trend.

The cyberspace illustrated in Figure 4.53 was designed to favor human activities as if they were real, but this total equivalence cannot be obtained and this is not necessarily harmful.

Final Remarks and Conclusions

Chapter 4 describes the potential use of recent media for communication, first considering the well-known character of Don Giovanni and his many distinctive descriptions. Different channels are used to broadcast images, concepts, and even ideas, by means of a variety of media. Don Giovanni is a working example with which to compare the exploitation of traditional media to the new strategies optimizing efficacy and efficiency of information transmission.

Figure 4.53 A private living room from Second Life.

Five different issues have been covered with reference to Don Giovanni, followed by an extended description of present-day practices, namely:

1. Representation modalities to exploit the visual channel.
2. Content structuring to profit from the simultaneous use of different media.
3. Key strategies (metaphors and icons) to convey meaning.
4. The role of usability within human interaction, including social networks.
5. Telepresence, virtual reality, and role definition to enable the manipulation of virtual worlds.

In the first part, authors and spectators (interchangeably) are allowed to describe and promote, accessing and interacting with information. These new channel opportunities were not available in the recent past, mainly because of the lack of the Internet. Because a great number of users are involved in any public communication, new techniques for annotating and retrieving documents are explained, including emotional or impressive messages. Remediation is a technique that positions old contents in a different media, whereas repurposing makes use of existing known brands for advertising in media. The evolution of communication in advanced societies gives rise to a number of devices that capture human behavior on a large scale (known as ambient intelligence), offering new interactive functions. In this connection, an impressive achievement is to be able to both see and be seen by anybody, anywhere, at any time, even from different vantage points.

The second part considers a pictorial composition by Madox Brown, illustrating *The Finding of Don Juan by Haidee*, followed by a series of primitive functions described by a Da Vinci pupil on the basis of his master's directions. The essential principles, contained in the earlier descriptions, were meant to enable a good image communication: when to add a new channel, specifically when to add an image to text, as well as how to manage and organize picture details.

The third part considers new communication alphabets and their relative composition rules. New metaphors and icons are employed daily as needed by new technologies, such as smartphones and social networks, to improve the exchanging, and understanding of messages within multicultural audiences. An example of using well-known icons from a film poster related to the Don Juan character is the one of speared hearts to convey his many female conquests. Another popular example in computer science is the office desktop metaphor depicting tools and data typical of an office. Furthermore, the blending concept is briefly reviewed to formalize and explain the role of iconic communication primitives.

The fourth part covers the subject of usability, and its fall over on social and human—computer interactions. It also touches on the relevance of visual communication for complex and voluminous data sets to be seen and easily managed. Two different paradigms to display data relationships are introduced: a horizontal one (employing pie charts) and a hierarchical one (using tree graphs). To make the most of such graphical representations by the largest population, accessibility has been considered and demonstrated with a few examples.

The fifth part deals with the most advanced graphic and pictorial facilities establishing the borderline between realism and illusion, defining presence and augmented reality/virtuality. Games are next described, because they represent today one of the richest markets, employing sophisticated software that have high-definition images, avatars, and full-immersion representations with strong interactive capabilities. A second important commercial market is the one of animated film creation, which is also briefly presented. Science fiction has introduced new artificial worlds that have, in turn, generated an inhabited cyberspace (cyberborgs).

Summarizing, the different ways to improve channel exploitation have been described both textually and visually with specific examples aiming to establish guidelines that content providers should use in their everyday work. Both contents and targets are becoming worldwide, and their distribution is pervasive. Conversely, the development sites are concentrated in few places due to their cost and the required specialization of their members. Furthermore, the complexity and sophistication of the available media make the new targets and tasks extremely hard and in need of a deep technological culture.

References

[1] R.S. Heller, C.D. Martin, N. Haneef, S. Gievska-Krliu, Using a theoretical multimedia taxonomy framework, ACM J. Educat. Res. Comput. 1 (1) (2001) 4—22.
[2] B. Shneiderman, Designing the User Interface: Strategies for Effective Human—Computer Interaction, Addison Wesley, New York, 1987.
[3] T. Berners-Lee, W. Hall, J. Hendler, N. Shadbolt, D.J. Weitzner, Creating a Science of the Web. *Science* 313, 11. See the Web Science Research Initiative, http://www .webscience.org/, 2006.

[4] C. Le Roy, Visual rhetoric and affective images: Part 2. BC Sustainability Education, http://communicatingsustainability.blogspot.com/, 2009.

[5] Available from: http://www.worldwidetelescope.org/Home.aspx

[6] R. van Kranenburg, 2002, The Internet of Things, Institute of Network Cultures, ISBN 90-78146-06-0.

[7] M. van Doorn, End-user programming of ambient narratives for smart retail environments, PhD Thesis, Technical University of Eindhoven, 2009.

[8] P. Mistry, P. Mae, L. Chang, WUW—Wear Ur World—A Wearable Gestural Interface. CHI '09 extended abstracts on Human factors in computing systems, Boston, USA, 2009.

[9] M. Weiser, The computer for the 21st century, Sci. Am. 265 (3) (1991) 94−104.

[10] P. Milgram, A.F. Kishino, Taxonomy of mixed reality visual displays, IEICE Trans. Inform. Syst., E77-D **12**, 1994, pp. 1321−1329.

[11] R. Datta, J. Dhiraj, J. Li, J.Z. Wang, Image retrieval: ideas, influences, and trends of the new age, ACM Comput. Surv. 40 (2) (2008) 1−60.

[12] Available from: http://www.w3.org/2001/Annotea

[13] Webnotes, http://www.webnotes.net/

[14] Diigo, http://www.diigo.com/

[15] P. Bottoni, S. Levialdi, P. Rizzo, An analysis and case study of digital annotation, in: N. Bianchi-Berthouze (Ed.), Databases in Networked Information Systems, LNC, Springer Verlag, Heidelberg, 2003, pp. 216−231.

[16] M. Addisu, P. Bianchi, P. Bottoni, S. Levialdi, E. Panizzi, Annotating significant relations on multimedia web documents, in: M. Maybury (Ed.), Multimedia Information Extraction, MIT Press, Cambridge, 2010.

[17] W. Mann, S. Thompson, Rhetorical Structure Theory: A Framework for the Analysis of Texts. IPRA Papers in Pragmatics, 1987, pp. 1−21.

[18] P. Bottoni, S. Levialdi, A. Labella, E. Panizzi, R. Trinchese, L. Cigli, MADCOW: A Visual Interface for Annotating Webpages, in: Proc. AVI 2006, ACM Press, New York, 2006, pp. 314−317.

[19] J.D. Bolter, R. Grusin, Remediation: Understanding New Media, The MIT Press, Cambridge, 1999.

[20] P. Levinson, The Soft Edge, Routledge, London, 1997.

[21] U. Eco, A Theory of Semiotics, Indiana University Press, Bloomington, 1976.

[22] C.S. Peirce, in: C. Hartshorne, P. Weiss (Eds.), Collected Papers of Charles Peirce, vols. 1−8, Harvard University Press, Cambridge, MA, 1960, pp. 1931−1958.

[23] M. Imaz, D. Benyon, Designing with Blends: Conceptual Foundations of Human−Computer Interaction and Software Engineering, The MIT Press, Cambridge, 2007.

[24] P. Duchastel, Illustrating instructional texts, Educ. Technol. 18 (1978) 36−39.

[25] M.I. Posner, Orienting of attention, Q. J. Exp. Psychol. 32 (1980) 3−25.

[26] J. Raskin, The Humane Interface, ACM Press, New York, 2000.

[27] W. Wahlster, E. André, W. Graf, T. Rist, Designing illustrated texts: how language production is influenced by graphic generation, in: Proc. Fifth Conf. of EACL-91, Germany, 1991, pp. 8−14.

[28] J.R. Levin, On functions of pictures in prose, in: F.J. Pirozzolo, M.C. Witrock (Eds.), Neurophychological and Cognitive Processes in Reading, Academic Press, New York, 1981.

[29] W. Winn, The design and use of instructional graphics, in: H. Mandl, J.R. Levin (Eds.), Knowledge Acquisition from Text and Pictures, Elsevier Science, Amsterdam, 1989.

[30] M. McLuhan, Understanding Media: The Extensions of Man, 1964reissued 1994, MIT Press, Cambridge.

[31] R.S. Heller, C.D. Martin, A media taxonomy, IEEE Multimedia 2 (4) (1995) 36–45.

[32] M. Gray, J.D. Foley, K. Mullet, Grouping and ordering user interface components, Technical Report Series No. 94-3, GVU Center, Georgia Tech, 1994.

[33] H. Lieberman, The visual language of experts in graphic design, in: Proc. Eleventh IEES Symposium on Visual Languages, Sept. 95, 1995, pp. 5–12.

[34] E.L. Hutchins, J.D. Hollan, D.A. Norman, Direct manipulation interfaces, Hum. Comput. Interact. 1 (1985) 311–338.

[35] G.D. Abowd, R. Beale, Users systems and interfaces: a unifying framework for interaction, in: D. Diaper, N. Hammond (Eds.), HCI'91: People and Computers VI, Cambridge University Press, 1991, pp. 73–87.

[36] L. Tondl, Problems of Semantics, Reidel, Dordrecht, Holland, 1981.

[37] P. Bottoni, M.F. Costabile, S. Levialdi, P. Mussio, Defining visual languages for interactive computing, IEEE Trans. Syst. Man Cybern., A 27 (6) (1997) 773–783.

[38] R.V. Miller, Human ease of use criteria and their tradeoffs, IBM Technical Report, TR 002185 IBM Corporation, Poughkeepsie, New York, 1971.

[39] J. Carelman, Catalogue des objets introuvables, Le Cherche Midi, Paris, 1969.

[40] J. Brooke, SUS: a "quick and dirty" usability scale, in: P.W. Jordan, B.T.B.A. Weerdmeester, I.L. Mac Clelland (Eds.), Usability Evaluation in Industry, Taylor and Francis, London, 1990.

[41] N. Bevan, K. Holdaway, User needs for user system interaction standards, in: C.D. Evans, B.L. Meek, R.S. Walker (Eds.), Technology Standards, Butterworth Heinemann, London, 1993.

[42] Standard ISO9241, http://www.userfocus.co.uk/articles/ISO9241_update.html, 2009.

[43] H.D. Offenhuber, J. Donath, Function follows form—the social role of virtual architecture, in: S. Doesinger (Ed.), Space, Between People: How the Virtual Changes Physical Architecture, Prestel, USA, 2008.

[44] SemaSpace project homepage: http://residence.aec.at/didi/FLweb/

[45] Visualization Showcase: http://vis.mediaartresearch.at/webarchive/public/view/mid:6

[46] Ars Electronica homepages: http://infosthetics.com/archives/2009/09/mapping_the_archive_30_years_of_ars_electronica.htmlhttp://www.aec.at/prix_about_de.php

[47] M. Porta, M. Turina, Eye-S: a full-screen input modality for pure eye-based communication, in: Proc. Fifth Symp. on Eye-Tracking Research and Applications, Savanna, ACM Press, 2008, pp. 27–34.

[48] The Eyewriter homepage, http://the189.com/art/eye-graffiti-called-the-eyewriter

[49] Wave homepages http://wave.webaim.org/ and http://webaim.org/

[50] R.W. Thomas, L.A. Da Silva, A.B. Mac Kenzie, Cognitive networks, in: Proc. First IEEE Int. Symp. on New Frontiers in Dynamic Spectrum Access Networks, Baltimore, MD, USA, 2005.

[51] M.K. Johnson, S. Hashtroudi, D.S. Lindsay, Source monitoring, Psychol. Bull. 114 (1) (1993) 3–28.

[52] T. Kim, F. Biocca, Telepresence via television: Two dimensions of telepresence may have different connections to memory and persuasion, J. Comput. Mediat. Commun. 3 (2) (1997) [Online], Available: http://www.ascusc.org/jcmc/vol3/issue2/kim.html

[53] W. Barfield, S. Weghorst, The sense of presence within virtual environments: a conceptual framework, Hum. Comput. Interact. 2 (1993) 699–704.

[54] M. Lombard, T. Ditton, At the heart of it all: the concept of presence, J. Comput. Mediat. Commun. 3 (2) (1997) [Online] Available: http://www.ascusc.org/jcmc/vol3/issue2/lombard.html

[55] R.M. Held, N.I. Durlach, Presence: teleoperators and virtual environments, Telepresence 1 (1) (1992) 109–112.

[56] C. Heeter, Being there: the subjective experience of presence, Presence-Teleop. Virt. Environ. 1 (2) (1992) 262–271.

[57] B. Thuresson, Interactive Storytelling for Creative People, Deliverable Number: D3.1.1 Workpackage: 3 of *In Scape Storytelling* 2005.

[58] D. Grigorovici, C. Costantin, Virtual Environments and the Sense of Being There: An SEM Model of Presence, Presence 2003, Aalborg University, Denmark, poster 45, 2003.

[59] *getstuff* application: http://entertainment.howstuffworks.com/computer-animation1.htm.

[60] W. Gibson, Burning Chrome, Omni, Bulverde USA, 1982.

[61] Second Life homepage: http://secondlife.com/?lang = en-US

[62] ACM SIGCHI, Curricula for human computer interaction. Chapter 2, section 3, last updated 2009, http://old.sigchi.org/cdg/cdg2.html#2_3

Printed in the United States
By Bookmasters